Sixth Sense

from the columns of the *Bucks Free Press*

2011-2016

Sixth Sense

from the columns of the *Bucks Free Press*

2011-2016

Colin Baker

FABULOUS BOOKS

www.fbs-publishing.co.uk

First Published in the UK April 2017 by FBS Publishing Ltd.
22 Dereham Road, Thetford,
Norfolk. IP25 6ER

ISBN 978-0-9932043-7-1

These articles first appeared in the *Bucks Free Press*
from 2011-1016

A CIP catalogue record for this book is available from
the British Library.

Cover design and illustration by Owen Claxton
Text Edited by Alasdair McKenzie
Typesetting by Scott Burditt

This book is dedicated to Barry Burnett, who has been my agent for the majority of my working life and who has never failed to make me laugh or to support me when it was needed or appropriately chastise me when it wasn't.

Introduction

I am struggling to come to terms with the fact that the two previous compilations of my weekly newspaper offerings to the citizens of a small town in Buckinghamshire were published respectively seven and eight years ago. Since then, of course, I have been continuing to delight and/or appal the readers of the *Bucks Free Press* with my opinions on the widest possible number of issues, local and interplanetary, world-shattering and parochial in equal measure. At least, that is what I fondly hope. The newspaper editor has either not noticed that I am occupying the outside edge of one of his middle pages every week, or he finds my presence there acceptable at least.

I am delighted that Theresa Cutts and Will Hadcroft—the discerning and clever proprietors of FBS Publishing, who made such a lovely job of publishing my daughter's first book, *Rhino Wants a Wife*— have agreed to publish this latest selection of my ramblings. Their list is full of such delightful work that I feel distinctly honoured to be added to it. And they are lovely people. Natch! Furthermore, they are hoping to satisfy the dissatisfied thousands (well, a few people did mention it in passing) clamouring for the first two books by republishing them soon.

It was July 1995 when I wrote my first column, and I am rather irritatingly smug about the fact that I have never missed a week since then. No 'Colin Baker is on holiday and his column this week is written by Brian Locke' for me. I am unashamedly going for the world record of uninterrupted weekly column writing, so if someone could tell me what it is, I would be very grateful/eagerly anticipatory/deeply depressed/ or give up (delete as appropriate).

Thank you for buying this book. Or if you stole it, then thank you too. I am flattered that someone wanted it enough to purloin it.

Colin Baker.
February 2017.

2011

7th January 2011

There has been a strong reaction this week to a story in *EastEnders* in which a young mother, on finding her baby dead, switches it with the living baby of a friend.

Quite strong stuff. The stuff of drama, and not just any drama, but a soap.

I don't think that *EastEnders* has any pretension to be a modern *Play for Today* in airing sensitive and powerful issues in a drama-documentary way. It is a soap opera.

The trouble is, however, that many viewers become so used to seeing the characters in their living rooms that realities can become blurred. Just read the comments about the programme claiming that it depicts 'real life' in a gritty and truthful way. No it doesn't. Real life doesn't have dramatic events every half hour. *EastEnders* is as close to the real life in an East London square as *Midsomer Murders* is to the life of a West Country village.

Any human tragedy shown in a television programme is bound to stir up an emotional response in someone who has endured similar events. Imagine seeing an episode of a police drama immediately after you have lost a loved one in similar circumstances to those depicted on the screen.

My wife and I lost our first child, a son, to cot death in 1983. I wouldn't want to watch this storyline even now and I can only imagine how recently-bereaved parents would feel. But I would suggest that that is no reason not to include subjects like cot death in plays or television programmes. It can even be an opportunity to stimulate debate and raise the issue publicly. Of course, that is not the intention of the broadcasters. They are making television programmes and hope to increase ratings through sensational storylines.

The help they offer via phone numbers at the end of the programme is a consequence of the anticipated effect the programme may have, not their motivation for making it.

From what I've read about this particular treatment of the subject, my main concern would be that anyone should for a second consider that real mothers whose children have died suddenly and unexpectedly might conceivably then behave in the way that the character in *EastEnders* has. I sincerely hope that the programme-makers will take their responsibility to real parents whose babies have died as seriously as they do the drive to attract more viewers.

14th January 2011

My wife and I attended a funeral in Guildford this week. Her elderly aunt had died after several years of a debilitating illness which had left a formerly busy and bright lady unable to recognise her family or interact with those around her—an all too common and sad scenario. As a result, the funeral was truly a celebration of her life, which can be harder to sustain when someone dies suddenly and unexpectedly.

Sandwiches and drinks were served afterwards at a church hall in the centre of Guildford and, as we parked the car in a nearby street, my wife pointed to a building immediately adjacent, remarking that it looked familiar. She was right. It was the building in which we had first met exactly thirty years and three days earlier. We were rehearsing a play *Private Lives* and this building, which now houses a drama workshop for young people, was then The Bellerby Theatre, a popular fringe arts venue in Guildford. Completely unexpectedly, we had found ourselves back there virtually on the thirtieth anniversary of the day my life changed markedly for the better. I can only hope that she shares that opinion.

The temptation was, of course, impossible to resist. We were drawn to walk up to the windows and peer in. In a certain type of TV drama we might have seen our younger selves shyly (?) exchanging first greetings. But all we saw was a room that hadn't seen much in the way of paint or renovation in the intervening years. Then we heard 'Can I help you?' from behind us. The charming young man who ran the centre, having heard our story, was happy to let us in to revisit the now cold and bare room where a young and stunning girl with a bad cold, wearing a pink crocheted hat, bent down to pat the red setter that was at the time my constant companion, when I was in my 'me and my dog against the world' phase.

The rest, as they say, is history.

Our timing was fortunate, as the building is apparently scheduled for demolition.

But to find ourselves back there, particularly on a day when for very real reasons our minds were already reflecting on the more important things of life—family and relationships—was rather strange and special. Hence, I took the liberty of sharing it with you.

21ˢᵗ January 2011

Just when we thought that the country was moving away from the absurdities of political correctness and institutional practices dictated by the fear of possible litigation, yet more examples of public pottiness appear.

It seems no area of public life is safe.

A senior police officer claims to have been instructed by superiors that his use of the phrase 'as sure as eggs is eggs' was inappropriate on 'diversity grounds'. Do you share my incomprehension? Apparently, the phrase could offend women with infertility problems. Please enter this convenient darkened room with padded walls and have a good scream with me. The logic of that particular lunacy would tend to suggest that anyone asking for 'the parson's nose' whilst having Sunday lunch would be castigated for offending chickens, the nasally self conscious or the clergy. Or maybe the use of the yellow card in a football match should be abandoned for fear of offending people with jaundice or of a cowardly disposition, or the red card those with red hair or the permanently embarrassed.

Big Brother (*1984* rather than Channel 4 style) has reared his head in the Fenland district, where council staff have been instructed to notify their managers in writing if they are 'having a relationship' with a colleague. The reason? To stop 'intimate behaviour' at work. I suppose, once notified, the manager will then be monitoring their behaviour to ensure they didn't linger lovingly by the photocopier or play footsie over (under?) their sushi at lunch time?

'No cuddling or canoodling in the canteen, please.'

Even the theatre has fallen foul of the jobsworths. You'll love this. Nurse Poultice in *Robin Hood* in Glasgow was forced, after a complaint from the Red Cross, to remove the red crosses from his/her costume, as they breached the Geneva Convention and could 'dilute the neutrality' of that otherwise wonderful organisation. It's true, I promise.

Then there is the lollipop man in Sussex who donned a variety of festive hats while ferrying children across the road.

Apparently, the sight of Santa's hat or one in the shape of a turkey could distract a driver and constitute a safety risk. Leaving aside that his great big luminous lollipop was intended to attract the attention of drivers, who in this benighted kingdom really believes that the additional sight of a fluffy reindeer hat would cause a driver to lose control of his car?

Well, someone in East Grinstead, apparently.

28th January 2011

I have been lucky to work for the last forty years in a profession in which sexism is almost completely absent. Actresses will tell you that there are traditionally fewer good parts for women than there are for men, and that as they get older they are less likely to find employment than in their earlier years. That is undeniably true. But by the very nature of the job, men play men's roles and women play women's roles. There is no workplace tension or competition for jobs between the sexes. Furthermore, I have never witnessed any bullying or victimisation in the theatre or television world that was solely gender-related.

As a father of four daughters, and a governor of an all girls school, I am of course only too aware that there are still substantial pockets of resistance in other areas of society to joined-up thinking when it comes to sexual equality in the workplace and society. The numbers of female MPs or leaders of industry are evidence not of a disparity of ability between the sexes but a disparity of opportunity. Some of this arguably stems from the one major differential—motherhood. However much paternity leave is offered, men cannot actually give birth. Just as well, really. Can you imagine the fuss we'd make?

As a result, employers with an eye on budgets and continuity, even though such discrimination is contrary to employment law, will often find reasons to employ a comparably qualified male. This results in an inevitable slowing down of the career progression of many very talented young women at precisely the time when their male counterparts have no such restriction.

It is appalling, however, that in a (comparatively) more enlightened society we are still seeing and hearing evidence of stone-age attitudes to women who have dared to succeed in areas considered by these dinosaurs as being a male domain.

Come and sit with me at Adams Park and you will see as many women as men who understand the offside rule perfectly well. The lineswoman who has found herself at the centre of a media storm in the wake of Messrs. Keys and Gray's stupid remarks must clearly have been both qualified and excellent in order to reach the position she has in the testosterone—driven world of football, yet these two twerps have failed to evolve sufficiently to understand or acknowledge that. Shame on them.

4th February 2011

If we are to believe the results of a recent survey, it would seem that reading to children at bedtime is no longer as common as it was when my children were growing up. That may in part be because there are today many more one parent families or ones where both parents have to work long hours to make ends meet. But even so, it is a great shame that five or ten minutes cannot be found most days to ease their children into sleep by reading a book with them. And it works, too. And it works too—often on the parent! I was often prodded into wakefulness by a daughter demanding to know what happened next because I had lulled myself into sleep.

Bedtime reading can be a rare opportunity to have some one-to-one time, when all the other distractions of the day can be forgotten. Also, the child's reading skills can be developed in a less formal or pressurised way than in the classroom (where, however good the teacher, there is always the possibility of it being seen as 'work'). It brings the process of reading into the home in the form of a treat, a shared fun experience.

The bedtime story was a precious part of my childhood. There were no *Mr Men* books or Roald Dahl or Jacqueline Wilson in my childhood, but we did have Beatrix Potter and Alison Uttley (*Little Grey Rabbit*), which led on to the wonderful *Just William* books, which I devoured voraciously. Indeed, I still have the pre-war editions that were handed down to me by my elder brother. There was, of course, no television and only one hour of children's radio a day back then. Books were the only opportunity to explore the intriguing worlds and ideas to be found in the imagination of others.

It is perhaps because of my early introduction to, and subsequent love of, books that I am astonished when I find myself in a house where none are in evidence.

When my children were young, a lot of my employment was in theatre, so I often worked in the evenings and my wife did most of the bedtime reading.

In fact, I was once castigated by one of my daughters for 'doing too many voices'. 'Mummy just reads it properly,' she complained.

And I thought my Hobbit voice was rather good, too.

Critics everywhere—even in my own home.

18th February 2011

Whenever I tell myself that I really must move on from the frustrations of the deranged behaviour of councils and other public bodies and talk about something else, another thing happens that makes me wish that good old Scotty could beam me up forthwith.

I know I'm preaching to the converted (mostly), but how

can we have created a world in which a 70-year-old woman representing an independent health organisation in Wiltshire could generate a six-month enquiry costing tens of thousands of pounds by uttering two words? They were two words that caused the body to lose its funding when the complaint of the equality campaigner who heard them was upheld. What were those words? 'Jungle drums'. Anna Farquhar uttered them to refer to unwarranted rumours within the NHS. It is a common phrase used to describe the effect of oft-repeated misinformation, much akin to that other obvious no-no, 'Chinese whispers', Mrs Farquhar even apologised when she learned that someone claimed to have been offended. Who? A tree lizard, an orangutan, an unemployed drum maker? What person (other than the officious complainant who saw fit to imagine an implied insult when none was intended or could reasonably be expected to have been intended) might have conceived this as a racially motivated phrase? But the pusillanimous pen pushers who upheld the complaint were frightened of allowing even the nano-possibility of being seen as not supporting racial equality and, as a result, they allowed reason to depart through the cat flap of bureaucracy into the realms of barking bedlam. The charity for which Mrs Farquhar worked and its 200-strong volunteer workforce were banned from county council-owned buildings in Wiltshire. You don't believe it? No, neither did I. But it's true. And the Wiltshire County Council is run by people who were voted in by folk like you and me and Mrs Farquhar, whose record of voluntary community work is decades long.

No one elected in Buckinghamshire would be so anxious to appease the unappeasable and unreasonable as to bow down to the tyranny of the politically correct, would they? Well, let us fervently hope not and keep our eyes open and shout when it happens.

And don't get me started on paedophiles being allowed to petition to be removed from the Sexual Offenders' Register. The officious robot who dreamed that one up has probably never had to stand for election.

25th February 2011

In the twenty-five years I have lived in this area there have been several deaths along the B482 that runs from Marlow to Stokenchurch through Lane End. Regular users are familiar with the moving evidence provided by bunches of flowers that appear forlornly by the roadside on the anniversaries. I know two local families bereaved by the loss of a son and a mother killed within half a mile of Cadmore End School. I mention the school because it has, in conjunction with parents of children at the school and some local residents, been campaigning for a controlled crossing to enable families to cross this notorious rat run safely at school delivery and collection times.

Who would argue that a road which is sufficiently dangerous as to justify the placement of signs notifying drivers that there have been '17 casualties in three years' should not have a controlled crossing outside a primary school? Well, Bucks County Council apparently, whose Head of Transport labelled it a 'Non-Key Issue' and advised the Cabinet Member not to proceed with the scheme. The three-page letter explaining this decision offers several reasons, the first being the speed of the vehicles travelling along the B482. Even though the speed limit is 40 mph. the average speed of vehicles passing the school area is apparently 48 mph. This leads Transport for Buckinghamshire to conclude that the high speeds of drivers will lead them to 'jump or miss the red light'. Maybe for starters, then, move the speed camera that catches people as they leave Lane End, where there is no public risk, to the school area, where there is?

Other reasons include road design detail and what one suspects is the 'driving' concern of cost, estimated at £75,000. Clearly this is too much to spend to keep our children safe outside their schools and less important than spending £114,000 on the *Buckinghamshire Times Magazine,* which tells us all how wonderful our County Council is and goes straight into the re-cycling bin in most households.

The justification for not spending our money protecting children ends with the sentence 'The current collision record does not justify the provision of such a facility and the additional revenue money that will be required to maintain it.'

Seventeen casualties along a ten-mile stretch of road don't cut it, apparently.

Let us hope it doesn't take an eighteenth to convince them otherwise.

4th March 2011

If we are honest with each other, we are all Nimbys. We all want the benefits of services and facilities, but there are many of the necessary places and buildings that provide those services that we would prefer not to have in our own immediate vicinity. I use Britain's motorways quite a lot and have one within loudhailing distance of my home. But it was there, albeit two lanes wide and terminating just short of Oxford, when I moved in, and therefore I cannot really complain that it is still there and much busier.

You do eventually get used to the noise, although naturally, like anyone else, self interest makes me keen to campaign for any noise reduction measures that may become possible in the future via low noise surfaces. Some of us have got to live next door to rubbish tips, sewage treatment plants, motorways, pubs, football grounds, shops and schools.

If they were there before we were, then any strenuous demands that they be moved elsewhere seem perhaps somewhat lacking in merit. But there are people who move into houses immediately adjacent to primary schools and then complain bitterly because the children make noise while they're having fun during break times, as if their arrival next door should change the status quo.

There are people who buy a house next to a farm and complain of the smell; people who find their own rural idyll and then set about preventing anyone else from finding theirs in the immediate vicinity.

It is understandable that people who live in very close proximity, say, to the site of a planned superstore, sports stadium, abattoir, pub or even a new school might vigorously campaign against them. But all those things have to go somewhere and they need to be near enough to the population they serve to be of use.

The bulk of the protests might be diminished, perhaps, if proper compensation were to be paid. When the M40 was widened, those whose lives were affected received varying amounts of compensation, none of which reflected the actual financial loss incurred by the recipients, in even the most basic terms of the value of their homes. A lot of necessary development would encounter less resistance if the genuinely blighted, rather than being inadequately compensated, were properly compensated and even rewarded more handsomely for their pains.

Namby-pamby 'Nimby' might then become 'Pimby'— 'Please—in my back yard!'

11th March 2011

As the bill-payer at Baker Towers, and one tottering towards the obscurity of the post-retirement age actor, I had issued an edict banning the acquisition of any new furry or feathered dependents. We have enough to stock a small zoo already.

Despite this, I discovered this week that we have been giving a home for over a month to a pair of guinea pigs. A permanent home, it seems. They are now our guinea pigs.

They used to be someone else's guinea pigs, but they returned them to the shop from which they acquired them, indignantly demanding their money back.

It seems that the wicked, uncaring shopkeeper had not informed the poor customer that you could not go away on holiday and just leave great piles of food and pints of water in the guinea pigs' immediate vicinity and let them get on with it for the duration.

I suppose we should be grateful that these imaginatively challenged people decided to return the poor little creatures rather than try out their novel animal care regime.

The shop knew my wife as the willing (nay, eager) recipient

of other people's unwanted goats, chickens, rabbits and guinea pigs. We have received dozens of them over the last decade. So, Bill and Ben are now luxuriating in the glow of their heated quarters and being fed the cavy equivalent of champagne and caviar. I know my place.

But it is extraordinary how some people approach pet ownership. Animals have been returned to shops for such reasons as 'It looks evil', 'It did not bark or meow' (let's hope that wasn't a guinea pig, then) and even 'It didn't alert me when someone was at the door.' Other reasons for rejection include 'It wagged its tail while I was talking' (no, I don't understand that either) and a Great Dane being too big. One even returned a piglet because, surprise, surprise, it turned into a large pig.

The most appalling of all was the case of the woman in Essex who returned her Jack Russell terrier because it did not match her curtains. When the workers at the animal shelter (tolerantly, I'd say) suggested that she might consider putting the dog in another room, she responded that her curtains were very expensive and she wasn't having the dog spoil the effect.

Let us hope it was a lucky escape for that particular dog.

18th March 2011

Many years ago I gave a dinner party in London. I know it was many years ago because who gives dinner parties anymore? And I escaped from London in the early 70s, as soon as I could afford to buy both a house and a car!

On this particular occasion, I had invited two couples. I had known them a long time but they did not know each other. They arrived simultaneously and I opened the door to four people whom I had to introduce to each other. I could not remember a single name and floundered for a decade or two (it seemed) before, being good friends, they bailed me out. I still suffer from the same tendency to forget names at crucial moments, but at least I can't attribute it to the onset of Alzheimer's, as I have always been like that. Whenever I do a radio interview to plug a show, I have a cast list in front of me in case I forget the names of my fellow actors at the crucial moment.

This is a condition not unfamiliar to actors. We work with a lot of people over a career, and it is rare to work with the same actor more than a few times in a career. Hence the use of the word 'Darling!' which has attracted so much scorn from those who think all actors are 'luvvies'.

But 'Darling' is preferable to 'Thingy' or 'Whosit.' At least it conveys an acknowledgement of both recognition and affection.

I met a lovely man last week whom I had last seen thirty years ago. He was quite disappointed, I think, that I failed to recognise him at first or remember his name, however hard I tried. I ended up having no option but to admit my confusion. He had remembered me, because he had followed my career over the intervening years and I had had no such advantage with him.

But things can still go wrong. Kate Winslet momentarily forgot Angela Jolie's name when making an acceptance speech at the Golden Globes in 2009. And Ms Jolie is quite famous and arguably unforgettable!

I have chaired meetings in the past when I was unable to invite someone to speak because I couldn't remember their name. How the teachers or Speaker of the House of Commons manage I cannot begin to imagine.

25th March 2011

The old adage 'Give a dog a bad name ...' is so true. I have worked with many people over the years who turned up dragging their reputations with them like millstones and turned out to be perfectly pleasant but had perhaps tolerated fools less than gladly once in the past.

Sometimes the parts one has played as an actor confuse strangers. When I first started 'walking out' with my wife, her mother was very dubious about her associating with that awful 'Paul Merroney' from *The Brothers*, the 1970s TV series.

We are currently experiencing the same phenomenon with

our greyhound, acquired from Stokenchurch Dog Rescue. I had not realised that, as a breed, they seem to be viewed in the same way as many people view Staffies and the like: assume that they are vicious and lock up your poodles, or they'll eat them and spit out the bones. But like any breed, they are as user-friendly as their owners allow them to be. I have been amazed by the number of people who react adversely when she rushes up to meet their dogs (and their owners by default). Her instinct is 'Wow, another dog—great, let's run!'

'Is he vicious?' they yell, clutching their precious fluffy to their bosoms. 'No' does not convince them. And they all assume she is a he. The dogs who respond with a cheery 'Yes, come on let's run' provoke a wonderful display of free hurtling, resulting in two happy and tired dogs. But clearly the black javelin hurtling towards them gives some owners the wrong impression. If she were a Labrador, they would assume good intent. But she's a greyhound. They are trained to pursue and grab, aren't they?

To be honest, our diminutive Jack Russell/Poodle cross is more problematical. She thinks all other dogs want to eviscerate her, and screams in terror and runs home when she encounters them. But that doesn't mean the other dogs are vicious. It means she's a wimp.

But it's clearly an issue we have to address. We have very good friends who were initially wary and not disposed to liking our Susie, but revised their opinion when they met her, especially when they saw our cats walking across her while she slept on the sofa. I don't blame people. We all make incorrect assumptions. I only hope her sunny disposition eventually wins them over.

1st April 2011

I can report that my theory about the great airport gate conspiracy is holding up.

Since last week I have travelled to Australia, first Adelaide and currently Melbourne.

This has involved four flights thus far, all of which have

departed from the furthest gate in the terminal. Two were long distance and two were short haul, so it can't be related to the size of the aircraft. In one case, I even missed the flight I was booked on (as my luggage went on a tour of the airport, eventually turning up too late for me to make my connection) and the rebooked flight was right at the end of the concourse too. Are all the other gates dummies? Do they park decommissioned planes at them in order to create the illusion of a busy airport? Perhaps they want us exhausted and compliant before we are jammed into seats designed to provide a lifetime's work for osteopaths and chiropractors? Or are they trying to ensure that we pass every commercial outlet possible? After my first three-mile hike at Heathrow, my sense of impending doom deepened when I espied across the aisle a young couple with a baby.

Twelve-hour flights and babies are not a great combination. However, I have to report that the aforesaid baby ruined my story, not my night, by being the most amiable and sunny co-passenger with whom I have ever travelled. I wish I could say the same about the young woman in front who was never able to get comfy, apparently, and propelled her seat backwards and forwards throughout the night without a thought for any liquids on my fold-down tray, a selection of which now adorn my travel trousers.

The nice Indian gentleman next to me shared a sympathetic glance when my coffee sloshed violently at me on one of her sudden backward forays, and he offered me a very convincing throttling mime with a nod in her direction. The sympathy of strangers can sometimes be a solace.

We bonded even more when the lady in the window seat demanded for the fifth time to be allowed egress to the loo just as we had raised the first forkful of dinner to our mouths. Regular travellers will know the kerfuffle involved in allowing the window seat occupant out at the best of times.

Six more flights before I'm home. Per ardua ad astra, eh?

8th April 2011

Since last week's bulletin from down under, I have been arrested and trapped on an aeroplane. In between, I fraternised with versions of weeping angels, Doctors Who, vampires and a real Hogwarts' bad boy.

I was in Brisbane attending a media convention along with several convivial American actors from programmes like *Stargate* and *Buffy*. The undeniable hit of the event was a young actor called Tom Fenton who plays Draco Malfoy in *Harry Potter*, proving (if proof were needed) that young girls still have a penchant for bad boys. The queue of girls in their middle teens seeking his autograph stretched around the building all weekend. He was, of course, a delightful, friendly and modest young man, as those who play baddies often are. Playing those roles gets all the bad stuff out of their systems.

And yes, I was arrested. It seems jaywalking is a heinous offence in Queensland, as I discovered within minutes of leaving the hotel on the day I arrived. I crossed a road in front of two policemen when a red light was showing. There was no traffic visible for two hundred yards in either direction, so I strolled across. Bad mistake. My gun-packing prime interrogator neither believed nor cared that I was unaware that I had committed an offence. Why else would I have done what I did right in front of him?

When I raised a finger to emphasise a point, he accused me of being aggressive and disrespecting him, and threatened to summon backup. My new-boy-in-town status mattered not a jot. I got a ticket. So, tourists beware in Brisbane. Local residents told me that they did it all the time and had never heard of anyone being ticketed. That didn't console me much.

And when I left, I was pinned in my seat for three hours because a grandmother in the aisle seat (she told me about all her family) had discovered the joys of alcohol to such an extent that the paramedics were called when the plane landed and I couldn't get off until they had checked her out and moved her to another seat.

Now I am in calm, user-friendly New Zealand for the next week, busy changing my upcoming flight bookings to aisle seats and checking for local variations on the law that might trap the unwary tourist. All well so far.

15th April 2011

Having completed my-round-the-world-and-back-again odyssey to Australia and New Zealand and being safely back in the gentle Buckinghamshire countryside, my abiding memory is of the process of travel rather than the destinations. This is mainly because of the amount of space allocated to each passenger on an aircraft.

I am trying to find the right adjective to describe my body shape. I'd like to say strapping or beefy, even stout or portly, but will have to settle for big. I am big. But glancing round the interior of the plane, there were many bigger than me and very few indeed who were Kylie Minogue-sized. But the seats provided for us to sit in for 24 hours are built for Kylie and her little sisters and brothers. On a three or four-hour flight, this is tolerable, but when you have to eat three meals without the ability to move your elbows in any direction other than forward, life becomes a tad difficult. The gentleman who had the dubious pleasure of sitting next to me from Hong Kong to Heathrow was less 'big' than me admittedly, but was big-ish. We did not discuss the problem, but eating simultaneously with our elbows clamped to our sides was fraught with problems.

You can spear or scoop up the food, but getting it to your mouth—a fundamental and necessary part of the process—demands the dexterity of a contortionist. We arrived at an alternating high/low strategy, in the same way as the possession of the arm rest was ceded after a short period of occupation by a ceremony that might be called 'the folding of the arms'.

The arm fold was the only way too that we could attempt what one might (inaccurately) describe as sleep. And he, poor chap, had the problem of another six-footer on his right. I at least had the aisle on my other side, a dubious advantage confirmed by the bruises I carry, caused by the bony extremities of waitresses, sorry—salesgirls, sorry—stewardesses as they lug their trolleys up and down the narrow aisles. And don't get me started on the available space in the loos!

I know that making the passenger space even a little bit larger would push up costs, but on long haul flights maybe it would be worth it. Oh for a TARDIS, eh? Can I have it back, Matt?

22nd April 2011

I was watching *Country House Rescue* on TV this week and was intrigued to learn that interring one's relatives beneath one's own land is not the impossibility I had previously thought. The owners of the minor stately pile in question were landscaping their rolling acres and had to pay due respect to the fact that their grandparents had been laid to rest beneath the pergola.

Enquiries of my friendly funeral director chum elicited the information that there are, of course, several logistical official hoops that have to be jumped through before there would be the possibility, say, of my joining all our deceased dogs, cats, chickens, guinea pigs, rabbits etc. that now occupy Baker Towers' subsoil. Indeed, there would probably be little room for me, in fact.

Clearly, it is not an activity that should be entered into lightly. The resale value of our home might be adversely affected by the presence of yours truly lurking under the daffs. Not only that, but the family might also feel just a little reluctant to leave me behind when they cash in the insurance and head off to pastures new.

Apparently, planning permission is needed and the Water Authorities also need confirmation that the water table is sufficiently removed from the site of a proposed interment. But in principle, it is not impossible.

This led to me to enquire further about the waste of natural resources involved in burning ornate coffins and fittings along with the deceased and the possibility of, say, renting a showy exterior that encases a separate practical interior coffin. More economical in every way, I would have thought. Apparently, this would be illegal in the UK, but is both legal and popular in France. Wow! Something the French can teach us!

It is a very sensitive subject. We all say that we don't care much what happens to us when we are gone, but of course the whole funeral process is for the survivors, not the deceased. But without wishing to deprive my good friend of a proper reward for his excellent services, is it not perhaps time that the public aspect of the grieving and mourning process should be separated from the actuality of the interment or cremation?

Not very cheerful this week, sorry; so now I'm off to dig a hole for our misanthropic, one-eyed hen, Olive, who finally chickened out this week.

29th April 2011

The British spent hundreds of years jaunting all over the world and colonising other lands, irrespective of whether the indigenous populations wanted to be colonised. We were not alone in doing that. The Greeks and Romans did it first, along with the ancestors of the Swedes and Danes, then the Spanish, the Dutch, the French all joined in, imposing their religions, their laws and belief systems on peoples all over the ever-expanding world.

Since then, some of the colonised have accepted the invitation offered by that old empire-building initiative and come to join us in the UK. They came from the West Indies half a century and more ago and were followed by the Asians driven from Uganda by Idi Amin and many others since then.

We now have an ethnically diverse society and have benefited hugely as a nation as a result, in so many ways. But like any marriage, compromise and mutual understanding are necessary when diverse cultures and beliefs are brought together.

For hundreds of years, religions that preach brotherly love and tolerance have been subverted by minorities that seek control, dominance and power and who prey on the ignorance and fear of their fellows.

The pretext of religious differences within Christianity has resulted most recently in continued and bloody internecine strife in Ireland, just as murderous zealots are today using the peaceful and spiritual religion of Islam as a pretext to kill and maim. The murderous and poisonous continue to get their way when mindless morons are moved to vandalise the graves of Muslims who have been buried by their families in our town.

I suppose we have to imagine that the despicable vandals who did this believe, because some terrorists use the Muslim faith as an excuse for their violence, that the faith itself is evil. The Bible, the Koran and the religious books of all faiths have been used and traduced by the evil and cruel from the beginning of time.

The only way to break the cycle of mutual mistrust and hatred is if those of all faiths and beliefs unite in condemning the actions of these awful and misguided people.

They have brought shame to our town, and we can only hope that they have sufficient decency left to reflect ultimately on the hurt they have done to the surviving families of those whose graves have been desecrated.

7th May 2011

I have recently discovered Twitter, having previously been under the impression that it was as inconsequential and unedifying as the implications of the name might suggest. Tiny little unseen birds making a pleasant but uninformative noise in your immediate vicinity.

I am happy to admit that I was wrong. Twitter is perhaps not for everyone. Some people have not the slightest desire to share much detail of their lives with others.

And, indeed, many people should probably resist the temptation to share as much as they do.

But, unlike Facebook, which I quickly discovered was not for me when I tried it a year or so ago, Twitter is a rather wonderful tool that is as useful or trivial as you choose to make it.

You put information out there and access information

from those whom you choose to follow.

I follow friends, work colleagues, Wycombe Wanderers and its players, the *Bucks Free Press* (of course) and random people like Alan Sugar, the Dalai Lama and Danny Baker. You pick whose messages you see, and that's the joy of it.

On at least two occasions it has saved me considerable grief, as I am lucky enough to be followed by hundreds of people all over the world who are fond of *Doctor Who*.

When I was stranded at an airport in Australia and tweeted of my plight, messages went round the world and back to the man who was in the wrong place to collect me. If I have a problem with my computer, a benevolent anonymous well-wisher will advise me, and all in 140 letters or less—and therein lies the genius of twitter.

It is not the vehicle for lengthy soul-searching but rather a means of getting your message out there, of sharing the frustrations and joys of your day. Today I am trying to find a reasonably priced Wi-Fi-enabled mobile phone to send out to my daughter in Greece so that she can phone us more reasonably than via her UK SIM. I tweeted about my search five minutes ago and already have 20 or more helpful ideas.

And whereas I would never give my address or phone number out to the world at large, I am perfectly happy to share my Twitter address with all and sundry—it's @SawbonesHex, if you're remotely interested. I'll leave you to work out why I chose that particular pseudonym.

14th May 2011

There was jubilation all round at Adams Park on Saturday. Well, I say 'all round'; one curmudgeonly 'supporter' nearby did mutter. 'They'll be straight back down' and was firmly put in his place by the rest of us. There's always one, isn't there?

But despite doing it the hard way far too often, by conceding an early goal and then battling to a victory or draw, the Wanderers did a magnificent job of keeping at bay the several teams snapping at their heels over the last few nail-biting weeks of the season. They beat two very good teams in the last couple of fixtures, including doing the double over Bury, who finished second, to gain promotion by the slimmest possible point margin—one!

So huge congratulations to Gary Waddock and his entire team, on and off the pitch, to Nikki Bull, the best goalie in the division who was rightfully named the Player of the Season by both players and supporters and to Mr. Football himself the indefatigable legend that is Gareth Ainsworth.

With a certain degree of shamefacedness, I have to share with you a personal moment of high comedy. As the players did their lap of honour, the manager, Gary Waddock, leaped over the advertising boards, ran up the steps of the family stand and along the back row where I was standing with my wife and daughter. He manoeuvred past half the row and stopped when he got to me, and for a millisecond I confess I allowed myself to wonder why, at his moment of triumph, he wanted to share his pride and delight with me. Doh!!

Without looking at me, he interposed himself between me and the wall behind me, leaning over to where, sitting in the posh boxes, were what transpired to be an ecstatic group of his family and friends. He exchanged brief triumphal and well-deserved hugs and returned to the pitch.

My daughter said, 'You thought he was coming to see you, didn't you?'

I indignantly denied it at the time; why would Gary Waddock even know I existed, let alone where I sat? But I must admit to the hopefully human failing of allowing my surprise to lead me to wonder, for the briefest of brief moments, whether he might have been a closet *Doctor Who* fan, before I rejected the notion as preposterous.

Now I know how the *Who* fans feel in similar circumstances.

21st May 2011

I was saddened to learn this week of the death of former councillor and Marlow mayor, Jim Campbell, with whom I had the pleasure of serving until recently as a governor of one of our local schools. I knew him only in this capacity, but always tried to sit next to him if I could at meetings because I found him to be wise and insightful, as well as a thoroughly charming and delightful person.

He was one of those rare people who are happy in their own skin—an odd expression I know, but one that sums Jim up perfectly—an immensely likeable and warm man with the most attractive Scottish brogue and beguiling twinkle.

I would also like to wish Lesley Clarke well, now that she has stepped down as leader of Wycombe District Council, after nearly a decade in that post during a tough time in local politics. I have enormous respect for anyone prepared to surrender so much time to serving their community, and have no doubt whatsoever that the majority of them, Lesley included, do so for altruistic and idealistic reasons rather than for self-aggrandisement.

It is too easy for those who do nothing whatsoever for others to carp about those who do. I think it is partly because the notion of public service is increasingly alien to large sectors of the community that those who do still offer themselves are seldom widely acknowledged as doing the best they can for those who voted for them, according to their own political beliefs.

The often disgusting level of personal abuse that Cllr. Clarke has received in print and on websites (predominantly anonymously) from the conspiracy theorists and opponents of the stadium development goes way beyond civilised debate and criticism, and I hope it doesn't taint her memories of her time serving us. She should take comfort in the knowledge that her personal vote in her ward remained as strong as ever. And let's face it, no one stands as councillor for the money.

The Leader and Cabinet, whether we agree with what they do or not, are the ones who carry the enormous burden of responsibility for policy and decision-making on our behalf and take the inevitable flack, for a mere fraction of the financial recompense received by the professional chief executive of the council, who oversees the execution of those policies and remains largely unscathed.

28th May 2011

However you may plan ahead, if it's going to be one of those days, it is going to be one of those days.

Last Sunday I served as a marshal for the Wycombe Rotary Club's annual Pedal Push. Armed with instructions and a map, I duly drove off to the rural hinterland around Great Hampden, not (as will become apparent) an area with which I have more than a passing familiarity. I had blown up the map and brought only the section relevant to me, found my junction already adorned with a handy, yellow cyclist-friendly directional sign and settled down with my Sunday papers, issuing cheery greetings as cyclists began to speed by me. After half an hour, as I thanked one group for supporting Pedal Push, a rider shouted, 'We're not Pedal Push, we're ...' The rest of his words tailed off along with him. Ah!

Clearly, I am not a candidate for orienteer of the year. Further investigation led me to drive another couple of miles through leafy and winding lanes, until I found the junction I should have been sitting at, having passed another marshal, who told me that no one had been by yet—and that our cyclist-friendly directional signs were red! Nothing lost though, and I had even encouraged some other stalwart riders.

I spent four pleasant hours ducking the showers and encouraging the generous and mostly very fit riders who sailed cheerily past with only the occasional groan at the sight of yet another hill! This is High Wycombe, after all.

Having been told by our leader that I could stand down after the next few riders had passed, at the appointed time I packed up my folding chair and returned to my car, to find that listening to the Grand Prix while marshalling had not been wise. I had a flat battery. And no signal on my phone.

Were it not for the generosity of the lady to whose house I trudged for succour, who had both jump leads and the kindness to drive me back to my car, I might still be adorning that windy (in both senses of that word) roadside in Hampden. I shouldn't be allowed out, really.

The good news is that the lycra-clad efforts of all those generous cyclists raised over £4,000 for Scannappeal and Thames Valley & Chilterns Air Ambulance. Well done all.

3rd June 2011

I visited Amersham Hospital this week with a family member, whose appointment was for 9.15 a.m. The consultation was finished by 9.30, so the appointment system is working well, although at the beginning of the day one might reasonably expect that to be the case, I suppose. A prescription was written out that could only be filled at the hospital. The hospital pharmacy didn't open, however, until 10.00 a.m., which enabled us to sample the delights of the adjacent coffee bar for half an hour, although we hadn't planned to do that.

The car park at the hospital is a pre-pay car park; you have to estimate your stay and pay accordingly. Whilst I am far from being a conspiracy theorist usually, it did enter my mind that there was a synchronicity here that had the potential to produce additional revenue for the hospital. Lull the unwary into thinking that an hour of prepaid parking should be enough for an expected short appointment, and then construct systems that guaranteed a somewhat longer stay? 'Surely not', I hear you cry. And you're probably right too, for very good reason. The reason I am not usually a conspiracy theorist is precisely because I doubt the ability (more than the will) of most large organisations to plan so meticulously to part us from a little extra cash and get away with it. So, presumably this has simply not been thought through. In which case, may I make a suggestion on behalf of the patients?

Might it just not be a good idea to align the pharmacy opening times with the times that patients are being seen by doctors who might write out a prescription for them? There were several appointments in the department we were visiting before ours, and there was a queue of patients bearing prescriptions when we arrived at the pharmacy's locked doors.

And might it not be an idea to set up a parking system which allows car owners to pay in arrears for the time they have actually used, rather than have to estimate something which is by definition resistant to accurate estimation: how long one may have to wait to see a doctor in a hospital.

In the event, we arrived back at the car five minutes after the ticket had run out, and there was indeed a parking attendant walking in our direction as we got there. We just made it.

10th June 2011

I should give up hoping that we might gradually return to being a society where common sense prevailed in the face of the creeping defensive inertia that has paralysed our nation. But I can't. Each year I look for signs that the voice of the majority is being heard, but until the pettifogging, pusillanimous minority who cocoon us all in endless restrictions and regulations wake up and smell reality, we continue to be hogtied by their robotic urges. I say 'robotic' because it is as if we've programmed some bureaucratic robot to protect humans at all costs and they have taken the instruction so literally that we'll end up motionless in cotton-wool pods, being fed from sterile tubes.

In the last month, the following have been reported. A woman who reported a stray dog in her garden was sent a form to fill days later and a warden arrived two weeks after that. A stationmaster in Lymington with 27 years' service spotted a supermarket trolley on the track. He asked the signalman to turn off the power to the track and went down in his protective gear to remove it. The power had not been turned off; he was sacked.

A South London school has banned ALL physical contact between children. Residents in Surrey have been warned by police that they could be sued by burglars injured by the installation of wire mesh to protect their garden sheds.

And tipping the balance even further into Lala Land, a professor of Animal Ethics has recommended that we abandon the use of the word 'pet' in favour of 'companion animals' and substitute 'free-roaming' for 'wild', a word that has 'unpleasant connotations'.

Not only do these people not read my column, but they don't read the expressions on the faces of the 99.99% of the population who no longer think it's a joke to be constrained by the whims of the frankly potty.

Go after the benefit cheats, the illegal clampers, the gangs of teenage yobs with knives, the drug dealers and the lowlife thugs who prey on the elderly and vulnerable by defrauding them as fake plumbers, builders, drive layers and gas men.

Leave the rest of us alone to climb trees, protect our properties, play sport, enjoy our pets and follow our professions without constant meddling from the rule-bound.

Join me in saying 'Why', over and over again until they wake up.

17th June 2011

The Italians haven't tried to sell off the Coliseum or La Scala for redevelopment, nor the Egyptians the pyramids, nor the Greeks the Parthenon. Covent Garden and the Theatres in Drury Lane and Shaftesbury Avenue are left alone, so why on earth are we allowing the BBC to sell the BBC Television Centre for development, even as a 'cultural quarter'? Is the iconic studio site that produced almost every great television programme aired in half a century to be sacrificed on the altar of the great god-regionalisation? It seems so. Gradually, programmes that have been produced there for decades have been hived off until the once great and vibrant building now languishes half empty. I recorded all my *Doctor Who* episodes there. Now, I am very fond of Cardiff. My mother lived there for the last thirty years of her life. But I am told that the studios in Cardiff, where *Doctor Who* is now made, do not have the same facilities as those in London. The soundproofing is markedly inferior and production stops when a plane flies over or when there is heavy rain. Dressing rooms are often temporary structures in the car park and there is a fraction of the space available. The facilities in Shepherds Bush are demonstrably superior, but anxiety about funding generated a nod to political correctness, and there was a commitment to share the output of our national broadcaster around the regions; as a result, changes are being shoehorned into the organisation, seemingly arbitrarily. The great majority of those who work in television live around London, because that's where the work was. Employees and performers now have to move or lose their jobs.

Can you imagine the national broadcasters based in California and New York being told that they had to make their programmes in Bismark, Montgomery or Topeka? No? Nor can I! To turn the Television Centre into a housing development or multi-use environment is rank philistinism. The complex may lack the antiquity of the Coliseum or the Parthenon, having been built in 1950, but they only survived because successive generations thought them worth keeping, even after their original use was discontinued. Could we not accord the same courtesy to the world's first purpose-built centre for television production, which gave us *Fawlty Towers, Monty Python, Doctor Who, The Forsyte Saga, War and Peace, Blue Peter,* and *Top of the Pops?*

24th June 2011

After three mobile phones rang during a concert that he was conducting, Sir Peter Maxwell Davies, the Master of the Queen's Music, recently suggested that people who use mobile phones during classical concerts should be fined. He likened them to 'artistic terrorists.' And although it would sadly be hard to police to administer such a system, one does have a certain sympathy with him. I have been on stage on several occasions when a mobile phone has gone off, although it was only on one of those occasions that the owner of the phone got up and walked out while conducting a conversation on the wretched thing—a conversation that started with the words, 'Oh hello – look, I'm in a theatre at the moment the reception isn't very good. Hold on for a second while I find better reception,' as he left the auditorium. I was talking at the time so his words were relayed to me afterwards by another actor on the stage.

I have also been in the audience while people have been texting repeatedly during a show. While this doesn't have the noise distraction of an actual conversation, nonetheless the light pollution of several screens between oneself and the stage doesn't help in the process of involving oneself in the story the actors are telling us.

I have heard tales of performers fighting back and even frogmarching people and their wretched phones out of the building, but whatever temporary satisfaction that may give performers and audience alike, it does interrupt the flow of the performance somewhat.

Clearly, there are enough people who lack the decency, common sense and desire to respect the probable wishes of those around them to suggest that self-policing isn't working. Most theatres now have announcements requesting that phones be turned off and most people oblige. But there will always be those whose lives are so very important that they leave their phones on, maybe turning the volume down and leaving them on vibrate which is still audible for several rows in each direction.

They are the same people who eat and rustle their way through films, or who conduct loud phone conversations on trains. Maybe we could refit venues with chairs like the one used by Graham Norton in his chat show and propel the offenders into the basement where a suitable new resting place for their mobile can be found. Any suggestions?

1st July 2011

I am not sure whether radio programmes have phone-ins (phones-in?) in order to satisfy their public service obligations or to demonstrate once for all that the majority of people should not be allowed the vote, although it would appear that more people are prepared to rush to the telephone with their half thought-out takes on some current topic than are ready to amble down to a school/village hall in order to participate in what we like to call democracy. I am a fan of spoken-word radio, but would much rather listen to experts in their respective fields discussing current issues, whether I agree with them or not, than hear the random prejudices of people who seemingly have time to hang on for half an hour, only to be cut off for the road report when they're halfway through their stuttering 'point', peppered with 'Y'know what I'm saying?', 'Well this is it.' and 'As I was saying to your researcher ...'

Sadly, people who do have fully fledged joined-up-thinking points to make also get cut off mid-sentence, because enough time is never allocated to any subject to allow sensible discussion.

As I drove to Lincoln yesterday to start rehearsals for my next play, the news came through of the two police dogs that died after being locked in their handler's car in the heat. Clearly, a very sad incident that serves to remind us all that heat such as we experienced this week is a potential killer for animals in non-ventilated spaces.

This topic was being discussed when an imperious woman with a cut-glass accent called in to ask what all the fuss was about for heaven's sake and complain that we cared more as a nation about animals than we do about children. Sigh! Yes, that old non-argument—the absurd one that suggests that anyone who cares about an injured animal would, for that reason alone, not care about an injured child.

Interestingly, the point is instantly disproved by the fact that you don't get the alleged 'bunny-huggers' complaining to the media about children being disproportionately protected at the expense of animals.

Could that be because people who care about animals are likely to be less selfish than those who do not, and can extend sympathy in every direction, not just to their own species?

Anyway—be careful in the heat and enjoy it while it lasts.

8ᵗʰ July 2011

Last year a greyhound called Susie decided that my family could offer sufficiently comfortable accommodation and cater to her needs to an appropriately high standard as to persuade her to leave her comfortable quarters at The Stokenchurch Dog Rescue Centre and take up residence in Baker Towers. It has proved an excellent arrangement.

We were impressed by the degree of checking carried out by the excellent (mainly volunteer) workforce at the centre and happy that we passed muster. Susie is an ex-racing dog who contrived three sixth positions in her three races, we discovered via research based on her ear markings, and was then cast adrift and found wandering the highways of Bucks. She has integrated with our rather strange poodle/Jack Russell cross well, in the sense that she doesn't interfere with the latter's sole raison d'être—chasing anything spherical thrown by obliging humans. Susie has adjusted to the fact that we have cats, rabbits, hens, goats and horses, and vice versa.

The cats now walk between her legs and rub round them. There are still folk out there who react as if a black greyhound is the spawn of Satan and will eviscerate and dance on the remains of their canine charges, but that has to be their problem, I'm afraid, as in the main our Susie has won over the local dog walkers, as well as our family of animals.

And like our other dog, she views my wife as the Pied Piper, Easter Bunny and Mother Christmas all rolled into one. Regular feeding and long walks—and simply being there—work every time.

Stokenchurch Dog Rescue does a brilliant job caring for stray and rejected animals and (very importantly) responsible rehoming. They are holding their Summer Fair on Saturday 16th July from midday to 4pm and I was hoping to be there, as Patron of the charity (ahem!), to help out with their Auction of Promises. But, alas, I cannot, as it is the production weekend of my new play, which starts touring the following week. But I would urge anyone who can to pop in to the kennels in Stokenchurch next weekend and see what wonderful work this local charity does for 'man's best friend', whilst enjoying all that a Summer Fair (not 'Fayre', thank goodness!) has to offer and also maybe win one of the great prizes that have been donated.

15th July 2011

This week the national newspapers have been contorting themselves to varying degrees in an attempt to put as much distance between themselves and the alleged practices of the late and (by me) unlamented *News of the World*. However, I suspect that there is a lot of 'tidying up' going on in and around Fleet Street. Many computers will probably have a little more space on their hard drives and filing cabinets and drawers will be a little emptier.

I was on the receiving end of the *News of the World*'s creative journalistic practices back in the 1970s when I was playing a high-profile character on television. Having declined an interview with them for obvious reasons, I foolishly fell for the 'Ah, we have a new editor who wants to concentrate more on the creative arts and get away from our previous more sensational reputation.'

They sent a senior female reporter to speak to me, a respectable middle-aged lady, who interviewed me for half an hour about the series I was doing—*The Brothers*. She then tucked her notebook in her pocket and, as I escorted her out of the BBC, started talking about her teenage daughter, who had moved in with her boyfriend, whom she had only known for a few weeks. I tried to explain to her (talk about naïve!) that young people were more liberated in their relationships and advised not to push her daughter away. 'Well, would you sleep with a girl you'd only known a few weeks?'

'Who knows? Anything is possible.'

The subsequent article spoke almost exclusively about 'Baker' bragging of his many conquests of girls he barely knew.

Compared with what has been going on recently, this is very mild stuff, but served to make me aware of the nature of that particular beast.

My depiction as callous stud was probably written before the interview took place. By agreeing to meet her, it was her word against mine.

It is therefore a delight to be working for a local newspaper with a mission to report the news, not make it, and whose journalistic campaigns are mounted with the support and at the instigation of the people who live in the area the paper serves, not a billionaire owner on a yacht in the Bahamas.

It will be interesting to see how much more corruption surfaces as more stones are overturned.

22nd July 2011

A few weeks ago my daughter damaged the exhaust of her car on a local road, as a result of significant subsidence to one side of the road that meant the crown of the single-track road is at a height that equates roughly to the under-car clearance of most small cars. The road even bears the evidence of other sumps and chassis that have been gradually removing the upper surface of the tarmac, hopefully less expensively.

I reported this incident to the highways authority with the prime intention of ensuring that other motorists don't suffer the same expensive damage to their vehicles. To date nothing has been done, except that I have received a lengthy form offering us the opportunity to claim against Bucks County Council's insurance.

It makes it very clear that it is very unlikely my daughter would succeed, but we can have a go if we like. The legal defensive imperative rules, as always. My knowledge of the law is sufficient to tell me that this is unlikely to be a successful claim unless we have evidence that BCC already knew of the damaged road, and I suspect they are not likely to volunteer that information.

But you only have to drive around a few miles of local roads to realise why nothing has been done yet. Any driver will know how many tyre, wheel and suspension threatening potholes there are on the roads of Buckinghamshire at the moment.

Many of the holes are even surrounded by the circles of yellow paint that indicate awareness, at least, of the need for action. But despite recent sporadic promises of a rolling programme of road repairs, there doesn't seem to be an awful lot of action, to be frank.

I do not recall, in the first thirty or forty years since I

started driving a car, ever having to pay as much attention to the conditions of the road surface in order to avoid damaging my vehicle as I do now. And, of course, we should all be paying attention to what is on and around the road while we are driving rather than be distracted by the need to constantly monitor the condition of its surface.

The answer that there is more traffic today doesn't wash either, as there are therefore more motorists contributing to the exchequer via fuel taxes and all the other indirect taxation on the motorist.

29th July 2011

Well, it seems the Booker Prize has not gone to Wycombe this year. I may be in a vilified minority of those who have been vociferous on the subject, but I thought it was an exciting project, worth exploring for its potential ultimate benefit to the community at large and not just the football club of which I am a season ticket holder. I fully accept that there were many people who felt differently on the subject of the stadium for a variety of reasons, from the cost to the public purse to fear of the effects of such a large development on green belt land near their homes. I live near enough to have been moderately affected by the development, but took the view that it would be a huge asset to future generations. I hope that the decision of the new WDC cabinet will not be the source of community regret a decade from now.

And the housing development associated with the stadium? New houses will be built in large numbers in the near future somewhere in the area and undoubtedly the people living close by will complain. We all want our little bit of England to stay the way that we like and that suits us. Of course we do. But the population is still growing. More homes are needed and more facilities for the people who live in them.

A new sports facility that could provide a sustainable stadium share for the Wycombe Wanderers and Wasps, enabling the future stability of both clubs at the same time as offering modern facilities for the use of the whole community, seems to me a laudable dream for a football club owner to have. And when did the notion of a risk-taking entrepreneur making a profit become a justifiable subject for abuse? Characterising those who have the entrepreneurial skills and drive to bring exciting projects to fruition as merely money-grabbing opportunists is too easy and usually, I would suggest, simply wrong. Most multi-millionaires would stop when they made their first couple of million if that were the case.

It is the drive to innovate, to make a difference, that characterises most wealthy and successful entrepreneurs. I would certainly jack it in after the first million and enjoy the things that wealth can buy. That is one of the many reasons why I will never become a millionaire.

5th August 2011

It's the first week in August, and football is returning to Adams Park on Saturday, when Scunthorpe kick off the Wanderers' first home match in their new season back in League 1.

I am experiencing a mixture of emotions. Because our summer began and stopped in April and has only just poked its shy nose around the door again this last week, the onset of the football season brings with it an inescapable feeling of a headlong rush into autumn before we've had enough time to start complaining properly about the heat. In an ideally constructed seasonal world, we would have been sated with barbecues, Pimms and hot summer evenings by now and looking forward to the post-harvest easing into the cooler autumnal weather that comes with the football season.

I know of at least one person, the wife of a good friend, who believes so strongly that football really shouldn't start until September that she refuses to go until then. So, as a football fan, I can't wait to lock horns with my friends again in our Fantasy Football League, which occupied more of my time than it really should last year (and to being higher than third this year!).

I can't wait to see what the new Blues team is like after the many interesting-looking signings of the summer. I look forward to catching up with the usual suspects who sit around us in Adams Park on a fortnightly basis, when I am not prevented from being there by a matinee somewhere. It is quite exciting and a time when hope is irrationally allowed to override caution, and small dreams of further advancement up the League are indulged in. But at the same time, one cannot help but be aware that another summer is coming to an end and the days are getting shorter again.

I am currently working in the theatre and touring the country, so I enter the stage door in daylight and leave in darkness, unaware, at the moment, when that transition takes place until each Sunday when I do not work. But my seasonal 'disaffective' disorder aside (and all seasons do actually have their unique charms), the prospect of watching our local team demonstrating their fitness to be in League 1 and inspiring dreams of loftier climes one day is one that I eagerly anticipate. So bring it on Gary, Gareth and boys.

12th August 2011

There was a heartening story from Tehran this week. Seven years ago, an Iranian woman, Ameneh Bahrami, declined to accept a proposal of marriage from Majid Movahedi. His response was to throw acid in her face, so that no other man would have her if he could not. She is now severely disfigured and has lost her sight. Under Iranian law, she was entitled to demand retribution in kind. Last week, Mohavedi was moments away from that retribution being carried out by the dripping of acid into his own eyes.

However, at the very last moment, Ameneh, who is clearly a remarkable woman, relented. She pardoned her attacker, when many who had suffered as appallingly as she must have done for a prolonged period of time might well have not been as forgiving. She explained her change of heart later, saying, 'I did it for my country, seeing that all the other countries were looking to see what we would do.'

A salutary example to all of us. To paraphrase Rabbie Burns, the gift of seeing ourselves as others see us is one that might easily and swiftly lead to a rethinking of many practices around the world that most other cultures find repellent. And we have no cause for smugness in the UK, either.

I remember several years ago listening to *From our Own Correspondent* on Radio 4. A rebel tribesman in Afghanistan, after threatening to kill a car full of journalists, on discovering that they were from the BBC, invited them to his home where he insisted, under his code of hospitality, that they share his very meagre supply of food and drink.

During their conversation, he asked if it were true, as he had heard, that when our parents are too old and feeble to care for themselves we send them away into institutions where strangers care for them. On hearing that it was true, he was appalled, saying 'And you in the West call *us* uncivilised?' Hard though it sometimes is, we do need to try to understand that other cultures are different; and different does not always equate with wrong or evil.

That is why when I visit other countries I always try to conform to the customs of that country, whether or not at first glance they seem sensible or not. I will not, for instance, 'jaywalk' in Queensland again.

19th August 2011

There was an awful lot more going on last week in our inner cities than can be explained or understood completely in a week's worth of phone-ins, political posturing or articles like this one. But, just because the problem is complex, it doesn't mean that we can't draw one or two small conclusions about things that haven't helped people who, for whatever reason, feel disassociated from society to see that rampant and random pillaging is not the best way to express themselves.

We have created a society where the very young learn that they can pretty much do what they like without fear of instant (or indeed any) retribution because parents, teachers and adults in public places are afraid to challenge any kind of antisocial behaviour for fear of what will happen to them.

Whether it's the ten-year-old who knows his rights and

your legal position if you challenge him, or the legally defensive mindset (that successive governments have done nothing to dismantle despite all pre-election promises) that means a savvy school child can get a teacher off his back by accusing him or her of grabbing, shoving, threatening—even shouting. The teacher will then be suspended for months while investigations proceed at a funereal pace.

I know it's an outmoded cliché, but the one time I ever complained to my father about a teacher giving me a whack, I got more of the same from my father. But is the new formula, whereby the parents come steaming in to schools threatening teachers who have dared to stand up to their undisciplined offspring, an improvement?

Every single day I see parents with children behaving appallingly in all areas of life. They halfheartedly tell them to 'stop it' and then when they continue to offend, shrug helplessly and take no further action, leaving the children with the inescapable message that adults don't mean what they say and don't care much what they do. Great lesson learned for a pre-school child. What chance do the teachers then have?

But, at least, this week we have seen the value of public CCTV systems. How many of the looters and arsonists would have been caught without the wide publication of their images in the media, I wonder? If police numbers really are to be so drastically reduced despite the clearest evidence to the contrary, then thank goodness for CCTV.

26th August 2011

Are lie detectors available commercially, I wonder?

I confess to a fondness for gadgets. Fashionable clothes, cars, even holidays leave me largely unmoved, but tell me that there is a new 3 or 4D television around and my mind immediately computes the current demands on the domestic budget to see if it might be within my grasp.

Show me the latest state of the art mobile phone with the processing power of a dwarf star and I covet it uncontrollably. Yes, I know it's odd that cars don't figure on my list, but basically they are just an essential (at least where I live) that is embellished with a whole host of non-essentials that are really the gadgets—the sat-nav, the CD player/radio, the rear-facing camera that stops you from demolishing the back wall of the garage. And no, I don't have one of those, at least partly because we do not have a garage, although there are some public car parks where such a gadget would obviate the necessity to get out and check where my invisible boot really does end.

A neighbour showed me some pictures on his iPad recently, and all I saw was not the photographs but the sleek means by which he was showing them to me. But, struggle as I may, I cannot justify acquiring one when there are so many other, more mundane artefacts that would enhance the life of the population of Baker Towers.

I did succumb to a small wireless CCTV system a couple of years ago, principally so that we could keep on eye on the assorted quadrupeds housed in the outbuildings around our house. That one got approval from my wife, as she was able to reassure herself that Holly the mare, Perky and Tigger the Shetland ponies and our three goats were still alive/asleep, lying down/standing up or eating/not eating, as appropriate.

And lie detectors? Recently, I was discussing an incident from our shared theatrical past with a good friend and colleague. My recollection differed substantially from his. One of us is clearly misremembering and I wondered if a lie detector could resolve the conflict. Possibly not, perhaps, as we both think we are telling the truth. So what chance do historians have when all they have to rely on are contemporary sources? What credence can we then attach to what they write? And are autobiographies likely to be any more accurate?

2nd September 2011

I am considering offering my services as a freelance product designer and marketing advisor. To establish my credentials for this post, I shall give a piece of free advice to the manufacturers of electrical goods generally. I suspect that, like me, you have had occasion to need service or parts for something technological in your home. It is never a simple matter of looking at the front of the thing.

My current requirement is very simple—a pair of plastic clips for the interior sliding tray in our dishwasher, without which the plate rack collapses during the washing process and with it all the plates. The original clips have broken. In order to convince the manufacturers to send me these small—but I suspect probably disproportionately expensive—items, they very reasonably require me to tell them the model number of the dishwasher.

Where they were less reasonable was in the design and manufacture of the wretched thing. It is a built in dishwasher, and having checked all the accessible surfaces, external and internal, there is no indication whatsoever of anything other than the name of the company that manufactured it. That is emblazoned across the front. Never miss an opportunity to advertise, they say. But no model, registration number, type? Nothing.

So the information that I, the consumer, now need is nowhere to be found unless, I presume, I get my toolbox out and undo all the retaining brackets and haul the thing out to scrutinise its back, whilst straining mine. Will the German manufacturer pay my osteopath for the remedial work required if I do that? I suspect not.

Had I been involved in the design stage of this very efficient piece of white goods, it might just have occurred to me that vital information that may be needed in the future should perhaps appear on the front of something that is designed to be built in, or inside the door or anywhere that is visible without hauling the thing out into the room.

We had exactly the same problem with an oven earlier in the year. The name of the manufacturer was writ large on the front; the model number was inside the door, blackened and baked by the after-effects of several years of high-temperature cooking. The vigorous treatment required to clean it also removed the information I needed. In the end I emailed a photograph of the part I needed to the manufacturer.

9th September 2011

I was following a Megabus that was on its way to Cardiff on Sunday and, as we crawled lethargically onward out of London, my eye was drawn to the large advert on the back tempting us to use their service—'Fares from £1' in mammoth letters. Lower down, in much smaller type, were the words 'plus 50p booking fee.' Why? Why not charge £1.50 and not run the risk of the disappointment and irritation, however small, that the sudden discovery of a 50% hike in price might bring? Yes, it's only 50p, but the 'onlyness' works both ways. 'Tickets from £1.50' hardly sounds a deal-breaking price-too-high, so why not start with the actual honest price and then there's no need to sneak in little additional increases.

And where did this habit of springing unheralded booking and admin fees on us come from? It is particularly prevalent in the theatre now. They advertise tickets at, say, £30, and when you turn up at the box office they slap a booking fee and sometimes even an administration fee on top.

Imagine going into a clothes shop, having seen an item in the window priced at £30, to find you are then charged an additional fee for the privilege of buying it. For that is in effect what some theatres are doing. If the ticket prices are not sufficient to pay the box office staff for the few seconds it takes them to take your money, then put the ticket prices up.

There is no consistency, either. Some places charge different add-on fees for phone bookings, online bookings, credit card bookings and even cash bookings. Then there are the ticket agencies who sell you a ticket for £50 and when you collect it, it has £40 written on it. Why anyone uses ticket agencies for simple bookings of theatre tickets, when all theatres have their own box offices, defeats me.

Some airlines, too, lure customers looking for a bargain to book by advertising seemingly lower prices than their competitors, only to gradually increase the actual price the passenger pays by a variety of add-ons for checked-in luggage, hand baggage, food and drink. It becomes impossible to budget sensibly without spending hours researching options and permutations. 'Oh, you want a seat too? And air? Will you be using the walkway to the plane, sir? In that case, there will be a surcharge of …'

16th September 2011

When I became an actor, it was not for the fame, the girls or the money—the unrealistic holy grail of all those *X Factor* wannabes. It was because I wanted to act. I had found something that I could do and hopefully do well enough to earn a living, and I gave it my best shot. I was lucky and am still earning a reasonable living from doing a job that is predominantly enjoyable and rewarding.

I had never anticipated as a possibility, let alone longed for, being immortalised as a poseable figure on sale in the shops. When I played Doctor Who in the 80s, there was some merchandise around, but the BBC was not as commercially-minded as it has been obliged to become lately in order to survive. In fact, there was almost an air of corporate disdain at the Beeb for anything that smacked of common commercialism. Now, however, the institution has realised what a wonderful commodity it has in *Doctor Who*, and they are emulating the football clubs who change kit every few weeks to maximise fan income. There is not just one small and very well made figure of yours truly, but five now. Heaven knows how many David Tennant and Matt Smith versions there are!

And yes, it is very weird to see a young child approaching me at a fan event clutching a mini-me for me to autograph (with difficulty, it has to be said, given the contours!). The merchandising department have been kind enough to let me have a figure of each of the 'Classic' Doctors (I don't get the really desirable new guys). They stand in various tableaux on a shelf in our downstairs loo. My daughters delight in creating varying scenarios that usually glorify my incarnation at the expense of the other doctors. They're loyal, my girls! Tom's Doctor for some reason, has a removable head (a bit like Worzel Gummidge—should have been Jon Pertwee?)

The other day I was treated to the beguiling vision of Old

Sixie (my Doctor) holding up Tom's head like a futuristic Perseus holding the Gorgon's head aloft, with his prostrate decapitated form at my feet and Peter Davison and Sylvester McCoy grovelling before the conquering hero.

It's quite odd to think that one day, when I am long gone, I might have some value as an antique figure 'in original mint packaging'.

23rd September 2011

I had been driving some time when yellow lines, meters and controlled street parking signalled the end the halcyon days of the free for all 'park where you can' car culture. Later generations are perhaps less surprised when the enforcement of parking restrictions is timed to the second.

Last week my theatre tour took me to Worthing, a venue I had not visited for two decades. Sadly it is rare that one revisits a place to find it greatly improved. This was no exception. Vanishing theatre subsidies from cash-deprived councils and audiences feeling the financial pinch have left their mark on the theatre, and the town too appeared less loved than I had remembered from previous visits.

I arrived at 5.53 p.m. and saw that street parking charges stopped at 6.00. I had no change, so took my bags into the theatre to cadge the 20p I needed off a colleague. Returning at 5.57, I found two meter enforcers attaching the £50 (£25 if paid in 14 days) penalty ticket to my windscreen. The want of 20p had cost me £25.

In the words of the Daleks, (and by comparison the plunger-wielding aliens seemed a friendlier option at that moment) 'Resistance is useless.' I later learned that the streets are full of parking attendants in the minutes before six. Fertile ground, obviously. I confess to expressing my sadness that they considered the dying seconds of the charging period as an opportunity for shooting fish in barrels, but am not sure why I bothered. They're used to it and presumably go round in twos for sound practical reasons of self-protection.

During the week I learned that the principal beneficiaries

of Worthing Council's decision to use contractors to enforce their parking regulations are the out-of-town superstores and shopping centres that increasing numbers of shoppers frequent, and that the town centre shops are as a result struggling. That, I guess, would explain the tumbleweed I saw blowing down the high street. If town centre visitors fall foul of such inflexible enforcement attitudes within seconds of arriving in a town, what impression does it leave?

Yes, I know the law is the law and I got what I deserved, but the other side of that coin is that Worthing will reap the eddies of the whirlwind when no one wants to go there.

Somewhere between rigid enforcement and a free for all lies a happy medium.

30th September 2011

There are several words that I find alarming or that flag up a warning about the user. Some are based on nothing but prejudice and personal history, but others have a sounder basis for my antipathy.

For instance, my resistance to the words 'nourishing' and 'refreshing' are more about former uses of those words and the situations in which they were used than any logical reason for finding them twitch-inducing. They both bring memories that are not to do with 'yummy' or 'tasty', for instance. My knee-jerk reaction to actors who pepper their conversations about their 'craft' with descriptions of the 'journey' is to clench whatever I have about me that is clenchable and hope that no one thinks I am with them.

It may be that my approach to playing a part is identical to theirs, but I am of the old school perhaps and think we should keep our 'journey' to ourselves—not just to preserve some of the mystique that used to exist about the acting profession but to lessen the widespread preconception of actors as self-indulgent narcissists. To hear someone who has just entertained me go on about the emotional investment and agonised creative journey that led to that performance leaves me, and I suspect many more, cold. It also feeds into the notion of acting as self-therapy, which for a professional is frankly naff.

And don't get me started on the notion of giving 110 per cent. Yes, we know what you think you mean, but it's meaningless and sloppy!

Coming from a different angle, there is the use of 'targets' for everything now, irrespective of whether the activity concerned is sensibly susceptible of having a target ascribed to it. Education in particular is awash with 'targets' and their abundant offspring SATS and League Tables. So much time that could be spent teaching or preparing to teach is devoted to formalising what most good teachers have been doing perfectly well for years by making them fill in endless forms and grids with a mind-numbing battery of ever changing acronyms attached to them. Nobody has convinced me yet that the desire to teach better and have students learn better is helped by the ever increasing battery of targets ascribed to each child and each teacher.

I am only grateful that theatres haven't given 'louder, funnier and faster' targets to actors.

I shouldn't have said that, should I?

7th October 2011

My paternal grandfather died when my dad was just four years old. Had he lived longer, he may well have taken my father to see their local football team play, and team loyalties being tribal (particularly back then), that team would have become my team.

This would have meant that today I would probably be a Colchester United fan, as my father was brought up not far from the town whose team is the long-term rival of, and provides the far-from-'local' derby match for, Wycombe Wanderers. There's a thought, now. But, perhaps because my father had no real male influence while he was growing up, he had no interest in sport whatsoever. As a result, my interest only surfaced when I went to secondary school.

My primary school years were spent in Rochdale, so

again, if my father had been football-orientated, I suppose the Wanderers' defeat at Spotland on Saturday might have been a reason for exultation rather than the slump of disappointment I suffered on Saturday evening as I came off stage to get the footie results after my matinee in Basingstoke.

I went to secondary school in Manchester, so along with my contemporaries I supported and went to Manchester United, and that's when my love of football was born.

Years later, in the days of Lawrie Sanchez and Brownie and Rhino, a friend took me to see Wycombe Wanderers play in Reading (yes, that long ago!) and my support of my local team began.

Supporting a local team is much more satisfying (as well as less expensive!) than supporting a Premiership team. The lows are counterbalanced by highs that the supporters of Premiership highfliers never experience. Man United and Chelsea fans expect to win and therefore never, or rarely, experience the wonderful high of the truly unexpected victory. When the Blues triumphed over Sheffield United a week ago, we were all a thousand feet in the air above Adams Park. Our lows are there too, but not as low possibly as, say, the Arsenal supporters are currently, because they expect and have had years of success.

Wanderers' supporters dare to hope; sometimes, the hope may get overinflated perhaps, but occasionally a ram does bring down a million-kilowatt dam, and we all want to be there when it does. For many Premiership fans it's just 'more of the same'—for us, each day is a new day.

21st October 2011

The reason that websites like Compare the Muntjac.com, Go Quite Spare, U-twitch etc. are so successful is because the Insurance and Utility providers have constructed tariffs that defy comprehension by anyone outside their industries, apart perhaps from the wonderful Martin Lewis, who fights a lone battle against the baffle 'em and rip 'em off culture.

If he has done nothing else to wring a cheer from all

sectors of the population, then David Cameron's promise to work to create an energy market that is 'trusted, simple and transparent' might do it. Let's hope it's more than just words.

Last time I tried to decipher the tariffs for electricity, I retired hurt and finally changed almost randomly to one that seemed better to my befuddled brain, whilst fondly remembering the days before choice, when power was one simple comprehensible price.

The great deity Choice hasn't worked always in the way that it was intended, i.e. to bring prices down. At its simplest form, just look at prices in supermarkets, where they label similar adjacent products at cost per 100 grams and cost per kilo in an attempt to befuddle the shopper. Energy providers offer tariffs that are capable of true comparison only if you spend an hour with a mathematician analysing the implications in relation to your past bills and consumption. The days of x shillings a pound or y pence a therm are long gone, alas. And small print bedevils all deals. They never put the good stuff in small print, do they?

Today, I spent an hour renewing my car insurance, which wouldn't have been too bad had I not spent an hour doing precisely that on Friday last. Having had a letter confirming the renewal at price A yesterday, I received another offering me a renewal at price A minus two hundred pounds today. When I phoned to query this, I was told I had no insurance at all.

Having checked the computer, they apologised, said yes I had renewed it but the computer had somehow failed to register that fact (entirely their fault—sorry) and I would have to start all over again. In the event, after grumbling mightily, I saved another hundred pounds. Why that price wasn't available in the first place is a mystery. But I had to pay in full again and wait for a refund of the first higher premium.

Go Quite Spare is right.

28th October 2011

This week, my wife spotted a blackboard outside a pub bearing the words 'Sunday Lunches available'. A simple enough message but, as she remarked to me, one that could be construed as suggesting that there were other things on the menu that were much more the ticket, but if you really insisted, you could have Sunday lunch.

It's a bit like when a broadcaster realises they have mentioned a product and therefore feels the need to add 'other providers are available' just to cover themselves. As far as inducements go, it was a bit halfhearted and did tempt us to jam on the brakes and nip in to book a table for the following Sunday.

Sometimes, people responsible for giving out information to the public just don't give the wording enough thought. And I am not just talking about the variants on the plurals of potato and tomato, beloved of greengrocers nationwide.

For instance, I recently saw a single urinal with a sign attached above it advising the user that the water was not suitable for drinking. You don't say?

This, of course, is another example of signs erected for legally defensive reasons so that the very stupid can't claim not to know that leaning over the wall on the promenade might lead to a rapid descent into the sea below. Other examples of the idiots leading the idiots include 'Caution: water on road during rain', 'May cause drowsiness'—on a bottle of sleeping tablets, 'Indoor or outdoor use only' on Christmas lights, and 'Pedestrians please pass either side' on a bollard in Oxford Street.

Whereas the publican and the 'available lunch' were possibly written quickly, all those other signs were discussed, planned, approved, manufactured and installed. Presumably no one with sufficient clout to suggest a rethink was involved at any stage after the original instructions were issued, so we are advised that a birthday card for a one-year-old is not suitable for children aged 36 months or less, that a microwave oven is not suitable for drying pets, that potty putty should not be used as earplugs, that children should be removed from pushchairs before they are folded up and that a TV remote is not dishwasher-safe. My favourite was on a butcher's knife—'Do not use in children.' A translation issue there, I think.

4th November 2011

You would never believe that we, as a nation, are supposed to be tightening our belts in order to get the economy back on its feet, if you were visiting any of our supermarkets in the last week or two. The amount of Halloween merchandise on display has been mind-boggling; and you can be pretty sure that the canny buyers employed by those organisations would not have stocked up with all that garish, ghoulish tat if they didn't believe that they could shift it and make a substantial profit in doing so. It doesn't seem to tie in with the gloom and doom we are hearing on radio phone-ins about the lack of money out there for the basic necessities of life.

The whole Halloween thing is an artificial construct, as we all know. Yes, it may have started here back in the mists of time, before it was imported back again from the USA after having been completely forgotten in the UK for generations. But its revival a few years ago was generated for purely commercial reasons and at a time of year when we already have an existing 'fun' event in the Gunpowder Plot, the failure of which is celebrated a mere five days later.

I suppose the very reasonable Health and Safety concerns about the sale and use of fireworks have diminished the appeal of small private bonfire parties on Guy Fawkes' night to the extent that the whole Halloween thing has gradually been allowed to supplant it.

The range of available merchandise for Halloween has greater potential too, which serves to make it much more attractive to the retailers. So move over nasty, dangerous fireworks and naked flames to make room for the marginally less worrying option of children roaming the streets, wearing scary masks and knocking on doors in the dark, demanding treats with threats of reprisals if their hunger is not satisfied. Yes, it's all basically just harmless fun, but the supermarket I visited in Somerset last week had a staggering four long aisles devoted to it.

But I am not alone in being concerned. Some local authority nurseries have been advised to give witches pink rather than black hats and conversely dress fairies in dark colours to avoid negative associations being attached to black, which might encourage racism. Tell that to the All Blacks! Well done, New Zealand, by the way.

11th November 2011

I don't envy the young people entering the world of employment that our generation has created for them. When I left drama school, work was by no means guaranteed, but we all knew that if the notoriously fickle entertainment industry couldn't offer us work, there were plenty of other short-term employment opportunities to tide us over to pay the rent.

During my early years as an actor, I worked at various times as a hardware shop assistant, low loader driver, taxi driver, opinion pollster, shirt seller, house painter and cleaner. My competence in those roles was varied, which was reflected in the amount of time I was allowed to continue doing some of them. But without the opportunity to earn between acting jobs, I may well have not been able to continue in that profession.

Now, there is so much competition for every job that an actor 'filling in' would not be a very attractive prospect for most employers. There are too many people chasing long term, full-time work. As a result, more and more young people are still living with their parents long after my generation had left home, usually for rented accommodation for a few years before comparatively easily getting their first mortgage. Today, even people on good salaries need to raise such a large percentage of the purchase price of even the most modest home as a deposit that the prospect of them becoming homeowners is receding way beyond the age we were able to do it.

Selfishly, I am not unhappy that my four daughters are still in residence and I don't have to deal with the empty nest syndrome. It is another sign of the age in which we live, but my relationship with my children is a lot less constrained than mine was with my parents. There were many areas of my life that I chose not to share with my widowed mother; but there are fewer fundamental no-go areas these days, which serves to make sharing a house with young adults less stressful.

It is only for their sake that I worry about the employment and financial future they face.

I find myself having some sympathy therefore with the young people who have chosen to confront the way capitalism has shaped their world by occupying the steps of St. Paul's. Whether it will change anything is another matter.

18th November 2011

I spent most of last week working on a television programme with a group of people I hadn't met before. Among their number were a young male and a young female in their mid-twenties who spent more time gazing intently down at their mobile phones than they did interacting with the rest of us. I must confess that, after a while, those of us who been around a decade or two more than them began to find this rather irritating.

The young people concerned were in every other way very pleasant, friendly and professional, but the moment the cameras were turned off to relight or re-dress the set, the eyes went down, out came the Blackberrys or iPhones and the fingers started flying over the keyboards. Holding the wretched devices surreptitiously under the table did nothing to disguise what they were doing and was the equivalent of an ostrich hiding its head in the sand to convince onlookers it isn't there.

The fact that the process is silent compared to the even less inclusive act of making a phone call doesn't help either, as at least in that case most people have the courtesy to walk away to keep the conversation private. Texting, twittering and emailing can be carried out inches away from you, and therefore inevitably is. I suppose it is the modern equivalent of my generation whispering in the corner and giggling, which irritated the older generation of our day so much.

It suggests too that the people they are with are insufficiently interesting to deflect them from the desire to chat about heaven knows what with their contemporaries. And because it is so easy and can be done silently, they perhaps don't consider it to be disruptive in any way and therefore expect it to be acceptable.

It is all about manners in the final analysis, and sadly fewer and fewer children are taught the basics of good manners any more.

I have noticed when I am rehearsing for a play, too, that during a tea break all the young cast members rush off to get their phones and spend the entire time texting or talking on them. I can never think of anyone to ring and have considered pretending to make a call so I don't seem like a Colly-no-mates.

I suppose they could be calling their agents, saying, 'Get me out of here!'

25th November 2011

And before the fireworks have faded from the sky, here we are at panto time again. While Lesley Joseph, who was at drama school with me aeons ago, was doing the honours turning the lights on in Wycombe, I was doing precisely the same thing in Mansfield in Derbyshire, where I am terrifying small children this Christmas. Not that that is what she is doing. I suspect that she is playing a more sympathetic role than I am. I am reprising the role of Fleshcreep, which I played in Malvern two years ago—the villainous henchman of the giant in *Jack and the Beanstalk*, necessitated by the impracticalities of having the giant appear before the plot absolutely demands it!

I was a little more careful this year in my utterances, bearing in mind that when I turned on Cromer's lights a few years ago, I got into terrible trouble with the burghers of Blackpool, whose magnificent display I pretended was inferior to the modest offering in Cromer. It never pays to underestimate the potency of civic pride.

Suffice it to say that Mansfield, a town with which I was hitherto unfamiliar, put on a fine evening and, as I suspect was probably the case in Wycombe, the citizens turned up in their thousands to celebrate for once in these austere times.

I am normally reticent to acknowledge the existence of Christmas until December, but I think everyone needs a little relief from the relentless gloom that seems to be pervading the world at the moment, so the early onset of Yuletide jollity is for once very welcome.

I have been experiencing it in another way this week, too. I have been participating in *Come Dine with Me*. which was a most entertaining and interesting experience. I was persuaded to do it by my family and my agent, all of whom clearly thought I was being too indolent. As someone who hasn't cooked anything other than beans on toast and various combinations of breakfast for four decades, it came as somewhat of a shock, but in the event was great fun.

I met some fascinating people that I can't name and ate some great dinners that I can't describe. The programme will be aired on Channel 4 from Boxing Day onwards, if you are curious as to who was in it, what they cooked and which charity ultimately benefited. Tune in and have a laugh at my expense.

2nd December 2011

I wrote here a few months ago about the time I was conned by the *News of the World*, as a naïve young actor, so I won't go over the details of that now happily defunct publication's duplicity. But the revelations by a succession of high-profile people at the Leveson Enquiry have highlighted the heartless and unpleasant tactics employed by certain elements of the national press in pursuit of what is often at best scurrilous titillation for those millions who seem to want to read that stuff, and at worst, vile fabrication.

To characterise the current debate as being about muzzling a free press misses the point hugely. Many of those who have been giving evidence and who might be considered justified in so wishing have made the point that true investigative journalism is and must remain inviolate in a free society. A state-muzzled press would be appalling. But what happened to the McCanns and the Dowlers in particular must never happen again; and to ensure that it never happens again, I believe we have to acknowledge that self-regulation by the press has simply not worked.

I mention the McCanns and Dowlers first because they were people who were in a place that none of us can imagine or would ever want to experience, and they were then subjected to the most callous and inhumane treatment by an out-of-control element in the 'comic book' end of the print media. But star actors and sportsmen who have also suffered deserve some protection too. The notion that because you do a high-profile job you automatically crave publicity is, for the majority, completely untrue. Very often they are contractually obliged to do interviews and appearances and would much more happily just do their job and go home.

Even at my low level of 'fame', I often have to explain this to people who want me to do something and add, as if it were an enticement, 'It will be good publicity for you.' They seem to think we wouldn't help them unless there was something in it for us, and this incorrect assumption that we are looking for a quid pro quo is actually quite offensive sometimes.

If there is anything to be learned, it is not to believe everything you read in certain nationals and to reflect how you'd feel if it were you they were pursuing so voraciously.

9th December 2011

Over the decades, judges have provided us with a selection of statements that have served to underline the popular preconception that they inhabit a world slightly more rarefied than the rest of us live in. The most famous (although perhaps, it now appears, apocryphal) example is the judge who, in the 60s, professed to be unaware who the Beatles were, at a time when even a bushman in the Kalahari might have heard of the Fab Four.

There have been other classic examples of apparent judicial naiveté—the judge in 2007 who didn't know what a website was and only recently, when Mr Justice Harman was informed that Gazza was a very well-known footballer, he asked 'Rugby or Association? Isn't there an operetta called *La Gazza Ladra*?'

But these instances of evidence of a judicial disconnect from the real world have decreased significantly as the law has opened up to a wider and more representative intake, and it could now be argued that the pendulum has swung too far the other way. The appropriately named Judge Bean is clearly keen to show how in touch he is with popular culture and social behaviour. It seems that swearing at policeman is now so commonplace as to make it acceptable. The expletives directed by a young offender at officers who were searching him for drugs would not have resulted in them being alarmed, distressed or harassed, according to Mr Bean, because they were words the policemen would hear everyday in the course of their work.

If Judge Bean doesn't see the inevitable consequence of the removal of this layer of protection for our police, then he perhaps will start to do so when defendants start addressing him in similar terms in his court. After all, why should he be considered as more worthy of protection from verbal abuse than the policeman on the beat?

And if verbally abused judges hide behind the fiction that it is not them as people but their judicial office that needs to be protected from abuse, then the same should apply to Her Majesty's Constabulary.

I have an aversion to violence in any form, and barrages of obscene abuse are a form of violence and often go hand in hand with actual physical violence. Anything we as a society can do to make public places family friendly again will get my vote. Judges who protect the foul-mouthed don't!

16th December 2011

I was contacted by a radio station this week. They were running a phone-in, offering people the opportunity to have a good moan and, for some reason, thought I would be a fertile source of grumpiness. I seized the opportunity, of course, and banged on relentlessly about all the things that regular readers of this column will recognise—people who put on those rear fog lights when there is a mere wisp of mist blinding everyone behind them, compensation-chasing legal firms that induce exaggerated insurance claims, litter, political correctness, the nanny state, the disappearance of the words 'please' and 'thank-you' and parents that expect schools to take over their role of disciplining their children.

When I put the phone down, it struck me that it is much easier to think of things to complain about than it is to celebrate the good stuff, those moments when life surprises you positively rather than negatively. I suppose that is unsurprising because things that really get your goat tend to linger on in the memory whereas, sadly, those rarer, more uplifting moments tend to get quickly forgotten. So I decided that this week I would try to allow the spirit of Christmas to inhabit me for a moment and count some blessings.

Funnily enough, it is the things that previous generations would truly have taken for granted that are unusual enough to delight this flinty heart. The checkout girl who chats to you as if you are an old friend and seems to genuinely believe that each customer is important, the girl in the distant call centre who actually does ring you back and sort out your problem without making you feel you're an irritant, the people who do thank you when you hold a door open for them.

I offer a tiny incident that highlights how easy it is to let the sun shine in. I was checking the oil in my wife's car at the weekend when a man came past with his dog. I looked up and said, 'Good morning' and he responded with a smile and raised his hat to me. When did you last see that? What a lovely thing to do; an action that would have been so commonplace as to be unworthy of comment in my grandfather's day.

I never wear a hat and find myself wishing that I did so I could emulate his courtesy.

23rd December 2011

Whenever I tell anyone that I am appearing in panto, the immediate response is usually 'Oh no, you're not!' This is not to suggest that people assume that I'm a liar or that no one would employ the likes of me to perform in panto. It is simply a conditioned reflex that confirms the still very strong part that panto plays in the Christmas celebrations in this country. Since 1970, when I played Lord Growlie (who he?) in *The Wizard of Oz* in Guildford, I have appeared in thirty-one pantomimes in places as far apart as Cork, Truro and Hull.

This year I am in Mansfield, being Fleshcreep, the giant's evil henchman, in *Jack and the Beanstalk*. A henchman is de rigueur in this case, given the practical difficulties of having the giant appear too often. Credible dwarves are easier to find than giants, though if you read the papers this week it would seem that times are tough for Snow White's little chums in Wolverhampton this year.

The nature of panto has evolved over the decades that I have been aware of it. It seems that some subjects are more popular than others, irrespective of who is appearing in them. I am told that if a story has been Disney-fied, then the box office receipts tend to be better. So *Peter Pan, Snow White* and *Cinderella* are audience attracters for theatres whereas good old Dick Whittington is fading, sadly. And when did you last see a *Goldilocks* or *Mother Goose* being performed?

I went to my first panto in Manchester as a child, when I saw Jewell and Warris, Dickie Henderson and the greatest ever dame, in my opinion, Norman Evans, with a chorus of a dozen or more dancers, a full orchestra and Morecambe and Wise at the bottom of the bill. This was when pantos went on until March and the theatres were full for the duration. But there was little or no telly then. The season has shrunk and very few reach the end of January now, but the annual pantomime still remains the security that theatres have of knowing that for two months at least they can reliably attract much larger audiences than can be the case during the rest of the year. When theatres struggle to balance the books and subsidies are being cut, the annual pantomime can be a budget saver. Long may it continue.

30th December 2011

As we enter the year of the London Olympics, I am heartened to read of plans being made to ensure that we come out the other side of the international limelight unscathed. Scotland Yard have announced that they have anticipated a problem that less caring bodies might have overlooked. Apparently there will be twenty eight police officers accompanying the Olympic Flame and its assorted bearers on its seventy-day journey around the country.

Not only will these officers be running alongside the torch, but they will sleep by the flame at night, conjuring up beguiling images of fully uniformed PCs, truncheons in hand, pounding the pavements of the UK and then sleeping in shifts at night in lay-bys on the A40. Clearly, compared with their more mundane duties of confronting violent looters or drug-crazed hooligans, this element of their duties is considered potentially more onerous and risky.

After they have completed their journey, the officers will be given counselling to help them reintegrate into their more normal activities, like being harangued by the foul-mouthed youths, which a judge recently ruled was something they ought to be able to cope with without recourse to the courts. Running alongside a flame, however, could result in the stalwart officers struggling to get back to reality after being the centre of attention for so long.

Clearly, the genius who came up with this plan has failed to register that the flame and its series of temporary carriers are what we will all be looking at briefly as they glide by, not the impassive escorts. Does the army offer counselling, I wonder, to the soldiers who act as royal escorts during the trooping of the colour? I somehow doubt it.

This kind of nonsense will only stop when the courts adopt a more robust attitude to damages claims from people who try to blame others for their own mistakes or ignorance. It is fear of the success of these claims that led, for instance, Lincolnshire Police to issue staff with written advice on how to eat their lunch. How else would these police officers have known not to eat out-of-date food or leave their sandwiches in warm cars? And several Government departments have used the services of a company that teaches staff to walk. 'Heel, ball of the foot and toes—in that order' apparently! I wonder if they've told the flame escorts that?

Welcome to 2012!

2012

6th January 2012

I never thought I would be tempted to hold up the French as a model of good behaviour that might be followed by the UK. But their decision to offer their citizens free replacement of all PIP breast implants, whether these have already failed or not, is one that clearly puts public health well ahead of financial and budgetary considerations.

There have been a lot of knee-jerk, unhelpful rumblings suggesting that women who have had implants for reasons of personal vanity in private clinics should not receive assistance from the NHS. This argument is not only grossly simplistic, but also inconsistent. We offer medical care on the NHS to habitual smokers, drinkers and drug users, despite the perceived 'self-inflicted' origin of their diseases; and so we should. Even in that small percentage of cases when the breast enhancements have been undertaken for purely cosmetic or misguided vanity reasons, the recipients of non-medical standard implants have been the victims of a deception, as indeed have the clinics that performed the operations in the belief that the implants were appropriate.

Certainly morally, and hopefully by law, the private clinics that make very good money performing these operations, will accept the responsibility of any supplier of faulty goods, albeit in good faith, and do what they can to remedy the situation. The broadcast media have been full, however, of stories from recipients of PIP implants of an initial reluctance on the part of some clinics and surgeons to offer much assistance. Once again, it is the fear of possible expensive litigation that stops people behaving decently. We have a culture today of never admitting responsibility for anything until the lawyers or insurance companies have crawled all over the minutiae to look for a way out. Why can't the clinics say that they'll replace the implants and sort out the liability later? We all know the reason. Money. And the fact that the manufacturers who supplied deficient implants have gone into liquidation doesn't help, of course.

But there can be no doubt that those whose implants have already ruptured should receive immediate remedial treatment. And if the original clinic will not do it, then the NHS should step in, do it and then bill them.

The medical community has the opportunity here to demonstrate the falseness of the popular belief that it closes ranks to defend its own, whatever the circumstances.

13th January 2012

Now that I have shaken the dust of pantomime from my weary feet, I am able to look back at the week that immediately preceded it, when I took part in my first 'reality' TV show—" *Come Dine With Me.* We all found it exhausting, as being a one-camera shoot, each episode offers very little downtime to the participants. How the crew maintain the relentless pressure, I do not know. For example, on my cooking day they arrived at my house at 9 a.m. and the last person left at 5-30 a.m. the following day. For five 25-minute programmes, they shot over 90 hours of material. The editing must take forever.

I have always been reluctant to allow my own home to be used for filming purposes, not just for reasons of privacy (mercifully I am not famous enough for that to be a real issue), but more because I have seen how people's homes have been treated when I have been on location as an actor. But I was very impressed by the care taken by the *CDWM* team, and I learned a lot. Any pictures in vision (and we have a lot) for copyright reasons either had to get clearance from the artists concerned or had to be taken down.

My main worry, though, had been the cooking. I had genuinely never cooked a meal other than a breakfast fry-up or beans on toast since I married my wife, who cooks superbly. I was so scared that I actually did a couple of practice runs for my family in the weeks before the filming. Otherwise, I would certainly have floundered. Perhaps unlike the usual version of the programme, where they put together potentially explosive mixtures of people, in this 'celeb' version we all got on really well, especially given the increasing lack of sleep! Linda Nolan was great fun and made me laugh a lot, Bianca

Gascoigne and Danny Young were both smashing young people and delightful dinner companions, although they did perhaps lack the staying power of we oldies, and 'Nasty' Nick Bateman is a rather sensitive and gentle soul trapped to a certain extent by his *Big Brother* history.

To have won the £1000 prize for Stokenchurch Dog Rescue was a fabulous bonus, and totally unexpected. And I am more than happy now to pass the chef's hat back to my wife! I can't take the stress!

19th January 2012

I attended a Speed Awareness Course in Burnham this week. Anyone who knows that I endured a six-m-month ban under the totting-up procedure two years ago may be appalled to learn that I was recently caught doing 36 mph in Wycombe. But with all the best intentions I had after that experience, I still erred.

All of the other 27 attendees at the training session felt aggrieved at worst or unlucky at best at the individual circumstances of their being caught by cameras or radar traps.

I suspect most of us thought that four hours of being told how naughty we were would be a bitter pill worth enduring only because no points were being added to our licences. Thanks to the skills of the excellent presenter and the strength of the message, I suspect that most of us left much better informed and resolved to be safer drivers, especially the woman who admitted that on the motorway she just sat in the middle 'cruising' lane and never moved. She was genuinely astonished to learn the error of her ways.

I was shocked at the lack of knowledge within that small group of speed limits, road markings and stopping distances, although I doubtless surprised others with my lack of knowledge in other areas. I would have liked to take away a copy of the presentation to assimilate and share it with my family. For some reason, that was not possible. I would urge Thames Valley Police to make the content available (either online or on paper) to those who have completed the course.

I also asked if the course was available to non-offenders for a fee. I would gladly have paid for my daughters to attend it. The £95 fee would be cheap if it saved their or another person's life.

The huge impact of tyres with reduced, although legal, tread depth on stopping distances and grip in the wet was something that I had never before fully appreciated. I intend to take all the family cars into our tyre supplier on a regular basis rather than rely on the occasional quick look that had been my previous custom.

If there was one abiding message, however, it was that if we all drove at speeds that enabled us to simply stop within the distance we could see as clear ahead, accidents and deaths would be massively reduced.

26th January 2012

I have no personal axe to grind as far as the impact of HS2 on my life is concerned. It will be miles away from my home and therefore I cannot be accused of being a nimby if I say, 'Why?'

Why do we all need to get to places more and more quickly? Why, when those business men who want to go from London to Birmingham a bit faster can now use their laptops and phones (and they do, curse them!) on the trains, do those phones and laptops have to go to Birmingham in the first place, let alone more quickly? Weren't the myriad of communication and conferencing opportunities offered by modern technology supposed to reduce the need for so much careering around the country?

Why, at a time when innumerable more important and pressing demands on our cashed-strapped nation are jostling for our attention, has this mammoth undertaking been green-lighted for funding? Yes, as a lover of all things new and innovative myself, it would be nice to have a new sleek, fast train service, but is there anyone outside Whitehall who thinks it is something we need to have before we sort out a heck of a lot of other more pressing demands on our funds in this time of recession? What would we rather have—schools without crumbling and antiquated buildings or the ability to go from Birmingham to London more quickly?

I need hardly add other things we'd like to see higher up the agenda, but I will. Hospitals that are properly staffed, so that nurses can nurse again and patients aren't left unattended unnecessarily. Local hospitals. Police forces that aren't forced to cut their number when the public are crying out for more visible policing.

I know that these are always the arguments trotted out by people with an agenda and that comparisons can be invidious, such as the argument that children matter more than animals, therefore we should support children's charities not animal ones.

Clearly there is room for both. Yes, the transport infrastructure, like the schools and hospitals, is getting old and tired, but the nod in favour of HS2 is a disproportionately huge financial commitment at a time when every penny should be spent wisely and for the benefit of all.

Getting people from to A to B more quickly doesn't justify the level of expenditure required for HS2 in the present economic situation.

3rd February 2012

Even Solomon's famed wisdom would be hard-pressed to solve the current debate over the capping of benefits. On the one hand, it seems completely barmy to create a situation where people consider themselves better off by not working. For every citizen whose fierce pride won't let them ask for handouts, I suspect there are dozens who are perfectly happy to do so. And we know too that there are some who create false identities and incapacitating illnesses in order to defraud the rest of us, via the benefit system. But on the other hand, there are fewer jobs than people looking for jobs, and many recipients of state benefits would much rather work.

It is hard to quarrel in principle with notion of capping benefits. The proposed £26,000 does represent, after all, a pre-tax salary of £35,000 per year, a sum which many working families would love to bring home. I can imagine that families earning less than that and coping with difficulty might think that even £26,000 was on the high side. The trouble is that there are a wide range of people receiving state benefits; the work-shy scrounger beloved of the tabloids does not make up the majority of those who need state help to survive. For every couple who get £95,000 in benefits every year because they have ten children and gave up working to look after them, there are hundreds of single parents with fewer children who struggle after losing a partner or because of ill-health. We could not call ourselves a civilised society if we did not help them. Even the ten-child family—and of course we all say that it is insane to have ten children unless you know you can look after them—but even in that family, it isn't the children's fault.

Hand in hand with capping benefits, there are things that could be done to encourage people back to work, including affordable childcare and travel.

But in the context of the total national debt having risen to just over one trillion pounds—i.e. a billion pounds—equal to 64.2% of GDP , then something has to be done, across the board.

I must admit to being unsure who we owe the trillion to. If all countries owe other countries billions, why don't we just write each other's debts off and start again? That would save a bob or two in interest, wouldn't it?

17ᵗʰ February 2012

If you were thinking of breaking down on the A404 Marlow bypass, my advice to you is—don't. My own car was in the garage on Wednesday, so I used my wife's 4x4, which is mainly used on local journeys normally, to take my daughter to the airport. On the way back (mercifully, as if this had happened on the way there, the result could have been calamitous for my daughter's flight to Shanghai!) the car started to overheat and within seconds slowed to a crawl and stopped some 800 yards from Handy Cross roundabout. I was in the nearside lane and from the time I realised there was a problem to the time when smoke started pouring from under the bonnet and the engine committed hairy car-y, there was no opportunity to get off the carriageway. So there the car sat, blocking the nearside lane.

I put the hazard lights on and, mindful of the well-known risk to cars on the hard shoulders of motorways, let alone the inside lane of fast dual carriageways, I legged it up the road for about 100 yards and waited for my breakdown service to come. If something hit the car, I didn't want to be near it. For one and a half hours, I stood there helpless and watched some of the worst driving I have ever seen.

Many cars failed to register the flashing lights until they were a few yards from my car. Some swerved at the last minute in front of the traffic in the outside lane. Others sat there until a kind driver flashed to let them out. They all had a good half mile or more in which to register the obstruction in their lane. I have to commend the professional drivers.

The lorry drivers, perhaps in part because they were sitting higher than most drivers, all made allowances and moved over in plenty of time. Nonetheless, when after an hour and a quarter a police car arrived and parked 400 yards behind me with blue lights flashing, miraculously the drivers became much more sensible and considerate. Perhaps blue is more visible than amber? A cynic might think that the blue light carries more power than the distress beacon of the hazard lights. Whichever is the truth, I was mighty glad to see them.

Now comes the expensive bit. I await the news from my garage.

24th February 2012

One of the most successful marketing operations of the last decade or two has been the elevation of the hot drink, specifically coffee, to the same level as branded clothing and shoes, as an indication of the wearer/carrier's style and status.

I don't get it, I'm afraid. And I have never understood the desire to wear anything with the manufacturer's name emblazoned all over it, unless they were to pay me for being a mobile advertising hoarding.

But then I wear clothes and shoes for their comfort and practicality and am not over troubled by the desire to convey anything to the world at large beyond that. If for reasons of politeness to a host or for a formal or official occasion I would cause offence were I to do otherwise, I will don the suit and tie and formal shoes. That is a matter of simple politeness. But the rest of the time, one of the small pluses about advancing years is that one knows that one can please oneself more.

The boom in branded coffee shops is, for me, another example of the triumph of marketing over common sense.

Whenever I start a new acting job, there is a period of rehearsal that starts usually with a read-through, when all the cast meet each other for the first time. Every rehearsal room I have ever been in provides a kettle, milk, coffee and tea, usually free or for a modest contribution.

And yet, the majority of the cast will turn up carrying a takeaway cup of Kostalotta or Vastbucks coffee, which they have purchased around the corner for the same cost as two or three litres of petrol.

I am astonished that at the same time as we all complain about rising fuel prices, there are sufficient numbers of people prepared to pay around two pounds and more for a small cup of coffee.

It used to be estate agents and hairdressers that moved into the high streets when fishmongers and butchers were squeezed out by the supermarkets. Now it the ubiquitous coffee shops who have identified a lucrative opportunity and scattered comfy armchairs in their outlets to persuade the upwardly mobile and would-be trendy to buy their wares.

It is interesting that one of the major coffee outlets is now owned by a large brewery, which has thereby rather wisely switched liquid assets as the pubs struggle to keep afloat.

2nd March 2012

Anyone over the age of 50 will remember that before the Internet came along to make our lives so much easier, things like electricity and gas came from whoever supplied them in your area. As a young man, I recall my parents got their electricity from Norweb, because that was the company that supplied it in Manchester. And as far as I am aware, there was one price too.

Whatever the cost of electricity was, that was the price for everyone nationally. Yes, you younger readers, just sit back and imagine the luxury of not having to wade through a dozen different pricing schemes from a dozen different suppliers before committing yourself to a package you don't really understand that will change after a year, when you have forgotten all about it. In order to get the best value for what is, after all, exactly the same commodity, you really have to change supplier every year or 18 months depending on the 'deal' you commit to.

It's not like a car, say, which also does one thing inasmuch as it carries its owner from A to B, but it does it with differing degrees of comfort, speed, style, economy—you name it. So understandably a diverse and wide market has grown up.

Electricity has no variables in its use; it brings power into our homes and workplaces. That's it. So to bamboozle us into changing suppliers and buying exactly the same thing from a new source, they wrap the prices up in such complicated layers of obfuscation that you need a degree in pure mathematics to understand it.

That is how the comparison websites were spawned. They pick apart the complicated pricing and contract lengths to offer the consumer the best deal for them at that fixed point in time and in their area. So the consumer is inevitably paying for all those people to formulate all those labyrinthine pricing plans and for all the nice comparison helpline people to explain them to us and advise us which to take.

If they didn't bother with all that flimflam in the first place, the price of electricity would go down and stabilise and we wouldn't have to spend half a day and more picking our way through the impenetrable options every year or so.

I have a horrible feeling that the same kind of thing will ultimately happen to the NHS.

9th March 2012

Call me an old romantic, but I decided to push the boat out on Valentine's Day this year and bought my wife two tickets for last week's England v Holland friendly at Wembley. She decided to take me with her. My generous entrainment package included parking (for over twenty pounds) in the 'Wembley official car park', which turned out to be an industrial park almost a mile away from the stadium. We dined expensively too. For the same price as we could have had a lovingly prepared meal for two in one of our many excellent local pubs, we queued at one of the burger vans that line the impressive Wembley way and chewed our acquisitions under the bronze statue of Bobby Moore, whose arms seemed to be folded in mute disbelief as he gazed off into a more acceptable distance.

The stadium is impressive. And big. It has to be, I suppose. There were over 70,000 there that night, many of whom may have been football supporters; it was hard to tell. To reach our seats we had to climb up the equivalent of Marlow Hill in Wycombe and then back down again. We were six rows from the pitch-side, level with the penalty half circle. For both of us it was a first. It may be a last for me. I have always assumed that young males wearing the team's kit, with faces daubed with national flags, were likely to make a good crowd of supporters.

The ones around us spent more time in the bar than watching the match and when they were back in their seats, they weren't in them. They were standing exchanging laddish profanities with their mates. When an elderly couple behind us suggested they might sit down, they were treated with drunken, barely comprehensible contempt.

Sadly, I enjoyed the game a lot more when I watched it at home later.

Then on Tuesday night I returned to the familiar

surroundings of Adams Park and the anxiety and thrills of a Wanderers match, surrounded by familiar faces and friends who (in their different ways, admittedly) all do care about what is happening on the pitch. COYB!

'There's no place like home' (clicking together the heels of my two-tone blue shoes).

By the way, I know what you were thinking, but my wife had always wanted to see an England home match and was delighted to receive the tickets.

16th March 2012

So now fairy tales are considered to be too scary for the delicate sensibilities of today's children, if a survey of two thousand parents is to be believed. The Brothers Grimm apparently took their name too seriously in delivering fantastical tales for children for two centuries. 2012 marks the bicentenary of their first publication, in fact. But the brothers were collectors of tales that had been around much longer than that, tales that explored the darker aspects of what it is to be human, to be afraid and to question a whole host of things that we may well know a little more about today but which still exercise thinkers, philosophers and writers.

But in a world where people need notices to tell them that coffee can be hot and that knives can be sharp, what chance do Cinderella and Rumplestiltskin have to make it through the minefield of cottonwool that is being constructed around us all by those concerned for our well-being?

Cinderella apparently offers a poor image to children, as it depicts a young girl doing housework all day. Well, a small sample of my household would lead you to discount that lurking danger. My four daughters have seen me in *Cinderella* several times and watched the film, without it leading them to feel the slightest need to load the washing machine, iron or clean out the ashes from the fire. It's a story for heaven's sake!

Jack and the Beanstalk was deemed 'too unrealistic'! I am not sure who was surveyed, but I'll bet a bag of beans that they let their children go and see *Harry Potter* or *Narnia*—

cracking stories and different only in the conventions of the age in which they were written from the more basic and elemental stories immortalised by the Grimms and Hans Christian Andersen.

Our local genius Roald Dahl knew all about the need for young children to explore through imaginative and sometimes dark storytelling.

It is the very nature of these stories that makes them right for young children in their learning to process their fears and the difference between reality and stories. They are, in fact, more likely to believe that there is a platform 9 ¾ at Kings Cross, a familiar and contemporary environment, than that a princess might let her hair down from a turreted castle window to allow her boyfriend to climb up and free her.

23rd March 2012

One of the biggest corporate failings, it strikes me, is the lack of opportunity for front line customer service employees to use their initiative. Combine the fear of litigation and the culture of butt-protecting (not a pretty phrase, but it accurately describes the phenomenon), and you get a severe thickening of the oil that is supposed to ease the wheels of commerce.

All those call centres that we loathe so passionately are staffed most of the time by poorly paid employees with a script and very strict parameters to work to, with no latitude for flexibility or creative thinking – both of which qualities are prized by customers.

The whole phenomenon is neatly summed up by that wonderful scene in *Five Easy Pieces* where the young Jack Nicholson is trying to get a sandwich. If you don't know it, check it out on YouTube. Nothing has changed since 1970.

We all know of know of schools who have wanted to put on a production of a musical or play and have been told by the literary agent responsible for 'green-lighting' school productions that the subject is not available because 'a West End producer has plans for a London run or tour' and therefore no other productions can occur during that period.

This seems to suggest that a performance of *Seven Brides for Seven Brothers* at St Botolph's County Secondary for four nights might hit box office receipts in London. Of course, this is not the real reason. It is simply easier to administer a blanket ban than to spend time sorting the minnows from the competitive basking sharks who might want to genuinely muscle in on the action. And no one at street level in the organisation has the authority to see the PR value in allowing a school or youth production.

Occasionally, however, they do have that degree of generosity and common sense, as anyone will acknowledge who was lucky enough to see the WYSPAS youth production of Hairspray in the Kite Theatre at Cressex Community School this week. What a joyful musical, which as usual underlined the fact that the young people in our area have a wealth of talent if they are given the opportunity to show it. So hats off to WYSPAS (and whoever allowed them to do it) for giving them the platform to show that they are, in the words of one of the songs, 'The Nicest Kids in Town'.

30th March 2012

The opportunities offered by the Internet and social networking sites to communicate immediately and internationally have potentially huge benefits for humanity. It would, for instance, be difficult for most regimes today to conduct any kind of mass repression or genocide without the rest of the world at least knowing about it.

Whether the rest of the world can or, indeed, would then do anything about it may be a different matter, but it would be known. Television too has helped to make war anathema to most of us. Audiences worldwide could see the struggles of the freedom fighters in Libya and unpick some of the lies and propaganda peddled by Gaddafi's supporters and whilst the media can be hijacked by the despots, the stream of information on the Internet soon exposes the worst excesses. It is arguable that the two great wars that the previous generation lived through would have either been shorter or even less likely to start, had the kind of communication we have today been available.

However, all the benefits that humanity can reap from the free and instant exchange of information and communication are, as always, balanced by the opportunity afforded to the mindless, the cowardly and the evil alike to peddle hatred and hurt others at arm's length. The student who tweeted so disgustingly about Fabrice Muamba's sad plight, as the young footballer was fighting for his life, would possibly never have dared utter his vile thoughts had he not had (what he considered to be) the anonymity of the Internet between him and his audience. But the Internet is not a void. It is a world that is populated by people who we may never meet, but who have feelings and families and most of whom are reasonable and well-intentioned.

It is too easy for the coward and the bully to drive people to despair and even suicide by harrying them through social networking sites. It is to the credit of the judicial system that the student who thought he could say whatever hurtful things he liked on Twitter about a stricken footballer (for reasons unfathomable by most of us) has been sent to jail for 56 days to think about what kind of person he is.

Hopefully the lesson will not only serve to benefit his future behaviour but will serve as a warning to others that these sites can't be treated like the walls of a public lavatory.

6th April 2012

It was no surprise to learn that less than 7% of us actually read the 'Terms and Conditions', otherwise known as small print, which we all happily confirm that we have read when we agree to anything online. The real surprise is that as many as 7% do read them.

Yes, it is irresponsible not to read something before signing it—and for most things, as an ex-lawyer, I am a stickler for doing so. But those reams of small print that you tick as 'read' when you sign up to a credit card or service provider would defeat even the most pernickety of pedants. The Consumer

Association has now revealed that the small print that most of us falsely confirm we have read is, in the case of iTunes longer than Shakespeare's *Macbeth,* and PayPal's 36,275 words is longer than *Hamlet.*

I would suggest too that even for the least literate of readers, Shakespeare is probably easier to comprehend than the legal gobbledygook of most Terms and Conditions.

If they really wanted you to read them, surely they would be in much larger print? But they don't, do they? They want us to trust that there's nothing potentially disastrous for us in there and just tick the box and sign up for what they're peddling. I got caught once buying a gift and got locked into monthly payments for something I didn't want any more of after the first month. The length of the commitment was concealed in the small print.

It will need Parliament to ensure that the crunch issues buried in the acres of standard stuff must be more prominent, or that the main points have to précised in the body of the agreement. Such legislation is long overdue.

And it's not a question of following Jack Cade's agreement in *Henry VI part 2* to '… kill all the lawyers', because however much the law do tie us up in knots, they do so because legislation allows them to.

The law makers are the ones who can restrict their ability to do so unfairly or restrictively. Simplification was advocated when I was practising law in the 1970s; as far as 'small print' is concerned, it hasn't happened yet.

'To the Editor: by printing this you agree to give me the key of the executive bar and allow me free use of the *Bucks Free Press* private jet on alternate Saturdays.'

13th April 2012

When I was 16 years old and living in the North, I cycled with friends to Ladybower Reservoir near Sheffield, because the village of Derwent, which had been flooded two decades earlier when the reservoir was built, had emerged from the depths when the waters receded during that long hot summer.

It was, I recall, an eerie and sobering sight.

Despite the considerable difference in scale, our present water shortage was underlined when I visited a charity horse riding event at West Wycombe Park on the Bank Holiday. Last year, we watched the horses plunge through the run off from the swan-shaped lake that is fed by the Rver Wye.

This year we watched them walk through the muddy residue adjacent to a non-existent lake. It is the first hard evidence I have seen of the reality of the water shortage that has resulted in a hose pipe ban being implemented in April— at the beginning of what we would otherwise hope would be the driest season of the year.

With a population that is steadily growing in a country that is not by any means in a part of the world where water ought to be a problem, we should perhaps be more proactively considering the impact of a growing population and a predicted global water shortage.

Certainly, we need to address the fact that the majority of the population is in the south of the country and the majority of water is in the north.

I would rather see the vast sums of money that are designated for the financial sinkhole that is HS2 being spent on assuring our future water (and food) supply than getting business men to Birmingham a bit quicker. Water is needed by everyone. Whether we need new reservoirs, desalination plants or water extraction from our rivers at their point of entry to the sea, we cannot provide for the future just by not cleaning our teeth with the tap running, filling our dishwashers before turning them on or turning off our sprinklers.

These are mildly helpful short term strategies, but our need for water for our children cannot be met by them alone. All the alternative methods of water generation, storage and conveyance have very carbon hungry implications, I know, but some joined-up thinking is required now to ensure that we avoid a potentially arid future. Our small island should never have reached this point.

20th April 2012

What is it about musicians, actors, artists and writers that makes the rest of the world think that it is perfectly acceptable to ask them to do things for nothing all the time? The latest evidence of the disdain that the business and political sectors have for 'creatives' is that the Olympic organisers are asking musicians involved in the whole circus that is, and will surround, the Summer Olympics to give their services for free.

They go even further and offer that familiar ultimate insult of suggesting that they do it 'for the publicity and exposure.' If the musicians and bands concerned are good enough to perform at this major world event, then surely they should be treated no differently to all the companies, consultants and suppliers of goods who apparently wouldn't do their thing 'for the publicity and exposure.'

Asking for volunteers to help in minor marshalling and competitor shepherding activities is one thing—these are principally people like students and the retired who are being asked to do something basic and other than their normal jobs, requiring minimal training. Asking professionals who already are operating in a notoriously insecure industry to subsidise the nation's flagship event in addition to their contribution via the tax system is frankly shameful.

The costs for the project are already spiralling, as is evident from the fact that the security budget alone has risen from an initial £86m to £284m, *The Guardian* has reported. I won't name the company providing the security for the Games, as they presumably don't need the publicity and exposure but are, unsurprisingly, doing it for the money. Even the athletes who, we must believe, are principally competing for the honour of representing their countries and their sports, have financial assistance in these post-Corinthian Spirit days of the amateur.

But the performers that keep the crowds entertained before, between and after the athletic and sporting activities are uniquely (apparently) expected to forgo the right to charge for their work.

But then I am constantly being asked for free tickets for shows I am in and get blank stares when I ask them to come and ply their trade free for me. How they imagine theatres keep open and pay their performers, I cannot guess. Try asking a chef to cook a meal for you for nothing, or an estate agent to forgo his commission.

27th April 2012

David Cameron and George Osborne were characterised by one of their own backbenchers this week as 'posh boys who didn't know the price of milk.'

Well, I may not be posh, but I didn't know the exact price of milk either. It turns out that it's around six shillings a pint—that's 30p in new money. But unless you have little or no money at all and want milk, knowledge of the exact price is surely a detail the majority of the population wouldn't know. I bet, however, if you asked a car owner the price of petrol or diesel, you would get a very swift answer. And I wouldn't be surprised if Messrs Cameron and Osborne knew that too.

I don't necessarily see it as an advantage for our Prime Minister and Chancellor of the Exchequer to spend time being mystery shoppers in the aisles of supermarkets and corner shops to pick up the minutiae of pricing. I'd rather they were spending time making sure that systems were in place to keep our hospitals open and finding funding for health and education.

If they do those things efficiently and their taxation regime is fair and doesn't further penalise those least able to afford it, I don't care if they went to Eton or Scunthorpe Secondary Modern or whether they do the weekly shop or not. In fact, I'd rather they had someone else popping down to the supermarket (or indeed Fortnum and Mason)—so they had more time to spend sorting out the economy and getting Britain back to work. Party political point scoring is a distraction, especially when it is internal bickering.

And we do all know now that politics is not about parties anymore; most people can't distinguish what each party stands for today without reference to historical differences that in many cases no longer apply. Electability is all about not being the other lot and having an electable (i.e. personable on TV) leader.

Dave and George had no choice about the families they were born into, nor where they were educated. Their poshness is a detail, not a crime. Unfair taxation systems, doing little to enable young people to enjoy a fraction of the life chances our generation enjoyed—that's worth shouting about. Criticise what they do, not who they are.

And then ask whether you really believe the other lot would have done much better.

4th May 2012

Call me an old curmudgeon, but there are some aspects of modern parenting that make me dream of administering electro-convulsive aversion therapy to the perpetrators.

We tried to escape the effects of a lengthy power cut on Sunday after the drought—in its manifestation as torrential rain and gales—wrought havoc around the region. What to do? Baked beans out of a can? A takeaway eaten by candlelight? We opted for a restaurant that boasted both lighting and cooking facilities. At an adjoining table was a young family, comprising parents, a baby in a push chair and a toddler. I am all in favour of children in restaurants, as long as the parents don't ignore them when they scream around the place being jet planes or hide under your table.

I still remember the occasion when we took our four young children into a Chinese restaurant by the coast somewhere at around 6.30 p.m. and having been seated by a waiter were then very politely asked to leave by the manager in case other diners were put off by our children. I pointed out that we were the only customers in the restaurant and my girls were sitting quietly. He responded that other diners would be arriving soon and might not like the presence of children. We left. So, I am a champion of children in restaurants.

However, I want to wheel out the tumbrels when children are hauled by their earnest mothers to the busy waiters' collection point and laboriously prompted to ask for the bill.

'Can I—what? (whisper) have the (whisper) bill (whisper) please?' Yummy mummy beams with pride. Then the waiter forces an indulgent smile while the aforesaid four-year-old is guided through the lengthy process of tapping the numbers of daddy's credit card into the handheld machine.

I fantasised briefly that the child was heir to a fortune and they had kidnapped him and were milking his account—that would have been more tolerable than the awful truth, which was that some parents indulge their children without concern for anyone around them. Just stand in a lift while two children fight to be allowed to push the button, while everyone waits resignedly and the parent watches vacantly.

I know I'm overreacting—I blame a whole day without football on the telly. Another day I might not have noticed. The power came back as we went to bed. Natch!

11th May 2012

The trouble with insurance is that you either spend a lot of money and get no benefit at all because nothing bad happens, (which is a big minus and a bit of a plus of course), or something bad happens and you get some of your money back and sometimes even more than you laid out over the years of premiums you paid. That's what insurance is supposed to be about, after all. The lucky help out the unlucky.

Many years ago, when the finances were squeaking, I allowed my house insurance to lapse for two years until the squeak was oiled and I could start paying again. Mercifully, nothing untoward happened and I've always seen that as a few hundred pounds gained. But definitely not a risk worth taking. The stories of those poor people whose homes were devastated by floods and were uninsured are heartbreaking.

There are, however, some policies that I have never taken out. Pet insurance, for instance. We have cats, dogs, horses, goats, chickens, hamsters, rabbits at Baker Towers in seemingly vast numbers. The premiums would be humungous, so in effect we self-insure. The saved premiums on the majority who never need expensive veterinary attention more than compensate for the unfortunate minority who do. Ditto those policies offered when you buy any electrical item. If you added up the annual cost of covering them all—cameras, phones, televisions, washing machines, etc.—it would enable you to replace the majority of them every five years. I've never understood why anyone falls for that point-of-sale pressure.

The one that I have never regretted having is car breakdown insurance. I have benefited from the men in yellow vans' tender ministrations more times than I can recall now, as have my family over many years. And as cars get more complicated and less owner-friendly in terms of quick repair jobs, the more I value those mechanics who may not salute the badge today, as they did when I first joined, but they certainly have got me out of trouble on countless occasions. My daughter's non-starter was deftly cajoled back into life today by the same man who sorted my previous car out when it ground to a halt in West Wycombe many years ago.

And he told me that he reads my column. Now that really is beyond the call of duty.

Service like that is at a premium.

18th May 2012

My wife and I were talking this week about our early lives and attitudes to possessions that were prevalent in society when we were young. It is certainly true that the desire to own something and the likelihood of doing so did not coincide then in quite the same way as has been the case more recently. I recall seeing cars on the road when I was at primary school and never once thought that I might ever own one.

When television sets were appearing for the first time, like many other families we acquired ours for the Coronation and were very happy indeed, and marvelled at the black and white flickering images that captivated us from early evening to closedown—which was sensibly timed to coincide with the time decent folk should be bedward with their Ovaltine.

There has been a huge shift in expectations between my childhood and dodderdom. Now any exciting innovation is expected, almost as of right, to be available to all instantly. One of the main propellers of this has been the ease of borrowing.

Home ownership and car ownership for all mushroomed when mortgages and hire purchase agreements were more widely and easily available. My father had a pathological aversion to borrowing and hated having even a small mortgage. He never borrowed money for anything and I have seemingly inherited part of this tendency. I have always paid off my credit card each month and not used one unless I knew I could do that. I have bought all our cars outright, when I could afford them; as a result I have never owned a new car.

Nor have I ever regretted that, though I am currently contemplating something more modern and economical to run, which may result in my finally having to venture into the scary waters of rental or HP—and I am not speaking saucily here. But how many young people have been taught to save up for what they want these days? I am as guilty as many other parents in giving my children the things I was lucky enough to be able to afford, which my parents could not do. I don't regret that, but I hope that they don't blame me as things are getting tougher and personal finances become more problematical across the board.

We baby boomers had the best of times; but what have we left in our wake?

26th May 2012

I wonder if the presence of a TV camera will ever be so commonplace that even the most resolute moron will be able to resist the temptation to caper about, waving inanely behind whatever the broadcaster is attempting to show us? Every post-football match interview is punctuated by background distraction as grinning youths leap around like baboons in a wildlife reserve when the tourists offer the opportunity to plunder their vehicles. The difference, however, is that the baboons don't care whether they're on television or not. And they have smaller brains. Or do they?

The expectation generated by reality television that anyone and everyone can appear on television still encourages such irritating behaviour, but could perhaps eventually have the unexpected result that not being seen on television is more cool. Let us hope that happens very soon.

Watching the coverage of the Olympic flame setting out on its journey around the UK was punctuated throughout by the awareness that cameramen were attempting to change the angle of their shots so that gurning youths would not distract us from hearing the stories of the many remarkable people who have earned the right to represent their communities as the Olympic flame passes through their towns on its journey to East London. We also very quickly understood that the guardians of the flame running alongside the torchbearer were not just decorative, when an enthusiastic 'bear of very little brain' attempted to run too close to the torch. His disappearance into a heap on the roadside was encouragingly swift and effective. I suspect they will have a busy time for the next ten weeks.

The broadcasters have recently become very good at not showing any coverage of streakers and other disrupters of sporting and public events, which has undoubtedly served to deter the solely publicity-hungry from strutting their antisocial stuff.

But they have now seen the example of John Terry, who might justifiably have felt the need to keep a low profile in Munich when Chelsea magnificently won the Champions League against all logic and the odds. Despite his doing everything to banjax their chances by being sent off in the semi final against Barcelona, he behaved as if he had single-handedly won the darn thing. His camera-hogging, brazen lack of reticence serves only to encourage those of a similar nature to think the camera is there solely for their aggrandisement.

1st June 2012

I find the Eurovision Song Contest confusing in many ways.

At Baker Towers, we have a tradition of watching it as a family, with score sheets and a degree of preparation and ceremony normally accorded to family birthdays, Easter or Christmas. Every year, though, we are perplexed by the continuing dogged insistence of the viewing billions to vote, as we see it, on criteria resolutely unrelated to musicality, originality or talent. Even given cultural and individual subjective ideas of what constitutes a good song, the last few years have demonstrated a uniformity of voting patterns that are inescapably partisan rather than informed.

If there were a way to present the show without identifying the country of origin, I suspect the results would consistently be markedly different. As it is, only countries that are disliked as nations by the fewest people have the remotest chance of success. It would be the most blinkered of commentators that failed to acknowledge the possibility, the likelihood indeed, that the voting patterns were more politically and ethnically motivated than anything else.

And we're just as bad—it's always 12 points to Ireland!

In which case, why does the UK bother to take part? But we do still cling on to the possibility that things might change, don't we, in a triumph of hope over expectation?

I am also confused by the perceived opinion that some countries are desperate to avoid winning because of the expense of running the darn thing. If true, Spain and Greece in particular must be heaving great sighs of fiscal relief that Sweden has moved now into second place (behind the Irish) in the list of all-time winners and has the burden of hosting the 2013 contest. But I have always believed that the costs were shared by all the participating countries and that the UK, along with the original Eurovision partners, bears the bulk of the cost, hence giving us guaranteed entry to the competition. I am unable to find out whether this is still the case or how the whole circus is funded. But if it is the case that we pay more than other countries (echoes of the EEC here?), maybe now is the time to save the likes of dear old Engelbert from the humiliation of beating only Norway on the same night, ironically, as our football team achieved a similar victory by a whisker over that country.

8th June 2012

I think it very inconsiderate of Her Majesty to have her Jubilee in the same week as I opened a new play. I spent all of Monday and Tuesday closeted in a theatre, and missed all the bunting, celebrations and cake.

There has been a lot of activity on the phone-ins this week, where the researchers have pitched ardent monarchists against tumbrel-hauling republicans in a pointless bout of Lilibet-canonising and bashing respectively. It is unlikely, were you starting a constitution from scratch, that you would end up with an inherited figurehead in a modern democracy. However, we have been phenomenally lucky in comparison with other inherited dynastic monarchies, in having Queen Elizabeth II for the last 60 years. The best argument in her favour, aside from her success in being relentlessly careful, polite and uncontroversial for all those years (I wouldn't be capable of doing that) is that no one has yet come up with an alternative that would stop the political estate from having absolute sway constitutionally. Every suggestion ever mooted for presidential possibles has appalled as many as it has pleased.

Yes, it is illogical. But the logical alternatives are either dull or just wrong. Our Royal Family (and I refer to the Queen and her descendants) is currently one of the biggest pluses for the UK worldwide, in terms of tourism, publicity and kudos. In any other job, you would be unlikely to find an 80-year old carrying on with the same vigour and resolute devotion to duty. I have an instinctive disinclination to bow to anyone, especially if told to do so, but I raise my hat to you ma'am for a difficult job well done in the face of a few anni horribiles, premiers even more horribiles and overseas leaders that would tax the ability of Ken Dodd to raise a smile that wasn't a rictus of horror.

I was lucky enough to be asked to compère part of the

D-Day clebrations in Hyde Park some years ago and was hugely impressed by the level of briefing and preparedness of the members of the royal family that I met. And at most parties you or I can slide off and have a quiet glass of bubbly away from the madding crowd. They have to be 'on' all the time. I wouldn't fancy it, despite all the palaces and privilege. Would you?

15th June 2012

June is an unusual time to make resolutions, but I have just decided to make one. Why allow the beginning of a year to dictate when self improvement should commence?

I am going to try and keep my counsel a little more often. Before you all celebrate the demise of this column, I hasten to add that this side of the page will continue to contain my weekly ramblings for the immediate future at least. You, dear reader, do at least have the opportunity to ignore that. On some occasions, people are trapped.

I was in Wycombe Hospital this week and relieved to find it still open and functioning, with a rejigged canteen. I must admit to preferring the old cafe run by the lovely volunteers rather than the new franchised version, but I sat and had a sandwich while waiting for an appointment.

About five tables away, a grey-suited lady had a fifteen-minute conversation on her mobile, every syllable of which I am convinced could have been heard by the person at the other end without troubling the mobile network at all had she simply opened the window and leaned out. And I have the diminished hearing of your average chap in his sixties, as that is what I am. I wish I were able to blot out such distractions, when I am trying to read my paper, but I'm not. I seethed a bit and when she finished promising she would 'get on to it straight away and sort it out by Friday' (I do hope she did) I heard myself boom across the restaurant, 'Thank goodness that call is over at last!'

She looked around the room that had been stilled by my 'outraged of Wycombe' outburst and begged the forgiveness of the world at large if she had been too loud; she hadn't realised, she said. Everyone else immediately protested that they hadn't been bothered at all; in fact they hadn't really noticed she was there. Very British, of course, but it left me beached high and dry. Mr Grumpy had upset nice young lady.

In future, I promise myself (and you, if you're interested) that I will just put up with it and keep my mouth shut.

But I can't promise not to bang on about it in this column if the Editor (May his descendants thrive and prosper) continues to tolerate my querulousness.

13th July 2012

Not a good week for banks or computers. When computers really entered our everyday lives two or three decades ago, the received wisdom was that we would ultimately all be relaxing in our hammocks while they took over all those jobs that no one really wanted to do and generated oodles of wealth.

We could then all become creative and productive in areas that we chose rather than were compelled to work in. The Arts and Sport would flourish and humanity would relax into a new post-Information and Automation Technology Shangri-La. Well, something like that, as I recall. In the event, of course, the *Terminator* movies seem to have been more accurate in portraying the scenarios that might play out as a result of over-reliance on computers.

It is only a few years since the NHS was allegedly going to be revolutionised by a central database available to all practitioners when we needed medical care. A simple enough task, one might have thought, even back then. In the event, and after expenditure variably estimated at £12 billion or even more, the system was scrapped before ever fully commissioned. The only beneficiaries seemingly were the IT companies charged with setting the whole thing up.

This week the RBS group of banks was let down by its computer systems, which will cost it (and therefore ultimately us) millions. Chaos was generated so quickly when just one large company's IT systems failed. Can you imagine the effect of a mass commercial or utilities failure? Or international weapons systems?

I also heard a story that echoes rather disturbingly a sketch from *Little Britain* with which we are all becoming regularly familiar. A colleague told me of a friend of his who, having been diagnosed with terminal cancer, would be unable to work during his last few months. He went to his bank to ask if his mortgage could be changed to interest only, to ease his financial situation during that period, as having no dependants the bank would get their capital back on his death. He was told that that was not possible as the computer said 'No!'

And there we all were, naively thinking that computers would make life so much easier. And they had the potential to do so if those who program and operate the darned things had a modicum of common sense and allowed for flexibility when it was required.

6th July 2012

I had first-hand experience of the impact of the downgrading of the health service provision in and around Wycombe last week. My wife fractured her wrist when a friend's dog tumbled her to the ground unexpectedly. The friend took her for emergency treatment at Wycombe Hospital, but all subsequent (currently weekly) follow up treatment can only be offered at Stoke Mandeville. Having broken her wrist, my wife is unable to drive and therefore is totally dependent upon others or the public transport system to get her to Stoke Mandeville. As we live in a rural area, the latter is impractical, verging on the impossible.

Our daughters all work and I am currently touring the country with a play. Asking friends to give up the three or four hours minimum that it would take to drive her to Aylesbury, wait and bring her back is an ask too far. And the cost of a taxi exceeded the expense incurred by me driving back from Malvern in Worcestershire to ferry her to the outpatients fracture clinic and then return for my performance.

Everyone (except the decision makers at the Bucks NHS

Healthcare Trust) knows that the conurbation that is made up of Wycombe and Marlow and surrounding villages is more than large enough to justify having a hospital capable of providing all but the most specialised of health care. And until recently we did.

Expectant mothers and people with broken limbs are not unusual and should be able to be treated locally. A country that can afford bankers who waste billions and get millions as a reward should also be able to maintain the same level of healthcare for all that was available only a few decades ago.

Two excellent GPs of my acquaintance have left general practice early because they were obliged to sacrifice patient treatment and consultation time to the ever-increasing bureaucratic and administrative demands of government and the NHS Trust. The same trust allowed a local commercially-run pharmacy to open yards away from our doctors' surgery, resulting in the downgrading of the surgery and closure of its own pharmacy, the operation of which had allowed the local village practice to survive, until now.

We will one day look back at what successive governments have done to our health service provision and be appalled that political and administrative tinkering effectively crippled and then fragmented and dismantled a service that was thitherto the envy of the world.

13th July 2012

If you are in the public eye, it is undoubtedly true that you can be perfectly pleasant most of the time, but if you let things wind you up for a brief instant, that is the moment that will be remembered forever by those present.

So I always take with a grain of healthy scepticism any rumours of a particular actor's unpleasantness, as I have found most of the time that they are not as bad as their reputation would suggest. There are exceptions, as in any walk of life, and some people simply struggle to acknowledge that we may not want to grovel at their feet or accede to their every whim. And their names I will save for my autobiography, should I ever write one.

I was intrigued to read last week the reminiscences of the recently retired Wimbledon racket stringer (there's a wonderful job for the panellists to unravel (sic) on the old *What's My Line* TV show of the 50s and 60s—remember the wonderfully irascible Gilbert Harding?). I was, I admit, unsurprised to learn that the Williams sisters were the only tennis stars who, when asked to sign a charity fundraising item, declined to do so, saying they were 'too busy.' It reminded me of the time I encountered a tearful and very well-known BBC newsreader who had just been unceremoniously despatched with two brief words by Katherine Hepburn, when she asked for her to sign a similar charity item backstage at The Royal Variety Show.

Both the newsreader and I will forever remember that (possibly not only) example of the great star's disdain.

It's funny how these events seem to coincide with charitable occasions. There is out there a woman who will forever remember me for telling her that she had a big bottom.

It was not a gratuitous observation. She, a complete stranger, had just advanced up to me with her family at a fundraising event in Banbury and without pausing to say 'Hello', patted me vigorously on the stomach, intoning the words 'My goodness, you've put on a lot of weight since you were Doctor Who, haven't you?'

The words were bad enough, but the enormity of the molestation of my abdomen provoked my perhaps unkind response. I think both statements were true, however. But in a polite society, perhaps neither need have been uttered.

I rest my case.

20th July 2012

A near neighbour rented a small digger/tractor this week, which was kept overnight in a small field behind his house. During Sunday night the caterpillar-tracked vehicle was driven through his field and two larger fields which were connected by gates and then through a wire fence (which was cut for the purpose) onto a country track and then presumably loaded onto a trailer. It is, in all probability, now on its way to a port where it will be shipped to a Third World country. Unfortunately, the neighbour had not been informed that he had to insure the vehicle, which is worth around five thousand pounds.

Having only ever hired cars before, where the insurance is taken care of at the point of hire, he had assumed that this was the case for his digger. He is now personally liable for the cost of replacing the machine. This responsibility to insure is surely something that ought to be made abundantly clear at the time of hiring, particularly at a time when tractors and mobile industrial machinery are prime targets for marauding gangs all over the country.

Only last month, members of a gang in Lincolnshire were sentenced to varying terms of imprisonment after they were convicted of stealing half a million pounds' worth of farm machinery for illegal export to Iraq.

A local farmer friend has had to spend a great deal of time and money recently to protect his yard and machinery by installing motorway grade barriers around it after successive tractor thefts, when the thieves simply drove them through the surrounding hedges.

Given the value of these machines, it is surely not beyond the ingenuity of manufacturers to install systems that, say, set off banshee alarms if they are moved from where they are left by more than a few inches and which is rendered live by a device that the driver removes and takes with him? Cars, which are usually worth much less, are much better protected now than they were, and modern cars are much harder to drive away.

Another increasingly worrying phenomenon is the theft of drain and manhole covers for their metal content, which has the added element of endangering the lives of the next person or vehicle along. And the removal of cables and track on railway lines implies a level of disregard for other people's lives that beggars belief.

It is all very depressing.

27th July 2012

Earlier this week a young man, wearing a costume of protective gear similar to that worn in a film and carrying guns, entered a cinema where that film was being shown in Aurora, Colorado and shot dead twelve people, injuring around fifty-eight more. The death toll may well rise. The young man must, by any reasonable criteria, be deemed deranged, but he was nonetheless able to amass an arsenal of weaponry and bullets over a few weeks without alerting any responsible body to the fact or raising an inquisitorial eyebrow.

In the wake of the tragedy, the cinema chain, AMC Theatres, has announced, 'We will not allow any guests into our theatres in costumes that make other guests feel uncomfortable and we will not permit face-covering masks or fake weapons inside our buildings.'

This announcement has triggered a stunned response from many commentators along the lines of 'a man in fancy dress shoots seventy people in a cinema, provoking the immediate banning of fancy dress in cinemas.' It serves to highlight the impossible dilemma facing politicians of sound mind in the USA.

To even suggest a tightening of the bizarre gun laws of (what has been for decades at least) the most powerful nation in the world, spells instant death to a candidate at the ballot box. The right to bear arms is so central to the beliefs of middle America. Otherwise perfectly reasonable Americans of my acquaintance react with exactly the same level of horror and incomprehension when I suggest the removal of their inalienable right to bear arms as I feel about them having that right in the first place.

The right for an American citizen to carry arms seems a powerful, almost religious belief comparable with the rights claimed by faiths worldwide to wear certain types of clothing, to kill animals in certain ritualistic ways or revere and protect specific animals, or to pierce or mutilate their bodies. Many of the practices of belief systems alien to us perplex us, and were we to delete the 'belief systems folder' of the human hard disk and start again, I would hope that many of them would be happily forgotten.

It would take a brave generation of Republican and Democratic candidates to stand up to the backlash and transitional period, were they to cooperate in taking on this apparently insoluble problem. I am sure that many would love to but simply daren't.

3rd August 2012

My daughter was unexpectedly offered the chance of a holiday last week when a friend was unable to use one he had booked when work intervened—and in my business work always wins; there's not a lot of it about. All she had to do was pay £95 to change the name on the booking.

Even though that is a lot of money for a process that should take seconds only to accomplish, it is a small price to pay for a trip to an Aegean island. She then discovered that her passport had run out with a week to go before her departure to Thassos. No worry, there is a four-hour passport service available—at a premium, of course—but that's fair enough.

It costs £77.50 already, so the extra £52.00 is worth it if you're desperate. Now given that this is the busiest time of the year, one would think that the number of people requiring this service could be predicted and appropriate staff put in place. First of all, there is the usual ritual dance of ringing a premium number that sends you through several options and recorded messages before kicking you into touch with a cheery 'This service is not available at the moment.' Why can't they tell you that at the beginning rather than the end of the process? No prizes for guessing.

When she eventually got to speak to someone, she was told that there was only one appointment available that week, in Belfast. Desperate, she grabbed it. She was told, however, that she could keep checking, as there were often cancellations of appointments at one of the half dozen passport offices in the UK.

Eventually, she got an appointment in Durham two days before her flight. She filled the form in and signed within the box in black ink and took every piece of evidence she could find with her on the 600-mile round trip to Durham and got her precious passport.

It appears that so many jobs have been cut that the agency is in chaos. Union officials have been warning the government for months that this would be an issue in the summer but their warnings, it seems, fell on deaf ears. When I last checked there were no appointments available for at least two weeks in Peterborough, London, Bristol or Newport. So check your passports now if you are planning a holiday trip in the next few weeks.

10th August 2012

I am anticipating Olympic withdrawal symptoms. The rare joy of events being broadcast at times when we in the UK can watch without staying up to 3 a.m. has meant that we have immersed ourselves in the breadth and depth of the fantastic efforts of competitors from all over the world. And the age of the red button has allowed us to choose our excitement of preference.

I know that some countries use the efforts of their athletes to boost their national image in the world, which is why we see certain countries suddenly break into the medal-winning limelight while others continue to languish at the bottom of the medal table. Just compare the list of high-achieving nations with those of ten and twenty years ago and you will see what I mean.

But leaving aside the politicians' desire to use the efforts of all these remarkable sports competitors for nationalistic purposes, there have been some remarkable achievements on display in the superb stadia that we have produced for this year's wonderful games. I have lost track of the number of times that I have 'had something in my eye' when sharing the joy of achievement of remarkable men and women who have dedicated their every waking moment for years to improving and honing their sporting skills to achieve beyond even their own hopes and expectations. Of course, our own athletes figure prominently for us, but it is a measure of the Olympic ideal that most of us are able to enthusiastically applaud and celebrate the successes of all nations, and if anything can bring nations together in any meaningful way, it is the co-celebration of what constitutes the best in us. Maybe the heady rush of global solidarity cannot be sustained, as the memory of the Olympics fades, but at least we will be able to remember that, like Camelot, the bright light shone for a while.

We live in a world where celebrity is valued as a commodity that seems to be accorded to those who earn a fortune working in front of cameras and inhabit the gossip columns. These athletes are the real celebrities, although with a bit of luck they won't find themselves subjected for too long to the kind of tabloid scrutiny given to reality TV stars and footballers.

How they will begin to sort out Sports Personality of the Year this year, heaven only knows.

17th August 2012

My car broke down in London last week, ironically a few strides from Waterloo Bridge, where I was born. While the recovery man was going about his oily business, we became aware of an elderly lady wandering in the middle of the road, looking confused and anxious. We approached her—and a uniform does help in these situations—and she told us that she was worried about her husband, who had gone off hours earlier.

Several subsequent conversations, as she kept getting out of her parked Mercedes and telling us ever-changing stories about the absent spouse, prompted us to call the police, as my car was hoisted ready for its tow and we needed to be on our way. The police call handler asked to speak to the lady, who told him that she was 21. She was at least 70, and they eventually agreed to send an officer.

Forty minutes later, she decided she needed to go to the loo and set off to look for one. The AA man continued to wait for the police and I accompanied her. As luck would have it, we met up with two police officers on patrol and I explained and handed her over to them.

About to depart, we noticed a smart, suited man in his 70s looking anxiously up and down the street.

Yes, he was the husband. She was suffering from dementia, he told us. He had left her in the car with strict instructions to stay where she was, 'a mere two hours earlier.'

He seemed oblivious to our slack-jawed disbelief, as he hastened off to join the officers and his poor wife round the corner.

We then noticed the disabled sticker on the car. She was clearly his validation for a couple of hours' parking in London, while he went to a meeting.

An acquaintance of mine recently found a distressed and confused elderly lady in similar circumstances in Birmingham and took her to the address where she said she lived, only to find derelict land. Her subsequent anxiety and increased confusion led him to drive her to a police station, only to be told she wasn't their problem, he should try the local authority. Having already exposed himself to risk by helping in the first place, he replied with understandable asperity that it now was their problem and left the police station.

So much for 'Care in the Community'.

24ᵗʰ August 2012

It is only during my lifetime that suicide ceased to be a criminal act. Amazingly, until 1961 anyone attempting and failing to end their own life could be prosecuted and imprisoned. It is a myth that it was ever a capital offence in this country, or indeed any other, in the two millennia since the Roman Emperor Hadrian tried to prevent soldiers from committing suicide (as a means of avoiding having to fight and die in battle) by making their attempt punishable by death.

Even countries that have been what we choose to call 'civilised' for less time than us regard the act of trying to terminate one's own life as evidence that a person needs help rather than punishment. Many argue, with some justification, that one's own life is something over which the individual alone should have ultimate control, and the right to decide to stop living, for whatever reason, is no different essentially from the corresponding right to choose to live.

Religions worldwide, however, take a different view. If we have been given life by a god, then (they argue) only that god has the right to take it away. It is for this reason that we find ourselves in a position where those who are physically unable to end their own lives, through complete incapacity, are unable to ask others to assist them to end the lives that have become intolerable and incurably painful.

The case of Tony Nicklinson, who spent seven years paralysed from the neck down, highlights for many the cruelty of a blanket ban on allowing the terminally and painfully ill assistance in hastening their ends rather than prolong their agony. Mercifully, six days after hearing that the High Court could not allow him to authorise his own painless demise at the hands of sympathetic friends or family, nature intervened and his two thousand days of torment are over. Who can be other than thankful on his behalf?

Clearly it would be unwise to make assisted suicide too easy, for fear of the few abuses that might subsequently occur. The vulnerable must be protected. But in those most extreme cases of demonstrable agony and torment, it must be possible somehow to allow a gentle passage into that dark night. In the multicultural, secular society we live in, the only consideration should be the protection of the weak, not the prevention of the determined.

31ˢᵗ August 2012

In the last week, 34 striking miners were shot dead at a platinum mine in South Africa; an 11-year old girl with Downs Syndrome in Pakistan was arrested for blasphemy as a result of burning pages from the Koran; a US Republican candidate for the senate announced that women who were victims of 'legitimate rape' (whatever that is) rarely got pregnant, therefore abortion could and should safely be made illegal; soup kitchens became commonplace in Greece; Winnie

Johnson died, after a lifetime of agonised hope, without ever having the small solace of knowing where her son Keith was buried by the vile Ian Brady.

But none of these different but compelling events merited the popular media's attention in the forensic detail accorded to the 'news' that a young man, who happens to be a prince, has taken his clothes off while behaving as young people sometimes do in the company of friends, at least one of whom turned out not be much of a friend and shared an indistinct photo of the royal fundament with the insatiable millions who cannot resist this kind of offal when it is thrown in their general direction by the redtop papers (I cannot bring myself to call them 'news'papers).

Yes, it is only human to look. As we drive past an accident on the motorway, it would take a will of iron to the point of perversity not to slow down and glance at the evidence of someone else's recent misfortune. To accuse drivers of rubbernecking is not always accurate, unless they have altered their route in order to view the carnage, which I suspect and hope is rare.

But to go out to buy a newspaper in order to see a young man's bottom is different. First of all, it is no different to anybody else's, for heaven's sake.

The lad has the sympathy of the majority of rightminded citizens. Were his actions ill advised? Yes, like similar actions of thousands of young people every week.

Unlucky? Certainly; no wonder royals restrict their circle of friends so obsessively to those who would have just as much to lose from this kind of unwelcome publicity. We all have moments in our lives when we were mightily glad that there were no cameras or witnesses present, things that are ever p-ppresent for Harry, the poor chap. Let's hope he picks better companions next time.

7th September 2012

We had to face an uncomfortable truth last week at Baker Towers.

I was brought up in an age when we all left our doors open, and although the post-war years would be regarded as times of comparative deprivation by the current generation—no TVs, no computers or mobile phones, few cars – thefts from homes were rare, perhaps partly for that reason. So we have carried that trusting attitude through our lives. We live well off the beaten track and strangers are highly visible, but not at night, alas. Last week we returned home late to find that of the four cars outside our gate, two had been unceremoniously plundered. The unlocked ones.

Having got into my wife's car, the perpetrator had set about the fascia with an implement, trashed it and hauled out all the wires from the loom, presumably with the intention of 'hot-wiring' it. Our arrival must have interrupted his (or 'her'—I suppose, but doubt) clumsy hackings, because we found a bag of tools on the driving seat and items removed from the car scattered around on the grass.

Our neighbours had also had their children's games and music similarly strewn around their car. Fortunately for us, though not for the felon, he had damaged himself as well as the car and there was enough blood to afford assistance to the forensic officer who came the next day to do his NCIS thing. Our genius mechanic has contrived to join up all the wires untimely ripped from around the ignition and the car is now restored to functionality, if not its pristine cosmetic beauty.

Lesson learned. All locked and alarmed now. We have to reluctantly accept that we do not live in an oasis of peace and tranquillity but are part of the real, and occasionally nasty, world. The attentive and helpful officers who arrived soon after our 999 call tell me I am not allowed to wreak havoc on the miscreant when (and if) found. But my visceral reaction to realising that while two of my daughters were in our home this was happening outside has surprised me.

On a happier note—if you want to meet some nice, caring people, come and join me at Stokenchurch Dog Rescue's Summer Fair and Dog Show, which I am proud to be opening at 12 a.m. this Saturday Sept 8th. Lots of dogs, hopefully sunshine and something for everyone.

14th September 2012

In past years, the process of sorting out who should be accorded the accolade of Sports Personality of the Year has not presented too many difficulties. Usually there are one or two prime and obvious candidates. In the wake of this summer of Olympics and Paralympics, the British public have an unenviable job when the list of candidates is revealed in a couple of months. And it's a job that Andy Murray has just made even harder, if it wasn't impossible enough already.

Any other year, he and Bradley Wiggins would have been the two predictable contenders. Had the Paralympics not completely changed the public's view of both disability and disabled sport, any one of a handful of multiple gold-winning athletes or sportsmen from what has until now been regarded as the main event two weeks earlier would have been prime candidates. But I really cannot see beyond our wonderful squad of Paralympians this year, unless in the interim Clare Balding (another of the Olympic successes) were to take up sprinting and break Usain Bolt's world record for the 100 metres and 200 metres and then win a golf major with a blindfold on.

In common, I fear, with many others, I think hitherto I may have subconsciously half-regarded the Paralympics as a worthy bolt-on to the main event. I cannot recall watching much of the programming of previous Paralympiads. This is clearly a view still held elsewhere around the world, too. In America, I understand that there was no live coverage at all, except for those whose enthusiasm led them to seek it out via the Internet. A total of seven hours of televised highlights were shown on non-mainstream cable channels.

Having the events in our own country and having the opportunity afforded by a terrestrial broadcaster to watch almost every event has altered that previous position forever for me, and I suspect for the majority of the population. Even non-sports enthusiasts of my acquaintance have been captivated.

Three weeks ago the achievements of Jessica Ennis, Chris Hoy, Bradley Wiggins, Mo Farrah et al—good heavens, the list is endless—seemed definitively unsurpassable. But the joy and passion of the Paralympic sportsmen and women has been beyond remarkable and almost requires the invention of new adjectives that properly define the triumphant ability of some human beings to defy expectation, limitation and apparent handicap to achieve the impossible and more.

21st September 2012

The deaths of the two young lady police officers in Manchester serve as a salutary reminder, if one were needed, of the number of people in this country who regularly put their lives on the line for the rest of us. Those who work in all the emergency services know when they enter their respective professions that even though incidents like the one reported this week are mercifully rare, there is always that possibility that even a seemingly routine call-out could have the potential to present them with life-threatening situations.

This harrowing and horrendous killing happened only a couple of weeks after two young officers in the Thames Valley force came out to my house and dealt calmly and efficiently with my family, when we were more than a little jumpy on returning home to find our cars had been broken into and the perpetrator, having clearly been disturbed by our arrival, had decamped into the woods behind our house, leaving his possessions and tools behind.

This offender was not violent or murderous on this occasion, luckily. But the two young officers had no means of knowing that, any more than we did, but they came out to assist us in the wee small hours and calmly allayed our concerns and went about their business. For them it was routine, as presumably it was for WPCs Fiona Bone and Nicola Hughes when they went out to investigate a report of a burglary in the middle of the morning in a housing estate in Manchester.

WPC Bone was about to be married. Their pictures have now appeared on our television screens and we see them for what they were, two personable young women setting out to do their best in the service of the community.

Our hearts must go out to their families and friends and to their colleagues too, who now have to deal with the investigation of their murders.

Without the work done every day by our police officers, firemen, paramedics and all the others who protect us in our domestic environment, our lives would be very different.

The tragic waste of these two young lives at the hands, it appears, of one evil man serves to remind us all of how lucky we are that there are people like these young ladies who are prepared to make a career out of risking their lives for us.

5th October 2012

English is a living language, and therefore one has to be careful about trying to preserve it in aspic come what may. I am sure that many 17th century grammarians were utterly appalled by the demise of 'thou' as the second person singular pronoun when that vulgar upstart 'you' became widely used in its place. My parents' generation may have a similar attitude about the loss of 'gay' as a word for that particular kind of light-hearted, easy fun enjoyed when they were young, but we all have to accept that it now has a new meaning.

However, there is a difference between naturally evolving language and casually corrupted language. I only have to offer the insidious and widespread use of the appalling 'should of' as a substitute for 'should have' to make my point. It clearly came from the use of 'should've' being heard incorrectly. But to see 'should of' written widely on Twitter and in emails and heard in everyday speech is evidence of linguistic pollution rather than evolution.

Nor is it a matter of English moving on when someone, as I heard recently on the radio, referred to a 'mute point' instead of a 'moot point'. One can only imagine how the great guardian of our language and first director general of the BBC, Lord Reith, would view that. The word 'decimate' means to eradicate ten per cent of something, but is now widely used by the media to indicate wholesale destruction. There is a difference between the casually erroneous or the imperfectly understood on the one hand and the deliberate adoption of existing words to define the culture of a new generation on the other. So calling something 'wicked', indicating quite the reverse, is not the same, say, as using the word 'generally' by mistake when 'genuinely' is intended.

Correcting people who say 'less' instead of 'fewer' may be verging on the pedantic, but the words do mean slightly different things, relating to size/number; and most people use 'uninterested' and 'disinterested' as if they were synonyms, even though they do have importantly different meanings.

Another irritant (in more than one way) is the PAT test that we all have to spend hours and/or many hundreds of pounds on having done annually to equipment in schools and workplaces. PAT stands for Personal Appliance Test, so the second 'test' is redundant. Here endeth the lecture, or 'lecher', as I recently heard.

19th October 2012

Why is everything unnecessarily complicated? That is the question I feel compelled to ask, even though I know the answer. The answer is that it suits those who want our money, our compliance and our obedience to have us all wandering around in a haze of baffled incomprehension. I am talking about taxation, insurance, telephone and internet service, travel tickets, hotel prices, utility prices, even a cup of coffee. Everything has been made so complicated that we need a battery of explanatory buffers between us, the consumers, and 'them', although they are the ones who should be called the 'consumers', because they gobble up everything like corporate Pacmen as they make billions and pay teams of tax lawyers to ensure that they baffle HMCR as well. It has to stop.

I don't want to spend half a day each time we renew the insurance on one of our cars, disentangling ourselves from the multicar policy that promised savings and produced the opposite as each new car joined. I don't want to spend hours of multiple choice options followed by conversations with people who can't speak English properly or comprehensibly, when I am having trouble with my mobile phone. I don't want to read that neither Starbucks (with sales of 1.2 billion) nor Vodafone (which earns several hundred million pounds a year from more than 19 m customers in the UK last year) paid any tax to the UK treasury.

They all latch on to the buzzword 'choice' to explain the myriad of variable elements to what they sell us, even down to the supermarkets flimflamming us by pricing similar goods respectively in different weights/measures and pricing structures. Which is cheaper? Four baking potatoes for 75p or a kilo of loose ones for £1.50? We shouldn't have to bring calculators with us to do our shopping. And if they trot out that smug mantra about promoting customer choice, I say bring out the tumbrils.

I don't want to have to change my car insurer every time I renew in order to get best value. Lovely though the meerkats are, we shouldn't need to compare anything via a third party website because the industry refuses to simplify its operations and save us all money.

We are the only ones who can change things and I just wish I knew how. Ideas, please, to the Letters Page?

2nd November 2012

On the 15th November, we are being invited to vote for a Police Commissioner for The Thames Valley. I have received my voting card, but no information about the candidates. So, I searched online and, lo and behold, it is all there for the asking at www.choosemypcc.org.uk. I had not given much thought, I confess, as to the advisability or otherwise of having an elected Police Commissioner, instead of the present system, whereby basically a Chief Constable who has risen through the ranks answers to the politicians at Home Office.

The Police have had a rough ride lately. The Hillsborough disaster may reflect historical policing methods and a culture that we must hope no longer exist, but the recent developments in that case are another hurdle the police have to overcome in order to regain the high levels of public confidence they traditionally enjoyed when I was young.

Education and Healthcare have moved slowly away from being 'The State Knows Best' paternalistic organisations to making efforts to embrace freedom of choice and introduce more democratic procedures, so it is undeniably arguable that the Police should do the same.

But all the evidence is that we, the soon to be enfranchised public, are underwhelmed by the opportunity. The election has been structured unhelpfully. The Government talked the talk about attracting independent candidates, but then decreed that they must put down a deposit of £5000 and that there would be no state-funded mail-out of candidates' details or intentions. As a result there are inevitably fewer independent candidates, and the political parties are treating it like another strand of local government elections. I think I had thought—naively—that this would be a party politics-lite election. Having checked online, we have the usual four suspects fielding candidates plus two independents. The former four all had their statements prepared by someone at party headquarters. Only the two independents wrote and declare ownership of their personal manifestos.

Whatever an individual voter's party allegiance, this is surely a time when independence of slavish adherence to party doctrine could offer a creative and democratic overseeing of our police forces.

This is an opportunity for us to 'own' our own police force in a very real way. If the Commissioner doesn't deliver the policing we the public demand, we can remove him or her at the ballot box. I shall be hoping for an Independent Police Commissioner.

16th November 2012

When I became an actor, reality television didn't exist in the way that it does now. I suppose the first such programme was probably *Candid Camera*, in which practical jokes were played on unsuspecting members of the public and secretly filmed for our entertainment.

The first serious attempt to show 'real life' on a medium that had until then, virtually exclusively, trodden the separate paths of news and current affairs on the one hand and drama and entertainment on the other, was the remarkable *Seven Up* in 1964, which interviewed a group seven-year-olds from a variety of backgrounds and then repeated the process with the same group every seven years thereafter. This is firmly at what we might describe as the serious end of the reality TV spectrum. At the non-serious entertainment end are those dating programmes and search for a singer, model, chef, entrepreneur programmes which are, shall we say, much more manipulated than the fly on the wall programmes. And then there are the *Essex* and *Chelsea* lot. They have very high viewing figures and supposedly show us real young people interacting socially and romantically in their respective environments. They are not actors pretending to be real people; they are real people pretending to be themselves in situations with their real circle of friends that probably would never have happened had the production team not offered up scenarios for them to live their real lives in.

I can only imagine that the 'cast' get confused themselves and, indeed, some—very understandably—don't stay the course as a result. In the case of the *Chelsea* programme, their motives for participating are interesting. As they are all clearly wealthy young folk, it can't be just the money. Maybe to their jaded 21st century palates, it may just be for the heck of it.

Then there are the programmes where 'celebrities' are placed in a variety of challenging positions and the audience is invited to delight in their achievements or humiliation, depending on the show. The added attraction is that the participants are known already to the viewers, so provoking a spot of the good old schadenfreude.

But we actors, singers, sportsmen or public figures are all entertainers in our way and must adjust our skills for the times we live in.

As a young actor, I never foresaw participating in *Come Dine with Me*—or indeed any other reality programme.

23rd November 2012

By the time you read this I will be in Australia, taking part in ITV's *I'm a Celebrity Get Me Out of Here.*

First of all, I would like to assure you that the word 'celebrity' is one that I have never coveted. I became an actor four and a half decades ago because I wanted to act, not because I sought fame. And I would caution anyone who joins any of the strands of the entertainment profession that if fame is your prime motivation, it is unlikely you will acquire it. The most 'celebrated' singers, dancers, actors are those who simply want—no, need—to sing, dance and act.

So, if I ever utter that word in the course of the programme, it will, I promise you, only be because I cannot eat a live humming bird or dangle by my nostrils over a pit of alligators.

I am writing the day before I fly out, and there is in my stomach a lump of what feels like lead, as I contemplate what lies ahead and, just as importantly—what I am leaving behind. Once I arrive in Australia, I am completely cut off from my family and everyone at home. No contact is allowed until I walk back over that bridge to be affectionately mocked by Ant and Dec (now there's a job I'd like!).

I think this is my principal anxiety. I have never been out of contact with my wife for more than a day in the thirty-odd years we have been together. And I will worry, even though we have good friends and tradesmen who will help out when the boiler explodes, some jobsworth demands paperwork my wife can't find, or (as has literally just happened) the Sky television packs up and has to be rebooted.

The not-knowing that Baker Towers and all who dwell therein is safe and secure eclipses even the prospect of devouring aardvark droppings through a straw while standing on my head in a bowl of primeval slime, or being closeted with more creepy-crawlies than the average human meets in a lifetime, the majority of whom are trying to make a new home in your bodily cavities.

So why am I doing it? Because it's there! It's a challenge, once offered, that I cannot duck. And what a brilliant way to lose weight! I can't raid the fridge!

30th November 2012

Why is car insurance so ridiculously frustrating? The very clever marketing idea of creating a collectible toy that my daughter covets has induced me over the last couple of years to check through their website to see if I can get better value insurance for our veritable fleet of vehicles. We live in a fairly inaccessible place and all six of us need independent transport.

Annoyingly, it is very rare that the best value can be obtained by remaining with the insurance company that covered each of us for the previous year. The market is so competitive now that they are constantly tinkering and inducing us to tiptoe into their murky actuarial lair by tantalising us with lower premiums for the first year in the hope, presumably, that we won't do exactly the same thing the following year when they rejoin the ranks of the money harvesters.

The deals change, as they do annually with electricity, gas, all forms of borrowing and, of course, other types of insurance. The end result is that a population that is, in these hard times, compelled to seek for best value in almost everything is perpetually yo-yoing back and forth between insurers and providers of utilities. It is time-consuming on both sides, particularly in the case of car insurance when you have to get last year's lot prove to this year's lot that you are entitled to the no claims bonus you are claiming. Why can't they have a central data-sharing base, accessible to all insurers to save me (and millions of others, presumably) the tedium of spending hours getting your jilted insurer to send you the information required by your new cover lover—a process that will be repeated the following year ad infinitum while they are all competing in a saturated market.

My latest lot wouldn't accept the last-but-two lot's letters. They needed to hear from the spurned (now expensive) lot that they accepted the previous lot's no claims. The letter from the insurers two years ago won't do, apparently—only the last lot are trusted. Interestingly the spurned company have been much more helpful than the new recipient of my money. I have sent them the last-but-one lot's proof so they can send their confirmation to the new lot.

Are you following this? No? Me neither—so I don't blame you. Pass me a cockroach!

7th December 2012

I am writing this a month ahead of publication as a consequence of being incommunicado in a Western Australian jungle as the deadline passes. So I do not know who won the American election, how Wycombe Wanderers are faring in their battle to climb from the bottom of League Two and ensure survival, who our new Police Commissioner is or whether you are already wading through feet of snow back at home, or indeed about anything of moment that has happened anywhere in the world for the last three weeks. You will also (should you have been watching) have seen me bonding (hopefully) with a disparate group of people whom I had never met before, and doing things that no one of my advanced years should ever be asked to do and eating things that most sensible people would avoid like the plague.

That is a very strange feeling and one that I suspect I will never experience again. However, I do know that on my return home I will be heading off immediately to Bournemouth, where I open in pantomime a mere four days after my 24-hour flight back from Australia. If I am voted out early, I will have time to work on my script as I sit by the swimming pool (hmmmm ...), but were I to have won—and of course I would like to—I guess that takes care of the 24-hour flight back. No movies for me this time! And I think I've seen more films on planes in the last few years than I have in the cinema!

The rest of the cast will have been rehearsing solidly for a whole week without me and will then have to tolerate me stumbling, jet-lagged, into their midst to try and catch up in very short order. I know pantomime has the reputation of being heavily reliant on ad libs, but those ad libs have to be judiciously applied around a well-honed structure that may appear chaotic but is in fact carefully constructed in rehearsal.

All the great comics from Morecambe and Wise, Les Dawson and onwards may have appeared to have been freewheeling and making it up, but all their asides were very carefully worked out, usually.

Let's hope I can emulate them! If you're in Bournemouth at Christmas, come and see *Sleeping Beauty*, with me as Nanny Nelly and Su Pollard as the Wicked Queen.

14th December 2012

Well, I made it safely back from Western Australia, and three days later opened in panto in Bournemouth with a bout of merry seasonal lurgy and promptly lost my voice. Hopefully, as you read this the Baker tones will be restored after much steaming, consumption of proprietary and prescription remedies and every other cast member's pet cold remedy.

I am in no doubt that many millions watched my sojourn in the jungle. The evidence is in the number of people who stop me to ask about it. So if you didn't watch it, forgive me if I answer some of the many questions I am being asked. Yes, it is all completely legit. We were all on lockdown and incommunicado from the moment we landed in Oz.

Our phones, laptops etc. were all confiscated, and between then and the moment I walked across that metal bridge two and half weeks later, we really did survive on the meagre menu and did sleep in that jungle clearing, which is a lot smaller than it appears on telly. Given poor Helen from Corrie's terror of trials and the public's insistence on making her do more, we really did live on a tiny amount of beans (yuck) and rice (sigh) for five long days, until we finally worked out a way to cook the wretched beans so that they tasted less like cardboard. The luckiest thing was that given the extraordinarily wide range of people in the jungle, we did actually genuinely get on well together. They were a great bunch and we will all stay in touch. The two who attracted the most adverse comments (I learned later) were in fact the two who helped me the most when, as the out-of-condition senior member, I struggled on the jungle yomps and slumped. So I will hear no criticism of either Nadine Dorries or Eric Bristow, both of whom went the extra mile for me.

What was it like? Well, despite being told it would be tough, we all found it tougher than we imagined. We all found the experience of being completely cut off from our 'real' lives unsettling and difficult at times. And we all learned an awful lot about ourselves, as well as quite a bit about each other.

For instance, I never imagined I would ever get a thumbs-up from a Pussycat Doll after exiting (successfully) from the dunny.

21st December 2012

As my memory of jungle deprivations, excitements and trials fades, I am now in the throes of panto twice daily down in wintry Bournemouth. Christmas is everywhere to be seen and heard and this year I am, I have to confess, woefully unprepared. I suppose five weeks on the other side of the world followed by an immediate immersion into the fantasy world of *Sleeping Beauty* with Su Pollard twice daily, six days a week does not leave a lot of time for a measured and careful preparation for the Yule jollifications.

I am afraid, for instance, that the sending of Christmas cards has been a total failure this year. Every year I promise myself to organise my address book and grapple with the (I am told) simple notion of printing labels up to ease the whole process. I also intend to have them all done and ready to send by the end of November. Dream on!

But I also struggle with the whole idea of sending out hundreds of cards that are barely scrutinised before being jettisoned—and hopefully recycled—a couple of weeks later. Yes, there are people with whom one has little or no contact between each year's end, despite the hastily scrawled 'Must see you in 2013' messages, but whom one wishes to reassure that they are still in our thoughts. But, on the other hand, however much I appreciate the thought of those who send me a card, I genuinely do not notice if people don't send me one.

Anyway, I shall be emailing felicitations to many this year and hope they will understand the lack of investment in card and stamp.

And, of course, with two shows on both Christmas Eve and Boxing Day, I shall be savouring that one precious day when we sit down as a family and celebrate together in the way that has evolved over the decades and which my daughters regard as sacrosanct and immutable. And it will be doubly delightful for me this year after I have confirmed for myself during my bush tucker trip just how important my family is to me. I knew already, of course, but somehow that time to think in a jungle clearing reinforced my certainty about what really matters.

So, I hope you all have your best possible Christmas too and can share it with those who you care about and I thank you for dipping, even occasionally, into my inconsequential ramblings.

28th December 2012

This has turned out to be a problematical Christmas for many people in the UK.

The traditional picture of robins perched on snow-spangled branches while laughing children, warmly wrapped in scarves, make snowmen below has been dispelled completely by the deluge that has subsumed parts of the country. The West Country has taken a battering and transport links in Devon and Cornwall in particular have been very badly affected. Our hearts must go out to those people who, at this time of family and traditional celebration, are instead sweeping water from their homes and worrying about the likelihood of their insurers being less than helpful in the aftermath, especially in areas where there is a local history of rivers bursting their banks in the event of greater than usual rainfall.

If proof were needed that we humans exist within very narrow boundaries of climate and temperature, recent changes in our weather underline the fragility of our dominance of our planet.

Even in the 'High' Wycombe area there are those whose property is at risk in the area around the Thames in Marlow, as was demonstrated by the recent flooding in the Longridge area.

Several of my fellow pantomime performers will have struggled to get home to their families after the second performance on Christmas Eve because of problems with trains and other transport and will be obliged to stay in Bournemouth. I am lucky in that I can drive home and wrap presents like a madman in the wee small hours. Why don't I do it before then? Ah well, that's the downside of Internet shopping. Having been out of the country in the build-up to Christmas, I resorted to my laptop for the majority of my Christmas shopping this year and it has, of course, all been delivered to my home while I am elsewhere.

As I write this I count myself blessed that, yet again, I will be able to spend that one special day with my wife and all four of my daughters in our home in the way that we still all treasure. When I am in pantomime, that one day becomes even more significant for me, as the festive season is otherwise taken up by my entertaining others twice daily. No complaints there, but it makes my one day with my family very special.

I hope you all have or have had the Christmas that makes you and your families happy.

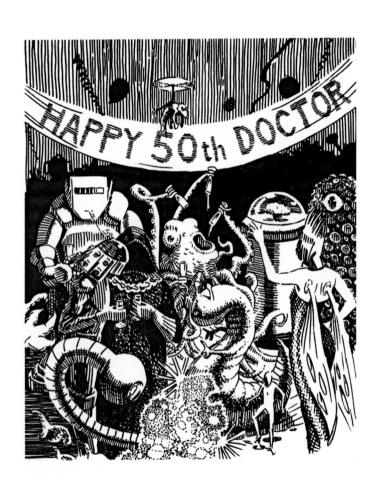

2013

4th January 2013

When I left the UK for my stint in the jungle, Wycombe Wanderers were bouncing ominously around the bottom of League 2 and had just suffered a home defeat at the hands of Oxford that left us on 12 points after 11 games. I dined on rice and beans for two weeks, unaware that the Blues were faring no better in my absence, although the tide turned at the end of November and the team is now climbing slowly back up towards the middle of the League.

I went to my first home game since October on New Year's Day and we lost to Exeter with an unlucky 82nd minute deflection off Wanderers' Kortney Hause, after goalkeeper Jordan Archer had made an excellent save. But this was a different Wanderers team from the one I had been watching earlier in the season. And I don't just mean that there were new players. The passion that Gareth Ainsworth seems to have instilled in the young players that he has brought on since poor results ended the managerial reign of Gary Waddock is impressive.

When a team is struggling, some fans find it hard to offer the unwavering support that it is arguable fans should always give their team in adversity as well as in successful times. But, despite the disappointment of a loss in a match that was pretty much evenly balanced and despite the otherwise impressive Joel Grant's regrettable failure to convert his penalty opportunity, I believe the fans were able to put their disappointment into perspective. The team is moving slowly and steadily towards safety and Gareth 'Mr Motivator' Ainsworth seems to have his dressing room firmly onside.

The club has had a testing time over the last months and the new directors have a formidable task ahead, presumably with little opportunity for significant transfer window investment; indeed, there is more likely to be a demand by bigger footballing predators for our star players, sadly. But the combination of firm and sensible control of the club— and a manager who oozes an energy and passion that would be envied by players a decade his junior—bodes well for the future of our local team. There were 3,679 fans there today.

They deserved a larger crowd, so come back, wrap up warm and exercise your lungs.

I wish my work allowed me more Saturdays off, but actors, like footballers, have Saturday jobs!

11ᵗʰ January 2013

My mother brought up my brother and me with the help of a book published in the 1930s entitled *The Motherhood Book*. It was, I recall a weighty tome. How much she relied upon its pages I don't know, but I do remember that there was a chapter on the importance of relaxation during pregnancy. Expectant mothers who found it difficult to relax were encouraged to take up smoking, which despite its 'tendency to make you cough initially', once you got the hang of it, it was a jolly good and effective aid to relaxation, the book advised.

It is sometimes hard to determine exactly what is or isn't good or bad for you, though I think no sane person would ever again suggest that smoking has any beneficial effect at all.

It has, for instance, been recently discovered from five hundred-year-old genealogical studies that eunuchs tended to live on average around seventeen years longer than their untampered-with male contemporaries. I explained this to our male kitten as I made the appointment with the vet. I don't know if he took it in.

But do you remember when we were all warned off eggs and the egg industry imploded—only recently, it seems? Well, that's all changed. A new study has revealed that eggs today contain 25% less saturated fat and 10 % less cholesterol and twice as much Vitamin D, a vitamin which is worryingly lacking in our diets apparently, resulting in a recent upsurge in cases of rickets.

And only last year we were being warned that having real Christmas trees in our homes can lead to shortness of breath, sinus problems and bronchitis, as a result of mould spores on the needles.

Beware of supplements, too. The fish oil tablets my generation were routinely forced to ingest by the generation of parents who read *The Motherhood Book* have zero effect on reducing incidence of strokes, unlike consumption of the actual fish—which is beneficial.

Chocolate, it is now claimed, is packed with antioxidant flavonols that help prevent certain cancers and dementia, keep your arteries from clogging and increase blood flow to the brain. Red wine also contains helpful antioxidants, and new research has also suggested that moderate beer intake can actually improve cardiovascular function.

Confused? Me too, but while I think it's a little late to benefit from castration, pass the bottle and the choccies, eh?

20th January 2013

The changes in the selection process for secondary education are a step in the right direction. At the end of secondary education, the preferred outcome must be that all will have achieved their potential. To distinguish between the two types of secondary education is of necessity a generalisation, but some thrive in the faster-paced, more overtly academic grammar schools, others in the upper schools, where the range may be broader and the pace more varied. I know children who have struggled at grammar school, having just achieved the requisite entry mark, while others with a similar score who attended an upper school were ultimately high achievers.

We are lucky to have excellent schools of both types locally and parents should visit them to see which might best benefit the individual that is their child, before making judgements either way. One size does not fit all.

Parents, who think they are acting in the best interests of their child, have their children coached to get them to a grammar school, where they may struggle. This is unfair both on that child and the uncoached children whose score was then lower, but who might otherwise have been more appropriately assigned to a grammar school.

The new system promises to try, at least, to level the playing field, so that children attend the school for which their natural verbal, non-verbal and mathematical abilities best suit them.

Yes, there may still be concerns. It is probably true that the wealth of data on each child that is amassed at primary school may be a better and more accurate indicator of the appropriate secondary education for that child. But this would put the primary schools and teachers in the firing line even more than they are already from the minority of parents whose expectations exceed the ability of their children to fulfil them. The independently marked and assessed test is a necessary buffer to protect all concerned.

We are told the new tests will be more widely based than the old 11+, and more varied, which must be positive. To those who complain about the eight-month lead-in time, it is the same for everyone and it is, after all, a test designed to measure ability, not what a child has learned from being given extra tuition. The ability of some to pay for extra tuition should not be allowed to affect outcomes in the state system.

27th January 2013

Head teachers and governors of our local schools have no chance of satisfying everyone when it comes to making the decision about whether to close schools in adverse weather conditions. They really are damned if they do and damned if they don't.

I have been a governor at three different schools over the last three decades and can attest to the fact that the decision to close a school is only ever taken with great reluctance when the consensus is that there really is no other safe option for children or staff.

As usual, opinions have polarised and 'outraged of Tunbridge Wells' have been protesting 'If I don't get to work, I don't get paid' and that tired old mantra, 'Teachers get two months off in the summer and now they're skiving off again.' As the father of a primary school teacher, I know just how hard they work, and suggest that few in the commercial sector would dedicate those hours for the salary teachers get.

Yes, things were different in my childhood, when almost every child attended the school nearest to their homes and no one drove to school. And you only have to factor in the impact of schools reopening after holidays on traffic conditions to realise the effect of school traffic on our roads.

Teachers, too, tended to live locally, which is not always the case today, given the need for teachers to move on more regularly than was formerly the case in order to advance their careers. And the idea of suing a school if a child fell over on uncleared ice in the playground would have been risible until the blame culture seized our nation in its paralysing grasp and the compensation lawyers moved in.

We are not yet a country that has the infrastructure to deal with the levels of snow that, say, the Scandinavian countries have. We may have to invest the many millions of pounds that will be required to achieve the ability to respond more swiftly and effectively in adverse winter conditions. Then the same people who complain about lazy teachers and school closures will undoubtedly complain about the huge increase in their local and national taxation.

I also wonder whether the reintroduction of the word 'accident' into our everyday and legal vocabulary might have a beneficial effect on decision-making processes, which currently are, of necessity, defensive to the point of paralysis.

1st February 2013

Very few of us now choose to live our lives without using the Internet. I would suggest that the majority of those only do so because they are intimidated by technology in much the same way as I know that ballet dancing and tightrope walking are not for me, although I greatly enjoy watching others do so. It would really be an un reconstituted Luddite that saw the opening up of information to the whole world (or a significant percentage of it) as a bad thing in principle. Like all great innovations, it has well-known pitfalls as well as huge benefits, and attracts the ungodly to attempt to subvert it for their own ends or personal gain.

More and more of us are conducting increasing amounts of our business, social and financial affairs on the Internet, involving the necessary use of passwords. Until last week, I was lazier about that than I should have been. I used only two or three passwords for the dozens of institutions and companies I access regularly. My wake-up call, thankfully, was minor in its effect but has propelled me to rethink my online security. I am on Twitter and find it a useful way of keeping in easy contact with friends and all those other kind people who choose to follow me. As a performer, it is an invaluable way of alerting those who are interested about any work or appearances I have upcoming and similarly I enjoy getting news of those whom I follow.

Last week I 'tweeted' some advertising about the benefits of a dubious berry on weight loss. Except that I hadn't done so. I had been hacked. I know now how it happened. Whilst I was on Twitter, I received a (false, as it turned out) message from them asking me to log in again as I had been 'connected for a long time' and, unthinkingly, I did. I recall now that the log-in page was laid out slightly differently but not to an extent that raised any suspicions at the time.

I quickly deleted the offending tweets and have now started a process of revising all my passwords. But the new dilemma I face is how one remembers them all without carrying around a little list, which is similarly vulnerable to loss or theft.

My default position now will be of suspicion, caution and double-checking with the alleged originators of unusual requests.

8th February 2013

Several months ago, the speakers in the front of my car stopped working. I duly trawled the Internet and found a car radio supplier/repairer in Wycombe and took the car to them. After five minutes' investigation, I was told that I needed a new radio, as it wasn't the speakers that were the problem but the factory-fitted radio itself. A replacement radio would also, I was told, improve the poor reception I was currently receiving on Radio 5, which I listen to a lot, being an avid sports fan.

As I was thinking of trading the car in at that time, I declined to install a new radio and went merrily on my way. Since then I have listened to the crackling and variable reception on the car's rear speakers only, and become increasingly frustrated.

I was in Blackpool last week on tour with *Woman in White*, the play that currently keeps Baker Towers from falling to the ground and its occupants from starving.

I decided after a frustrating and slow 230-mile journey in dire weather, enduring poor reception, to try my luck again with a car radio company there, just in case they could do something. They could and they did. I learned that the front speakers were blown and that the aerial I had been supplied locally was not up to the job. I left the car with them on a matinee day and saved some money in the bargain, as parking is horrendously expensive in Blackpool—even more than everywhere else.

I picked it up the following day and was told that two new speakers, a new aerial and some judicious electrical earthing had solved all my problems for a fraction of the cost that I would have paid for a new car radio.

This is mainly worthy of comment because it underlines the wasteful nature of our disposable society. No one can be bothered to repair anything. There appears to be more profit in replacing than repairing. The 'make-do-and-mend' philosophy of my childhood is long gone, it seems. But, thank goodness, it seems there are still businesses that see the advantage of giving the customer the service he or she wants, rather than the one they want to give.

My journey back home was considerably more enjoyable. I listened to a live football commentary and heard every word in glorious surround sound.

15th February 2013

Last week my daughter miraculously walked away from an accident that destroyed her car and could easily have injured or killed her. The fact that she survived with only bruises and a few aches and pains meant that it was a good day.

Because of my profession, there was media interest, and I unashamedly gave access to reporters to highlight the danger of the particular pothole that all witnesses agreed was the sole cause of my daughter losing control of her car on the A404. As a result of the media interest, the pothole has been repaired ahead of its scheduled repair date later in the month.

In my opinion, that is a good result. However, there have been suggestions on the BFP website that the publicity generated by my 'fame' is a bad thing. 'Why report this? Only because it's a BFP columnist ...' or 'an ex Doctor Who?'

But surely it would be perverse not use the opportunity presented by my being a moderately successful actor to achieve something worth achieving? My daughter survived that pothole; other drivers might not have been so lucky. A brief perusal of the BFP website shows that many other drivers recognised that the particular pothole was a disaster waiting to happen and were glad it has been highlighted, but there are always those who resent the opportunities offered to a lucky few to have their voices listened to. And yes, I know I am lucky to be afforded that opportunity, but do they suggest I should spurn the chance to do something worthwhile?

It is not for reasons of self-aggrandisement that I agree to lend my name to charities and local initiatives that believe (rightly or wrongly) that my public support will attract attention and interest in their organisations. I would, by nature, keep my head below all parapets and avoid the flack, but agree when I can to help, partly as a means of paying back in a small way for the good luck I have had in earning a living in a notoriously precarious industry. Yet there always those ready to accuse others of being publicity-seekers or self-interested when they use their fame for constructive purposes.

As I write this, Meera Syal and Jo Brand launched a Dementia Care initiative and people listened and may become involved because of who they are. They both had personal reasons for doing so. Is that a bad thing?

22nd February 2013

Thirty-two years ago when I was playing King Rat in *Dick Whittington* in Lincoln, I befriended a seven-year-old girl who was one of the young local dancers that traditionally play village children in panto. She was shy and seemed somewhat lonely, and apart from her more confident contemporaries. I used to chat to her in the wings and make her laugh. She became quite attached to me and I was even invited round to her home for tea by her parents, who appreciated my avuncular attitude to their daughter.

She, now a forty-year-old mother of three, came last week with her parents and her husband to see the play I am currently doing in Lincoln, and we met up and reminisced afterwards. She seemed pleased that I remembered her too, and thanked me for the kindness I had shown her all those years ago, when she might otherwise have struggled in the unfamiliar and pressurised environment surrounded by girls who seemed to her (and were) more confident and outgoing. I had forgotten a lot of the details in the intervening years, but they were very clear to her and her family. I do remember her tears on the last night of the panto when we said goodbye. We kept in touch by letter for some years afterwards, but gradually contact ceased.

What we all suddenly realised last week, however, was that a similar situation would be highly unlikely to arise in quite the same way today. A man in his thirties would be ill-advised to take a seven-year-old girl under his wing in similar circumstances. We also agreed that it was a sad indictment of the times in which we now live that the default position is not one of assuming the best in people but of suspecting the worst.

I cannot recall feeling in any way odd about befriending a seven-year-old girl; nor did anyone else at the time see it that way. But it is beyond doubt that it would be different today. Somehow, all men have been tainted by suspicion that is based solely on the perverted actions of a tiny minority, however much the incessant media attention might indicate otherwise. I deeply resent the fact that the vast majority of us can no longer show concern, say, for a lost and crying child for fear of being seen as a potential abductor.

1st March 2013

My wife was flicking through the pages of one of those unasked-for catalogues that arrive in the post (and which are usually instantly recycled), when she spotted a garment she liked.

Being a generous husband, I spirited the catalogue away and went online to order the said item. I was filling in the details required—address, credit card details, etc.—but ground to a halt when asked to fill in my date of birth. The table bore an asterisk to indicate that this was 'an essential requirement'. So I logged off and telephoned the company instead. I explained that I was ringing because I had been asked to give my date of birth when ordering online, which I considered unnecessary. I was told by the chap on the phone that this was 'a legal requirement because of the Data Protection Act'. I suggested politely but firmly that the Data Protection Act had no such requirement, as was witnessed by the fact that I had just ordered and paid for several items from another company without my exact age being either of interest or remotely relevant.

All I wanted to do, I said, is order one item, pay for it on my debit card—so no credit involved—and have them send it to me. I asked him how he would feel if he was asked for his date of birth when he bought a burger, or was acquiring a pair of socks from a high street retailer. He said that there was no Data Protection issue in those purchases. I asked him what Data Protection issues were involved in the purchase I wished to make from his company that were so different from those in any purchase from a shop or another online outlet that resulted in their unique need to know when I was born. We then got stuck in a Data Protection loop that served only to convince me that he couldn't answer my question.

So my wife will not be receiving a pleasant surprise and I am still perplexed by the logic of demanding personal information from someone wishing to buy a printed washable tunic from Kaleidoscope. I cannot be alone in finding that level of intrusion unacceptable.

Ask me for a password if you must, or my first pet's name to protect me, but don't prise unnecessary personal information out of me for nonexistent reasons.

15th March 2013

During the BAFTA and Oscar season my wife, who was an actress until we had children and she decided to concentrate on being a mother and send me out to work, commented that she had always felt uncomfortable about the smug, self-congratulatory nature of those events. Her point was that film stars and successful theatre actors have more than enough already in terms of job satisfaction, fame and income without the additional business of statuettes and ballyhoo at the celebrity junkets that surround those events.

I have to say that I struggled to disagree with her, despite the knowledge that (in the unlikely event that I would ever be nominated for any of those awards) I would not be averse to being a recipient of such a ringing confirmation of my worth.

But the whole thing does have that slightly uncomfortable air about it of giving to them that already have a heck of a lot. Having said that, it seems that there are still hordes of members of the public who want to watch these events and to turn up in their hundreds to touch the hems of the garments of the glitterati.

When I told my wife that I might write about the whole phenomenon this week, she commented that I would be accused of sour grapes if I were to snipe at award ceremonies for actors, given the fact that I have never had an award of any kind since I got the Penmanship Prize at school. And I only got that because otherwise I would have been the only boy in the class not to get a prize. My handwriting has always been rather unremarkable, verging on a scrawl.

So if in the future you ever see me gurning inanely and mouthing platitudes at such an event (dream on, Colin!), forgive my human weakness. Most of us, I suspect, would find it hard to resist accepting such a confirmation of our worth in the eyes of others. But in principle the whole business of 'Who's Best' in an arena that is already a hugely enjoyable and profitable one for the participants is fairly invidious and, of course, ultimately entirely subjective.

Prizes and awards for people who have no job satisfaction or significant financial reward seem to me to be much more acceptable, but sadly attract less attention from the media or the world at large.

22nd March 2013

This week marks the demise of the iconic building, the BBC Television Centre. I have been asked to appear on the *The One Show* on Friday evening to help celebrate the glory years of BBC Television. Whilst I am delighted to be able to share some happy memories of the wonderful programmes made by the Beeb over half a century, it is a bit like being invited to visit the home one lived in as a child to reminisce just before the demolition men move in to reduce your memories to rubble.

I was lucky enough to spend a large part of the Seventies and Eighties at TV Centre, when the classic serial (which is now a landmark event in the television schedules) was staple fare on our screens. In quick succession, I appeared in *Roads to Freedom* (an adaptation of the Jean-Paul Sartre trilogy), *War and Peace* and *Cousin Bette* by Balzac. It was perhaps naïve of me to think that this pattern would be continued in perpetuity. Looking back now, I realise just how lucky we all were to be working as actors and performers at a time when the BBC was at its most productive, a time when programmes were made by creative and innovative individuals and not by committees of administrators and accountants.

It was a fantastic place to work. The energy and buzz about the circular corridors gave you a spring in your step as you entered the building, and the eight studios were always busy and productive. Admin was minimal; creatives abounded.

Practitioners from news, current affairs, sport, drama,

music and light entertainment intermingled happily and were able to share their creativity with each other at a time before internal costing, political correctness and 'health and safety' stifled originality and freedom, before the programme makers were moved out to other sites and the administration moved in.

I can hear this all being dismissed as nostalgic nonsense—'Things were better in my day', but you only have to compare the output of those days with the programming today when there are hundreds of channels available to realise that programme makers, performers and audiences alike had the best of it back then.

At the back of my mind, too, lurks the nagging suspicion that a decade or two from now, someone will come up with the bright idea of building a dedicated creative media hub in London.

29th March 2013

Any illusions I may have had about greater press responsibility and self-r-egulation post-Leveson were swiftly dispelled this week.

A former producer of *Blue Peter* has chosen to publish a book about John Nathan-Turner, who produced *Doctor Who* in the 70s and 80s. In the same week as the programme is returning to our screens and the Post Office has issued stamps celebrating the programme's 50th anniversary, he alleges that Turner and his partner (another BBC employee) behaved inappropriately (and possibly illegally) on BBC premises.

The Sun and *The Mirror* published some of these allegations with pictures—on the front page—of John and myself with the respective headlines 'Pervs of Doctor Who' and 'Doctor Who Sex Scandal'.

Despite the addition in minuscule print, a fraction of the size of the blaring headline in *The Mirror*, that I was 'not involved', the casual observer in a newspaper shop would see only one image of a Doctor Who on which to base their assumption of whom the headline was accusing of being the subject of a scandal. *The Sun's* exclusion of me from the allegations was in paragraph twelve of an article on page six. The front page used the word 'pervs' and there were two images above it, mine and that of the producer, who was not a publicly recognisable face. What other conclusion would the casual observer arrive at but that I was a 'perv'?

I have protested and complained to the Press Complaints Commission—an organisation in transition pending any changes as a result of Leveson. I have already been on the receiving end of a shouted 'Pervert' from a bunch of youths in the street.

I would dearly like to take these two papers to court to answer publicly for this appalling implied smear, but they are very rich and I have four daughters still living at home who, to varying degrees, partly rely on me financially. They can chuck more money at their lawyers than I dare risk.

Despite the 'tomorrow's chip wrapper' maxim, there will still be people out there years from now who will remember the headline and not the detail, unless the truth is blazoned in the same size print as the casual smear.

Why did they use my image? Why not crop me out? *The Sun* even included a picture inside of me and Jimmy Savile! No prizes for guessing their reason.

5th April 2013

I was involved this week in a legal case three years after a minor collision when a car rolled into the back of another at a roundabout when the driver's foot slipped off the brake of an automatic car. The driver was adamant that the contact with the car in front was minimal; the complainants' legal advisers alleged whiplash and assorted pains that lasted up to eighteen months. It transpired in court that even the claimants were perplexed about large chunks of the claim, saying they had only felt the after-effects for less than a month; they had not, as claimed, taken any time off work; nor had they suffered some of the injuries alleged.

They had signed statements containing demonstrably

inaccurate claims because they had been told to by their legal advisers and had, by their own admission, not read properly the documents they were signing. When they were read out, to their credit, they acknowledged the untruth of some allegations. Those in both the medical and legal professions responsible for a raft of inaccuracies were not in court, as they had briefed a barrister to present the case. He did his best in the face of forensic dissection of the case by the defendant's barrister.

The judge was fairly uncompromising about the nature of some of the medical evidence presented to him, but nonetheless found for the claimant, as there had been at least some post-accident discomfort and the defendant had admitted contact with the rear of their car, although there was no visible damage.

The damages awarded were considerably less than had been claimed, and as the insurance company involved had offered a sum more than that awarded over two years previously, the defendant's costs were ordered to be paid by the claimant. The defendant's costs were around fifteen times the compensation awarded to the claimant.

Basically, the compensation culture on this occasion lured an unfortunate and badly advised victim of a very minor collision to press a claim too far and ended up with a pyrrhic victory, and no one was a winner, except perhaps the legal profession.

A judge was tied up for a day settling a claim that amounted to less than four figures, and the lawyers earned over five figures.

It is perhaps appropriate to call time on the 'whiplash' ambulance chasers who prey on the ignorance and/or greed of victims of road accidents.

12th April 2013

I am currently in Australia with other former Doctors Who celebrating the programme's 50th anniversary with the Time Lord's many fans down under.

One of our party believed that he had been deprived of his wallet and phone by a pickpocket while shopping in Sydney and it was only after he had cancelled all his credit cards, of course, that the shop in which he had left those items managed to contact him. This triggered reminiscences within our group of other incidents, both actual and imagined, of the felonious appropriation of wallets and handbags.

We recalled the story of the actor, well-known to all of us, who, whilst performing in a play in New York, ignored the good advice given to him by local residents and decided to walk the few blocks back to his hotel late at night after his show. His route involved walking through a narrow subway tunnel. Halfway through the passage he was nervous to see that there was a large, shabbily-dressed gentleman moving menacingly in his direction. He was apparently nervous, but saw boldly going forward as the only option.

They brushed past each other in the narrow tunnel, and when he reached the other end he discovered his wallet had gone. At this point, you or I would not probably have done what he did next. Having partaken of a beverage or three, he spun round and hared back down the tunnel, seized hold of the man, spun him round and loudly and aggressively demanded his wallet back. A risky strategy usually, but on this occasion the man, confronted by a frenzied English actor half his size, stared at him wildly for a moment before handing the wallet over and haring off at great speed.

It wasn't until the following day that the actor discovered that he had had his wallet all the time and was now the not-so-proud owner of his imagined assailant's wallet as well.

Sober now and contrite, he contacted the real injured party and abjectly apologised before arranging to restore his property to him.

Several valuable lessons learned there.

I shared this story with my family when I spoke to them on the phone later, only to be told that one of my daughters had had her handbag stolen while shopping in High Wycombe. And as I write this, no one has phoned to apologise or return it.

19th April 2013

Having returned from another trip to Australia and New Zealand with my fellow Doctor Who actors, I have had time to reflect on the business of world travel in the 21st century. I don't suppose there are many people who relish the process of 'getting there', even when the journey is short. I dare say that those who travel to holiday destinations with the prospect of relaxed days by aquamarine seas, sipping cocktails and dining in a warm breeze under the stars, are more disposed to endure with equanimity the stresses of air travel than those of us who travel at the behest of our employers and have to sing for our less exotic suppers in places of employment rather than leisure.

Even those of us who remember shorter, less stressful check-in processes are now resigned to the shuffling indignities of security checks and identity checks and luggage checks and clothing checks. But that resignation is born of necessity; we all know the excellent reasons for all those checks.

So there are increasingly more hoops to jump through to test our passive compliance. For instance, there are the tape-lined walk channels that we are obliged to trudge through in order to reach somewhere only four paces from our original starting point. As I approached one such, an official turned the eight serpentine twists into twelve with the flick of an imperious wrist. Eleven of the channels were empty. I smiled at her and said, 'You think I need the exercise, don't you?' She raised an amused eyebrow and went off to challenge other victims in another rat run.

The bored scanner operators wait till you take off your belt before telling you that you don't need to; they then ask you to put your phone, coins and wallet in the tray. On the next flight it's the reverse—they want, the belt not the coins.

It's all designed, really, to ensure utter compliance when you board the plane to spend fourteen hours ignoring the ever intrusive elbows of your similarly compliant neighbour in the silent battle for an extra millimetre of space. It's also designed to take your mind off the food, which is always prepared carefully with the sole aim of ensuring that you leave the plane with some of it on your shirt, due to the physical impossibility of guiding it accurately to your mouth, unless you're in first class.

26th April 2013

Many voters appear to have lost interest in the political process. This may be because of a perception that the two main parties are indistinguishable when the pre-election rhetoric has died down and the other parties are considered rank outsiders. Another ingredient today may be the feeling that the Lib Dems have sold their supporters down the river for a mess of potage. These are all perceptions that may or may not be true, but the predominant feeling among the electorate is one of resigned apathy.

The election for the Police and Crime Commissioner for the Thames Valley attracted 226,512 voters—a turnout of 13.3 per cent. This means that almost a half million residents of Thames Valley either didn't give a hoot who oversaw the police, or thought their vote was irrelevant. Clearly, had they all voted, those votes could have made a huge difference.

Next, we elect our County Councillors. There is a huge ongoing debate about whether we need so many layers of regional and local government, but at the moment we have County Councils, and they have a huge responsibility. The 49 councillors we will be electing have a budget of £845 million to administer; £845 million of our money. Aside from their record on potholes, we should perhaps be noting that they also have vital scrutiny over education, public health provision, planning and libraries.

This will be the first County Council election for some time that is not piggybacked onto either Euro elections (with a 40% turnout) or a general election, the last of which attracted 65% of us to vote. It may be, therefore, that the turnout will be poor, which would be a great shame for democracy.

I am a great believer in the principle that if you can't be bothered to vote, then you have no right to complain when whoever is elected fails to deliver. I know I would feel disenfranchised if I failed to join in the electoral process, however much we may feel that our one vote either way would make no difference.

I still wish that party politics were removed from local politics and we were offered choices of local people who told us what THEY stood for, not what their national party stood for.

But notwithstanding, I would urge everyone to turn up and put their mark on the ballot, even if to say 'none of the above!'

3rd May 2013

I wore a pair of odd shoes to a concert this week. I discovered when I returned home that I had spent an entire evening with friends and colleagues wearing one blue and one black shoe. None of them had commented. Too polite, perhaps? Probably not. At least one of them would have derived enormous pleasure in drawing attention to my fatal foot folly, had he noticed. It is more likely that, just as I had no idea what footwear they were sporting, they had similarly failed to deem it necessary to check mine out.

Even more likely, the quality of the music at Wycombe High School's Senior Concert on Tuesday night was of a sufficiently high standard to ensure our undivided attention. Even Boris Johnson swinging from the ceiling, wearing a Hawaiian shirt and juggling, would have failed to draw our attention away from these talented young performers. I'm not sure why I am still surprised when the young people of Wycombe prove yet again how talented they are. But I was utterly mesmerised by the standard of musical ability displayed by the girls of Wycombe High School. Both ensemble and individual performances were excellent, and some were simply outstanding. Violin, piano, guitar and vocal virtuosas abounded, and had I closed my eyes, I could have been sitting in the expensive seats at the Barbican.

But I was instead at the top of Marlow Hill, in my odd Crocs, applauding wildly.

And yes, I know that wearing odd shoes is bad enough

without compounding the solecism in the eyes of many readers by wearing what I have now admitted are shoes that are considered by the righteous to be unbearably naff. But I am already old, and wear purple on occasions, like the lady in Jenny Joseph's wonderful poem 'Warning', so I might as well go the whole hog and 'wear terrible shirts and grow more fat' while wearing my comfortable, naff shoes. My *Jungle* companion Hugo, former star of *Made in Chelsea,* was no more appalled when I outed myself as a Croc wearer than if I had confessed to biting the heads off kittens for fun or liking Justin Bieber.

But I am, I cannot deny, old: I wear purple and unfashionable shoes. Comfort over style every time for me.

But I also like good music and applaud talent in the young, so I can't be all that bad.

10th May 2013

It was initially encouraging to hear in the Queen's Speech that the government are planning to do something about 'Health Tourism'. I say 'initially', because a little research revealed that successive governments have made similar promises dating back to the days of Messrs. Brown and Blair.

I would hate us to have a society where genuine visitors to our country would be left lying in the street because they are unable to produce details of their medical insurance or a triple platinum credit card in times of dire need. On the other hand, I resent deeply that our taxes are paying for the cancer treatment or heart operations of people who have travelled from wherever in Europe for the sole purpose of getting treatment from our health service. Somewhere between these two unpalatable extremes lies a solution that means we are not as callous as some western nations are alleged to be, but not a soft touch either.

Maternity tourism is apparently an escalating problem. Women from other countries arrive in the UK on visitors' visas late in their pregnancies, often after detecting complications. They turn up in labour at hospitals who cannot turn the patient away; but when later presented with a bill, the women claim that the circumstances of their childbirth qualify as an emergency.

There are numerous examples of visitors arriving in the UK and turning up at hospitals with kidney failure and needing dialysis, which can continue for months.

A junior doctor at a hospital near Heathrow recently wrote, 'Every single week, I see people who have been flown in from all over the world with a variety of extremely serious health problems. Many of these people had to be wheel-chaired on to the plane because they were too unwell to walk on board. I understand the temptation to come to Britain, but we often have our Intensive Therapy Unit full of patients without NHS numbers who are there for weeks or months with no means or intention to pay, which impacts on our resources.'

It makes it even less acceptable when, for financial reasons, medical services are being reduced everywhere, as residents this area are only too familiar.

It is not callous or xenophobic to insist that protection should be afforded to those who pay their taxes and National Insurance contributions. If that means a stricter attitude to abuse by overseas nationals, then so be it.

17th May 2013

Do those of you over a certain age ever hanker for the days before plastic debit, credit, reward and store cards dominated all our retail and financial activities? I have such fond memories of only having to worry about the cash in my pocket and the cheque book which spent most of its time in my drawer at home. My wallet just contained money of the folding kind, and there wasn't always much of that in my first job, when my weekly salary was two pounds. Mind you, this was long before the pound coin appeared, and that wallet could have contained four ten-bob notes (ask your parents!).

I know the credit card is amazingly useful and we can't turn the clock back; in fact, I wouldn't want to, but I can't help harbouring a sneaking nostalgia for the simplicity of the shopping of my youth.

I have just counted the plastic cards in my wallet. There are twenty-three. They enable me to shop, travel, get books from the library or prove my entitlement to healthcare, breakdown assistance or discounts. I tried to cull, I really did. But there is not one of them that I do not use at some time to my benefit, although I did find that I had identical membership cards for breakdown insurance, for some reason. So, despite my best endeavours, net reduction, one.

If you want to separate your spending for ease of domestic and professional accounting later, then more than one credit card offers advantages. So I have several of them. Each of them has a pin code to remember, and I had to radically rethink my use of a single pin code that I used for many cards when one of them was compromised. So, now I have a little book with them all in, plus all the online and website log-ins and passwords for tax, for utilities, for the bank, etc. etc. But that little book is now my biggest security risk. Maybe I should use some code that would fool anyone purloining my little book, say: put down the code for the card above in the list. But then, of course, the more difficult it is for the thief to decipher, the more difficult it is for ME to remember.

It was so much simpler in my youth. You either had the money in your pocket, or you didn't.

24th May 2013

I have just spent two weeks in the USA. On my outward journey, the entertainment system was down and we got credit notes offering $150 off our next flight if, given the non-existent leg room, we ever used that airline again. And legs don't get longer with advancing years. Other parts of me may have expanded, but not my legs. On the way back, I was the only person whose screen was sullenly unresponsive. And the plane was absolutely full. There were seats available in first class, but they didn't deem an unresponsive screen sufficient justification to offer me one. So a three-film flight turned into a no film-flight.

They also made an announcement that a passenger was allergic to peanuts, and therefore no peanuts would be offered on the flight, and indeed no passengers who possessed peanuts would be allowed to eat or even open them. Now I know that a peanut allergy is a serious and life-threatening affliction, but I couldn't help thinking that I wished they treated my allergy to cheese in the same way. Not only did every meal contain the stuff, but I was surrounded by people who were tucking with gusto into what to me is a powerful emetic. I survived the nine-hour flight with a dry biscuit and a banana. Probably good for me, I know.

To heap insult to injury, when I arrived at my hotel in the USA, I opened my suitcase to find a note from the US Transport Security Administration perched on top of a jumble of my clothes and personal effects, saying that to 'protect me and my fellow travellers' they had tossed my clothing in the air and emptied all over the resultant jumble sale my boxes of pills (the ones that all men over 50 seem to be taking these days—no, not those!). They helpfully added that if my case had been forced open because it was locked—tough! Fortunately, I hadn't locked it.

That had never happened to me before. But it happened again on the journey home. Either red suitcases are targeted, or someone stateside didn't like the cut of my jib!

I'm going back to the US this week. I'd put a cheery message in my case, if I thought a sense of humour was part of the armoury of the folks whose job it is to check us out.

31st May 2013

I wish I could understand the people who are so adamant that gay men or women should not be allowed to formalise and celebrate their commitment and love for each other by getting married. The bill being considered at the moment specifically protects those religions that have objections to the notion of same sex marriage so that they cannot be compelled to act contrary to their agreed beliefs. Only religions that are willing to marry same sex couples will be doing so.

Those who would deny the gay community the right that straight couples enjoy employ a variety of arguments, none convincing. That marriage is all about bringing children into the world is clearly a non-runner, as childless couples would by implication have no need or right to be married. And plenty of children are born outside marriage and suffer no harm for that reason alone. Then there is the old chestnut, 'Why are they bothering with this unimportant issue when the economy is in such a mess?' That argument, if taken seriously, would preclude any legislation that didn't restore the UK's triple A rating with Moody.

And Norman Tebbit has really helped the debate with his talk of future lesbian queens providing heirs to the throne by artificial insemination, or the spectre of men marrying their sons to avoid inheritance tax. This is the best they can come up with to scupper a compassionate initiative designed to level the playing field so that all couples who wish to make a commitment to each other can do so, irrespective of gender or sexual orientation.

In a world in which a huge variety of religions approach their particular paths to salvation in many different ways, including attitudes to marriage, some religions will be more comfortable than others about same sex marriage; these are the religions that will be offering such marriages. None will be compelled to do so, and rogue members of the non-participating religions will not be allowed to embarrass their organisations by doing so.

The fact that there are so many couples in this country anxious to be accorded the same status as male/female couples is evidence that marriage is still a strong institution and seen as something worth having. It is not in the least devalued, as the antis would suggest.

7th June 2013

I received another lesson in how to travel painlessly this week.

I spent four days in Denver, meeting more lovely people who want to celebrate the 50th anniversary of *Doctor Who*, (about which I will expand in this column soon).

As usual, the destination and its citizens were delightful and welcoming.

The process of getting there, of getting anywhere today, it seems, was less convivial.

I have learned to minimise the contentious items in my hand luggage, all liquids removed or in my checked-in luggage, along with anything that might be deemed a potential weapon. I have discovered that putting my laptop in the suitcase that I check in is also a bad idea. Apparently, that is why my bag was opened twice last time I went over there and found that my clothing had been stuffed back in a jumble.

My mistake this week was buying a ham sandwich in Boots Airside at Heathrow. I did so because I have a cheese allergy, and bitter experience has taught me that more than 50% of airline food has cheese in, on or around it. There is no 'no-cheese' option that leaves me with all the other stuff I can eat. In fact, there is no 'no cheese' option available. So rather than survive on a dry roll or biscuit at 30,000 feet for nine hours, I decided to take a sarnie with me. In the event, unusually, there was a totally cheeseless meal available. My sandwich therefore was uneaten as I passed through immigration control in Denver. The official asked me if I was bringing food in with me, and I replied casually, anticipating that this was okay, that I only had a ham sandwich. He gave me a basilisk stare and wrote SANDWICH in huge red letters across my landing card and directed me to the customs hall, where I was ordered to join a queue for examination by the officers of the Agricultural Department. Forty five minutes later, I had my ham sandwich confiscated. When I resignedly suggested that I could have saved myself a lot of time at the end of long flight by eating the darn thing in the baggage hall, I was told that I would have been arrested had I done so, as eating in the baggage hall was a federal offence. Phew, thank goodness I don't chew gum or bite my finger nails! Traveller beware.

14th June 2013

This is already, and will continue to be, quite a year for *Doctor Who*.

In November, the programme celebrates its 50th anniversary. When I joined the show, it had just reached its 20th year. Who would have predicted that the old warhorse would be even healthier in 2013 than it was three decades ago?

Christopher Eccleston did the hard job of re-establishing the mercurial Time Lord in the nation's televisual heart after more than a decade off our screens. Aided by phenomenally good scripts and greatly improved production values, he did so assertively and excitingly. Then David Tennant charmed a nation and achieved the thitherto impossible task of getting women of all ages to embrace a science-fiction programme that had previously been predominantly the domain of the young and the male part of the population.

When David left, I was initially concerned when I heard that another young man had been cast in the role, hankering as I was for another Troughton or Pertwee to bring back some senior gravitas to the role. But in an inspirational piece of casting, we got Matt Smith, who enticingly combines youth and vigour with the wisdom of the ancients, the charm of Cary Grant and a wonderful eclectic randomness of the kind we oldies loved so much in Patrick Troughton, whose inspired first regeneration enabled the series to live on when William Hartnell left the show in 1966. Without him, indeed, this would be an empty column today!

Now Matt has announced his departure (is it really four years?) and the speculation begins about the next occupant of the TARDIS.

It is beyond doubt that white males have thus far dominated the incarnations, and I am one of the seemingly unpopular minority who would be intrigued to learn that the Doctor is in touch, say, with his feminine side. They won't do it, of course. They would fear the probable resultant drop in viewer figures, but I would applaud their bravery and honesty if they did.

But it is going to be a fascinating year. The anniversary is broadcast in November, followed by Matt's swansong at Christmas and the probable unveiling of his successor, who alas will have missed out on postal fame by not being immortalised on a stamp.

For this year has been the only time that I could truly claim to be first class—along, of course, with my fellow Doctors, bless 'em!

21st June 2013

All drivers have had experience of being tailgated by a lorry.

I had better confirm at the outset that most lorry drivers are sensible and professional. But that is of little consolation when an exception puts you in fear of your life. Last Saturday at around 11.15 p.m. I was driving down to Herne Bay, where I was working the following day. There are roadworks on the M25; the lanes are reduced and the speed limit is currently 50 mph. Having three points on my licence makes me very aware of speed limits, and the presence of average speed cameras sharpened that awareness. I was in the inside lane, driving at exactly 50 mph. Then a large lorry, multiple headlights blazing, came up behind me and settled in so closely that I could only see his headlights in my wing mirror. Not to put too fine a point on it, I was terrified. But I knew that if I were to accelerate to get out of his way, my explanations in court would have fallen upon weary and deaf ears.

There was a steady line of traffic in the lane to my right travelling at the same speed. There was nowhere I could go to get away from the murderous maniac behind me. So for several miles that seemed endless, I prayed that nothing would compel me to brake. He was so close that I doubt he would have seen my brake light anyway before his tonnage ploughed over my car.

When the road widened out again and I could accelerate legally away from him I did so; then slowed down to allow him to pass me so that I could get his registration number.

But what do I do with it? A serving police officer (not

involved with traffic) told me that he had had a similar experience recently which induced him to make a report at his local station. He was told exactly what I would doubtless be told. It's one man's word against another, so it wouldn't be taken further.

I may contact the company whose lorry it was, but I expect little solace from that. But perhaps I should, on the off-chance that a rare sympathetic person there might just have a stern word and save others from similar terror.

I am now seriously considering buying one of those rear window cameras in case I encounter a similarly criminally insane driver.

28th June 2013

I have been a member of the same car breakdown association since I was eighteen, and that's a long time. I remember when we had badges on our radiator grills and motorcyclists working for the organisation would salute while passing on the other side of the road. Clearly, health and safety considerations have altered the scenario. There are no motorcycle repairmen anymore and we have cards instead of badges.

I had occasion this week to call upon the services of my yellow van men in London. My car made noises that were sufficiently unusual as to persuade me that the expertise of professionals was required. I met my first patrolman at 1.45 p.m. A brief examination under my bonnet convinced him that a recovery vehicle would be required. He took my details, called into control and told me that one would be with me between 5 and 6 p.m. That timing was to fit in with my commitment in London and was perfectly acceptable.

At 5.10 p.m. a patrolman arrived, insisted on checking the first man's diagnosis and, having done so, concurred with his analysis. A tow was necessary. However, he couldn't do it. His van was not equipped to tow a car like mine all the way to High Wycombe. The first patrolman had given all the details of the car and its intended destination, but the phone operator had failed to communicate this to him properly. He would summon a colleague with a more appropriate vehicle. At 6.45 p.m. said colleague arrived.

We went through the same diagnostic procedure and then he solemnly informed me that he couldn't tow me to Wycombe, however, as he was due to go off shift in an hour and he wouldn't finish within his working hours. I was starting to get a little tetchy at this point.

At 7.30 p.m. I finally met up with a man with the right van, the right information and an available time span that could accommodate the journey to Bucks.

He told me that the phone operators were trained to answer the phone and had no detailed knowledge of the types of vans required for different jobs.

I got home at 9.30 p.m.

Every one of the four men I encountered had to fill in a form which I had to sign.

Before they started selling insurance, holidays and credit cards, I remember them as being much more efficient.

5th July 2013

Those of you who followed the saga last week of my ailing car and its repeated failure to be towed back to Wycombe until the fourth patrolman of the apocalypse eventually turned up to undertake the task will perhaps be diverted to learn that those worthy gentlemen's diagnoses were as lacking as their preparedness to tow. I could have driven the car home myself, it appears, and saved them all a lot of energy sucking air through their teeth, as the hideous knocking noise that prompted my calling for their services emanated not from the engine, as I and they had thought, but from the air conditioning unit. My mechanic was barely troubled for an hour before sending my quiet car humming through the lanes of Buckinghamshire again. Phew and ho hum!

And my week got even better when, in this 50th year of *Doctor Who*, with its celebrations and postage stamps, yet another exciting opportunity came along, one that I could never have imagined possible when I was a young boy dreaming of being an actor. Next Monday I shall be attending my first sitting for award-winning sculptor, Andrew Sinclair, at his Wendover studios, where he and his wife, Diane, run The Sculpture School. Andrew was the sculptor who recently helped refurbish the Royal Box at Ascot with a bas-relief version of the Royal coat of arms, and he created the wonderful life-sized dinosaur which was displayed at the Chelsea Flower Show, ridden by a sculpted fat unclad lady.

He has kindly offered to make a bronze resin bust of your doddering columnist, which will be unveiled later in the year in time for the programme's anniversary in November. He is also, over the same period, very generously creating a bust of another local person in the public eye, to be announced later. Sadly, my bust will be of me as I am now and not of the curly-haired golden youth of the 80s, and will therefore be requiring poor Andrew to employ somewhat more of the old bronze resin in the creative process. But I am relieved that the head and shoulders nature of a bust will remove the possibility of my far from ripped anatomy being immortalised.

And I am really looking forward to being able to sit still for a while without feeling guilty about the many things I really ought to be doing.

12th July 2013

At first I thought that HS2 sounded reasonably viable, until the cost was brought into the equation. And I don't just mean the financial cost, which is already rocketing before a meadow has been desecrated. I mean the real cost. I visited a sculptor's studio near Wendover this week. It was in a barn adjacent to a farm in the most picturesque of surroundings.

The vista was one that 18th-century painters of rural England would have been delighted to reproduce, as there were no signs of the three following centuries to distort or pollute the view. As I stood by the vegetable garden and listened to the birds singing in distant trees, I was told, 'HS2 will be going through here'.

Cue *Monty Python*'s large descending foot.

I don't live there, so I certainly can't be accused of being a nimby—but on behalf of those who do live and work there, as well as all the rest of who don't, I demand that we get the tumbrils out immediately for those who, for reasons unfathomable outside Lilliput or Brobdingnag, think we should tolerate this appalling vandalism just to knock less than 30 minutes off the rail journey from London to Birmingham.

We know that the financial cost, borne by all of us, will continue to rise exponentially and then double again at the last minute. Why can they never get a budget right and stick to it? It was only last year that we learned that HS1 had left the British taxpayer with an ongoing 4.8 billion-pound debt. Hardly a model we wish to repeat, surely? We also all know that the existing infrastructure could be improved to provide speedier transport, if we really must have it, without ploughing a noisy, festering scar through rural England. We know too that for a fraction of the existing budget for HS2 (let alone the eventual one), our steadily deteriorating roads could be restored to something approaching tolerable levels. In the age of the Internet and instant communication, do we really need to have all those men sitting on trains getting to Birmingham a tiny bit faster? With wifi, if their time is so precious, they can work on the existing trains, if they can persuade each other not to bellow on their mobiles about their being on the train.

We must make them listen to us this time.

19th July 2013

The e-petition on the Government's website that has attracted the largest number of votes ever is the one urging the government to think again about the proposed badger cull as a means of controlling the spread of TB.

At the time of writing this, 259,197 people have challenged the decision, made two years ago, to cull 70% of badgers in two test areas. Given the nature and importance of many other e-petitions that have attracted fewer supporters, it is clear that the public are really not happy about the plan to speculatively slaughter our wildlife on flimsy evidence.

This decision to cull was announced only four years after The Independent Scientific Group on Cattle TB reported that 'culling Badgers would have no meaningful effect on bovine TB in cattle' after they had conducted a cull of nearly 10,000 badgers and systematically gathered evidence of the effect of so doing.

TB is a nasty disease. My brother contracted it in his early teens and lost a year and a half of irreplaceable learning time at school. Our hearts go out to farmers who lose their livelihood because of it. But before we cull even more of our indigenous wildlife, we should be relying on evidence much, much stronger than we currently have to justify such drastic action.

The main problem, it appears, is that EU law prevents the UK from setting up a vaccination programme. The reason for the EU prohibition, interference with the skin test for contracted TB, is arguably no longer valid, as a different test could be used on vaccinated cattle. DEFRA claims that it would take five years to change the EU ban. But if they had started to try to do so years ago, it could have been changed by now. And vaccination is not necessarily a more expensive option than culling, as has been frequently suggested. It is becoming clear that the relative costs of both courses of action are very similar, but vaccination has the advantage of being in harmony with the public's wishes and would also not need policing. It has already been demonstrated in Wales and elsewhere that the public are willing to contribute to vaccination schemes that would benefit farmers, as well as wildlife.

Mine is not an anti-farmer stance, it is a pro-sense one. The same amount of energy spent sorting out the vaccination issue would be much more productive and countryside-friendly.

26ᵗʰ July 2013

This spell of weather reminds me of what I fondly believe were the summers of my childhood. Endless days of sun and blue skies, when I disappeared for hours on my bike with my brother and friends. We cycled to places miles away from Rochdale, where I lived, just for the heck of it. We even cycled the forty or fifty miles to Blackpool, spent the day there and then cycled home. I can't believe I was ever fit enough to do that, but I did, I can assure you. I cannot imagine that any sane parent would encourage a teenager to do a journey like that now. It is a far less cycle-friendly world that we hurtle about in today.

But is my memory of those long, hot, carefree summers a correct one, I wonder? Have I airbrushed out the rainy, dull days of my youth to hanker after a fictitious past where everyone was polite, people drove considerately along leafy lanes and the car breakdown men saluted their members, when everyone tolerated each other.

I remember the tarmac on the road bubbling in the heat; we used to pop the bubbles to release that sweet tarry smell that is one of the many aromas that instantly drag me back to my childhood, along with the intertwined smell of horses and bread, butter and milk. For many years our milkman delivered those items daily in a horse-drawn cart, and that wonderful hay-scented breath that horses have always makes me hanker for fresh bread and jam, which was our regular teatime treat in the summer.

But then nostalgia is a dangerous thing. The ringtone on my phone is the signature tune of *Housewives' Choice*, a record request show that was broadcast every morning on the Light Programme, which I listened to regularly with my mother.

But hankering for the past that my post-war generation enjoyed is pointless, as there will probably never be such carefree days again, when our parents' generation was taking a deep breath and starting to live again, free of the horror of a world war. We, in our blithe innocence, thought that it had always been like that and would always continue to be like that. We really did have the best of times, so perhaps the weather really was that good too.

Now, of course, I'm already moaning about the heat.

2nd August 2013

This week, one of my daughters was driving up Amersham Hill when her car ground to a halt. Scores of cars passed her as she stood beside the car with its hazard lights flashing. I was out of the country, but she phoned home for help, and while she and her sister and her sister's boyfriend were struggling to solve the problem, one driver stopped and spent some considerable time helping her sort the problem out.

He was Swiss and was in England for two weeks only, but despite being a stranger in a strange land, as a motor engineer, he felt unable to pass by a damsel in distress. A true 'Good Samaritan' tale.

It would be wrong to draw conclusions from this one incident about the British disinclination these days to get involved and the reticence that we all now have about exposing ourselves to the risk of accusations of improper behaviour. But in another incident that week, a different daughter was walking to her car from the station in Chalfont in the middle of a heavy rainstorm. A man was walking behind her and he had an umbrella.

He offered to share it with her as she walked along the road, adding hastily that she shouldn't be alarmed as he had just been granted British citizenship, which had made him very happy and he was anxious to adopt the customs, as he saw it, of the country which had so generously accepted him into its heart, by behaving like 'an English gentleman'. He spoke with what my daughter identified as an American accent.

It appears that, despite all evidence to the contrary, we are still seen to be exemplars of courtesy and chivalry, arguably long after those virtues have been driven out of the national psyche by the fear of being considered creepy at best or a potential molester at worst. How sad that the old virtues that were once considered to be embedded in the British population are now more likely to be found in strangers who wish to embrace those old courtesies.

Of course, there are still those of us who refuse to be deflected from succouring strangers as a result of the fear of our motives being misinterpreted or of future litigation, but the fact that these two incidents are worthy of comment says something about the way our 'Big Society' seems to be moving.

9ᵗʰ August 2013

It has been an exciting week in the world of *Doctor Who*.

It is 30 years ago exactly this month that I got a call from the then producer telling me to get into the BBC immediately because someone had leaked the secret that I had been desperately concealing for some weeks—that I was to be the sixth incarnation of the Doctor. A hastily-arranged press conference and photo shoot with my soon-to-be-companion Nicola Bryant launched me into the public gaze as the newest incumbent of the nation's favourite blue box.

It was an experience I shall never forget, and my life and career changed direction immediately.

It has always proved tricky to time the announcement of a new Doctor without it being pre-leaked, so it was very sensible to stage-manage the event and make a virtue of necessity, which the BBC did with great aplomb on Sunday. The name of the new Doctor was already the source of great speculation.

In 1983, I thought I was doing well when my being cast in the role got a minute at the end of the *Nine O'Clock News*. Peter Capaldi's arrival got a half-hour programme with a dramatic build to a spectacular entrance which was a reverse variation on the theme—'The Doctor will see you now'. And he handled it with a disarming, almost self-deprecatory charm.

There appears to have been a collective sigh of relief that the new Doctor will be the mature man that many with strong memories of William Hartnell, Patrick Troughton and Jon Pertwee have hankered for—older men with gravitas and an avuncular/paternal air. The selection of Peter Capaldi seems to have attracted nothing but praise and eager anticipation, as far as I have seen.

I think he is an excellent choice. He is an actor whose work I have admired for many years and has the ability to portray a piercing intelligence and quicksilver mind, with a hint of mischievous other-worldliness. After the excellent, very different, but physically youthful Doctors of David Tennant and Matt Smith, it is very appealing to have a return to the 'older' Doctors of what seems now to be called the 'classic era'. And another Scot, too—Sylvester, David and now Peter C.

The Doctor is in safe and exciting hands. I can't wait.

23rd August 2013

I have been asked to appear in several celebrity versions of popular game shows recently, in the wake, presumably, of my three weeks in *I'm a Celebrity ...* at the end of last year. At my age, there is no potential harm to what I like to think of as my career in doing these kinds of shows, which (for reasons only of prejudice in the eyes of those who might have employed me as an actor) I might have been wiser to decline when I was younger. But at an age when the sensible part of the population is long retired, I am more than happy to accept every opportunity to have a bit of fun, while hopefully earning something for myself or for charity. Stokenchurch Dog Rescue and St. Tiggywinkles in Haddenham have both been beneficiaries of my recent game-show ventures.

But I have been intrigued by the number of people with rampant TV snobbery, who don't like to admit that they have watched, but have to do so in order to share their opinions. As a result, the standard opening gambit is a variation on a theme of 'I never watch that programme (or those kind of programmes) normally, but ...' I can't tell you how nice it is when someone simply says that they saw the programme and enjoyed it.

But there is a prevalent subtext that performers need to be taken down a peg, as we clearly have a very high opinion of ourselves. (If only!) So as not to appear to be fawning fans, one's appearance, one's prowess and age are all, it seems, fair game to strangers, friends and acquaintances alike. I wish I had a pound for every stranger who feels able to comment on my weight or age!

And because I did *Mr and Mrs* with my wife, she is also fair game, it seems. Comments about her hair, her clothes and her appearances flow as freely as the denouncement of the programme as being silly or ludicrous. The same people would not do that to anyone 'in real life' about their jobs, uninvited. Why is it acceptable to do it for performers?

Some would suggest that we accept kind comments happily enough, so should put up with criticism.

And if I had asked for their opinion, that's fair enough.

But I was always taught that if you can't say something nice, say nothing at all!

30ᵗʰ August 2013

Bitter experience teaches most of us that it is very rare that officialdom ever reverses a decision that affects us adversely, whether or not logic dictates that they should. This week, however, the company running Wycombe Lido had the very good sense to realise that they really had no option but to rescind the £150 parking fines issued to many drivers in late July despite signs on the parking payment machines stating that the new parking regulations did not come into force until August.

It was small wonder that the motorists were infuriated and kicked up an almighty fuss; but more often than not in these circumstances, those who tick the boxes and fill out the forms force us to jump through innumerable hoops and threaten legal redress before they will even think of admitting that they got it wrong. During this time, many of us apparently will simply shrug, pay the fine and get on with our lives. This is what they rely on, of course. They have all the time in the world to ignore our complaints and file them repeatedly in the bin; and normally we have to have the dogged persistence of Frank Sinatra's ant with his rubber tree plant to have a chance of beating City Hall and getting justice.

In this case, the evidence was so overwhelming as to make it impossible for (Con)Fusion Lifestyle to enforce the fines, but we should still be thankful that they didn't protract the dispute. I went to court once to have an unjust ticket overturned, and succeeded—but it took me hours of my time, which others might consider not worth it. This was after I had gone into a police station in Hull to explain the circumstances in advance of why my car tax was not on my screen, but was paid for. The magistrates were very sympathetic, I am glad to say.

Let us hope that on October 15th and 16th the same common sense will prevail at the High Court in London, when the appeal concerning the wasteful and pointless HS2 will be heard. The appeal may be on the basis of the government's failure to undertake a Strategic Environmental Assessment before green-lighting the project (a failure described by one judge as 'egregious'), but it at least opens the doors for a major rethink.

One can only hope that common sense will prevail.

6th September 2013

When the computer sidled into our homes, we were all assured that our lives would get easier. Computerisation would ease the process of paying bills, shopping and organising our financial affairs. As the pieces of paper ceased to clog up our shelves and files were consigned to the recycle bin, a few moments in front of our screens at home would speedily and effectively transact all our business, freeing us up to enjoy our leisure time swinging in our hammocks or growing begonias.

Wind forward a decade or so. All that has happened to me is that it has become immeasurably harder to make contact with any of the companies or institutions that we used to be able to ring up or visit, and the computer invariably says 'No!' when you try get past the contact barriers.

When I received a printed bank statement regularly, I used to check it against my cheque stubs and I cannot recall one occasion in decades where there was an error. Since everything went digital, I confess I have failed to be as diligent. This week I needed to check a series of payments for a tax form, and while doing so, a payment to a company I had never heard of leapt off the screen at me.

Now £39.99 is not a massive amount but it was, it seemed, the first payment of a direct debit.

My bank gave me information about the institution raising the payment. That institution told me I had to contact their client company to ascertain what it was. So much for computers making things easier. It makes things easier for the monoliths who harvest our hard-earned cash and then make it as difficult as possible for us to contact them other than by email, which they don't answer properly, if at all. 'Making things easier for the customer' in my case means half a day spent already trying to discover who had taken my money and why, with as yet no definitive resolution.

When computerisation works, it is undoubtedly remarkably useful. I can, say, get a book that I urgently need and which is not in my local bookshop within 24 hours, without leaving home.

But the big boys can really tie us in knots if they choose to, safe in the knowledge that a percentage of us will shrug and write it off to experience. Lesson—check your bank statements!

13th September 2013

It takes a brief interruption of services to remind us sometimes how dependent we are on so many things that we might otherwise take for granted. At Baker Towers, we had no water for only a few hours last week because of a burst main, and that temporary deprivation served as a powerful reminder of the level of our dependency on essential services.

Another area that we take for granted is waste disposal. Waste collection disputes in the past have had immediate and unpleasant consequences for the areas in which those weekly collections have been interrupted. It is therefore with no eagerness that we are anticipating imminent changes to our refuse collection schedules.

The new multicoloured bin system and altered collection rotas and routes have already started in the Amersham area, and friends in that area are already concerned that what was working well and smoothly under the previous contract is now both confusing and less user-friendly or reliable.

Of course, there will be teething problems when a new contractor undertakes any major enterprise from another company. But in my area we have already seen the narrower 18-ton lorries that were sensibly used by the previous contractor to negotiate the winding roads of rural areas replaced by wider 26-ton vehicles that struggle to negotiate the lanes around where I live. Those of us who live where the local authorities won't repair our access roads will be facing the substantial added cost now of remedying the damage caused by these significantly heavier vehicles to our roads. As if the roads weren't bad enough already!

It is tempting to suggest that if a thing is working, why tamper with it; but the need to cut costs for local services leads councils to make decisions that inevitably have an adverse knock-on effect for us, the council tax payers. Recycling is good if it really does what it says on the bin and we are not just being bamboozled by the coloured bin bonanza. But I hope that changing routes and vehicles which have delivered an excellent service for years, so soon after being awarded the contract, may not be that great an idea for the rural householder in particular. I hope the fact that the contractor Serco dropped out of the FTSE 100 this week in the wake of contract problems with its prisoner delivery operation isn't a bad omen.

20th September 2013

There are many questions that need answers. Some bigger than others. So big that it is easier not to spend time trying to pick your way through the brain strain of processing them. Questions like whether the universe is finite or infinite. Either option perplexes even Stephen Hawking, so what chance do I have?

There are also questions that we all know the answer to, but cannot persuade those who have the power to join us on our journey of logic.

Examples? Well, HS2 for starters. If they really want to give employment to the thousands of folk involved in compelling business men to spend 20 minutes less on their computers between London and Birmingham, we can all think of a thousand potholes that need filling in, a hundred railway lines that are already there and need modernising, innumerable schools and hospitals that need upgrading, supplying and staffing. All these urgent activities would similarly boost the economy by getting more people to work on something constructive rather than destructive.

Here's another one. Do we really need parish councils, town councils, district councils and county councils? Both Wycombe District Council and Bucks County Council have been charged with mammoth swingeing budget cuts. Leaving aside the fact that somehow they will do it, begging the question why it wasn't done before, a simple way of effecting the required saving would be to merge those councils and add in a smaller Wycombe Town Council to sit alongside the parish councils.

At the moment, finding out who is responsible for a particular civic responsibility can take eons, as the respective authorities pass the buck at a funereal pace.

And then there are the smaller imponderable questions. Why do all clothing stores put the big sizes on the bottom shelf and the smaller on the top shelf? The customer with the 32" waist is more likely to reach the bottom or top shelves with more ease than the guy with the 46" waist. But who do they get to bend down? Why?

And how about my wife's experience this week when she went to Waitrose in Marlow. She parked in Dean Street Car Park opposite the Chapel Street entrance, but having completed her shopping, could not exit by the same door, necessitating a few hundred yards' walk in the pouring rain from the rear of the store in Liston Street. Why? Answers on a Möbius strip, please.

27th September 2013

Several times I have started to write about the wearing of the niqab and then decided not to stir up a potential hornets' nest. But I should expect the same freedom of expression as the wearers of niqabs expect from the rest of us. I am not in favour of banning things unless there are very real and demonstrable dangers otherwise. It is sensible to ban the widespread ownership of guns, for instance, or the sale of alcohol to minors. As far as clothing is concerned, we should all be allowed to wear whatever we like in public, or indeed not wear it.

I would advocate tolerance of the 'naked rambler', for instance, on the basis that the human form, whilst not always an object of visual delight, is no more offensive than some T-shirts people choose to wear.

I confess that I cannot understand why a woman's face might be considered capable of inflaming male passions beyond their powers of self-restraint. Angelina Jolie has managed to survive whilst fully visible. My instinct, too, is to reject objectifying women.

But there is a big difference between not liking seeing women as sexual objects that need to be concealed, and banning the concealment. Providing it is the free choice of the woman, then she has as much right to so dress as spectators at a cricket match do to come as Pinky and Perky.

But there are circumstances where identification is essential, so there must be times when the face cannot be obscured. In our schools, teachers rely on visual as well as spoken communication with pupils. When driving a car, full visibility is essential. The police have to be able identify people as part of their job, as do airport security staff. There are many public activities where the identity of the individual is paramount and the state must be allowed to proscribe that freedom to wear the niqab on those occasions, in the same way as the wearing of hoods. It should be done as sensitively as practically possible. But it must be done.

We should all try too to be less nervous about expressing our real concerns openly and calmly without fear of being accused of religious intolerance. Just as we can accept the niqab in most situations, those who wish to wear it must accept our need to discuss when it would be inappropriate in our society and legislate accordingly.

4ᵗʰ October 2013

My brother always used to talk about the first time he saw a banana, just after the end of 'the war', as my generation still calls it. We should probably start referring to that conflict more specifically soon, as there have been countless others since 1945.

My brother probably intended to make me feel like a privileged brat brought up immediately after the deprivations he suffered for his first eight years. And he had a point. But an incident made me reflect on the vast array of 'new' foods that have arrived in the UK in my lifetime. I was dining with friends whose other guests were from Sri Lanka and did not know what lychees were. I had imagined that being a lot nearer China than we were, that strange lapsang souchong of fruits might have reached them before it did us back in the 60s, when I remember very clearly going to my first Chinese restaurant, which had just opened in Manchester. We felt so exotic.

Food has moved on apace since my childhood, when my mother would routinely boil her vegetables into soggy oblivion, in common with her contemporaries. Fresh peas were very common then, and my Sunday morning job was to remove the little bullets from their pods and sneak the odd one raw when no one was looking. Who does that any more in these post-Birds Eye years? We had cauliflower, carrots, cabbage and broad beans (which I always thought tasted like sweaty socks). Where was broccoli back then? It must have been thrusting its now ubiquitous florets at us somewhere. Did we spurn it for its paler cousin the cauliflower? Every time I go to a restaurant now there seems to be a new vegetable that I have to ask the waiter to identify.

And what about fish? Cod was abundant and cheap. If

you were rich you bought skate, halibut or haddock. Where did the John Dory, pollock, bream, turbot and brill languish, happily unloved, back then?

And Scallops! They are very much the fishy-come-lately in every restaurant in the land, and they can be absolutely delicious. Were they skulking unnoticed in the lower oceanic depths all these years, thanking the mighty mollusc of the Sargasso Sea for their unloved status, until their scrumptiousness was discovered and ended their aeons of safety? What next?

And don't get me started on 'jus'!

18th October 2013

It appears that Next want to build a large store in Cressex. They have presumably decided on this location because of the comparative ease of delivery and customer access that might not be available anywhere in the town centre.

The owners of the Eden Shopping Centre are planning, apparently, to contest the granting of permission for Next to do so, presumably on the basis of some clause in their original agreement with Wycombe District Council to build Eden. I cannot think of any other possible grounds for contesting the application. Whatever the end result, a cash-strapped local council will be obliged to expend tens of thousands of pounds of our money defending their decision to permit the development. If they lose and Next move elsewhere, a whole raft of jobs will go with them.

The town centre problem is not going to go away. I tour the country regularly and am now sadly used to seeing a rising percentage of shops and offices on high streets boarded up as a result of the changing social and financial environment. And of course, once that becomes a familiar sight, people are less inspired to visit somewhere shabby and unloved.

Eden itself has several empty units now, which they do their best to make look attractive, unlike most high street closures, with bright hoardings and advertising. But they are, nonetheless, compelling evidence of the drop in demand for what those shops once sold.

I don't know what the answer is. We all mourn the closure of the local owner-operated shops we loved in our childhood, but we still only notice they've gone when we need something quickly and don't want to drive the few miles to the supermarket that gets the majority of our cash.

We have closed those shops by not using them and then whinge when they aren't there anymore.

It is a transition that I suspect we may to endure until we decide what it is we really want. But the clock can't be turned back for all those small businesses that have been absorbed by the ever-expanding and seductively price-cutting giants.

The small newsagent's days are numbered, I suspect. They cannot survive on newspapers alone and everything else they sell is festooned around the tills at the supermarket. When you can no longer walk to get your paper, it'll be too late to do anything about it.

25ᵗʰ October 2013

I am travelling to Newcastle this weekend.

Unbelievably, my cheapest and quickest option, door to door, is to drive myself alone in my car. And of course, it's the door to door element that makes the difference.

Yes, a plane to Newcastle would take around an hour— but we all know how much time you have to allow now to get to an airport and be processed. The train would be the most expensive option, if the cost of getting to and from the stations is added. My car enables me to leave when I want and go door to door, without the stress of passengers ignoring the 'quiet' carriage restrictions or hurtling their seats backwards, unexpectedly spilling hot coffee in my lap.

When I was a young man, even with a car, public transport was the first option I considered, because it was invariably cheaper and just as quick. In fact, you didn't bother looking at timetables, because you knew the bus to take you into town and the station would never be more than a few minutes away. My bus fare into Rochdale town centre two miles or so away was a ha'penny in proper old money, which I believe equates to 5p in our current decimal system. Try and travel a couple of miles on a bus now for five pence, without a bus pass!

The default position we all have now of using our cars to go pretty much everywhere will be hard to change even if public transport were to both improve and get cheaper—and I am not talking about headline-grabbing HS2 projects—I mean passenger-grabbing local lines reopening and buses to rural areas that travel at times and frequencies that real people need. But I venture to suggest a lot more of us would start to use them than do now.

Just look at the excitement generated this month by the reconnection by Chiltern Railways of the Chinnor and Princes Risborough Railway to the national network and the running of a regular shuttle between those towns for the first time in 57 years. Dependent on volunteer drivers and crew and masses of local support and energy, it showed what could be achieved if the will were there.

Now, if the Wycombe to Bourne End link, closed in 1970, were reopened, linking to Maidenhead, imagine the use it would get today.

1st November 2013

It would seem that my pessimistic prediction of how the new refuse collection would roll out this week was accurate.

Strangers and acquaintances alike are volunteering stories of disappointment and frustration to me. Otherwise perfectly intelligent friends struggle to understand the system. A garage receptionist told me that she had now unsuccessfully asked on four separate occasions for the new bins that we are now compelled to use. She's not alone.

Baker Towers was visited on Monday by two separate huge trucks (both bigger than the lorry that used to come up our unmade, potholed road every week). There were two drivers and four loaders involved, as opposed to the one of each in the smaller lorry that formerly collected our refuse. I hope I don't get them into trouble by telling you that despite not having the correct array of bins that have replaced the one we had before, they took what they could stoically, for which I thank them as front-line workers put in a difficult position by their employers.

We have known about this impending upheaval in our refuse collection for months. Serco have presumably known about it even longer and therefore had plenty of time to demonstrate their worthiness to take over the contract from the company who for the last number of years have successfully served the area.

When I telephoned Wycombe District Council, who awarded the contract to Serco, presumably on the basis that they would do a better job than their predecessors, it took around fifteen minutes to get through. No prizes for guessing why they were so busy. The very nice but clearly busy lady apologised for my lack of bins and told me that they were committed to delivering them 'within 48 hours'. I noted she didn't say that they actually would be delivered within 48 hours. And of course they haven't been, and we are still waiting. I asked her why it now took nine men to do the work formerly done by two and how this could be possibly be better value for the council tax payer. She told me the council had gone for the cheapest tender. How can it be cheaper to have more men and more and bigger vehicles churning up our roads? I'm glad I'm not a Serco shareholder.

I wonder if the men who do the job were consulted on how best to provide the service.

8th November 2013

Our new set of assorted receptacles that do not replace but add to my existing black refuse bin have finally arrived. The lady to whom I addressed my concerns about our continuing binlessness proudly volunteered WDC's commitment to deliver them 'within 48 hours'. In the event, it was after 196 hours that they finally arrived in their pristine and colourful glory. Now we are keenly studying the long list of dos and don'ts.

There is disagreement at Baker Towers about the correct receptacle for a plastic wheel that has come off a small wheelie bin of our own. Is this household plastic waste and therefore blue bin, or is it general rubbish—black bin? The debate continues. We will put it to the vote before our next collection day.

Maybe there is potential here for a new TV quiz show. *What a Waste* might be a good title, or maybe just *Rubbish*. Viewers get points for identifying the correct bin or bag for assorted items. The prize could be a visit to the recycling plant to see what really happens to all those bins full of plastic, glass and cartons. And the bumper prize could be for the contestant who successfully explains why shredded paper is no longer 'paper'.

I spent last weekend in Florida at a convention celebrating the 50th anniversary of *Doctor Who*. I landed at Orlando with some five hundred other travellers, predominantly families off for some holiday fun. After a nine-hour flight, it was with weary dismay that we beheld a queue of at least that number again, who had just disembarked from another flight. It took me an hour and three quarters to reach one of the three US Customs and Border Protection officers on duty with a dozen empty control points around them, while my luggage was getting dizzy on a carousel waiting for me.

I learned later that I was lucky. Three-hour queues are common. It is ridiculous by any standard, but when you are trying to attract people to come to one of the most popular tourist attractions in the world, Disney, surely the first experience of families arriving in the USA could be better managed by the most powerful country in the world. Mind you, they'll be queuing for just as long in Disney to be made to feel sick, so I suppose it gets them used to it.

15th November 2013

After writing about the new waste and recycling arrangement twice recently, it was not my intention to revisit the subject. However, the letter in last week's paper from 'Chiltern and

Wycombe District Council's' Joint Waste Team', publicly inviting me to spend a day with the collection team, misses my point so completely that I must respond. I do not doubt that the nine men who now collect my rubbish are working their socks off to fulfil the requirements of the new system. I do not need to watch them in action to know that. As always, it is the guys on the sharp end that have to make new systems work. To tell me that they are all 'dedicated, conscientious workers doing their level best under challenging circumstances' implies that I thought otherwise.

But it is the 'challenging circumstances' I was highlighting and not the prodigious efforts of the foot soldiers, who are always unjustly in the firing line. I spoke to a team in the street in Wycombe the other day, and they left me very aware that in their opinion the wheel has been reinvented unnecessarily. I asked whether the men who do the job every day had been widely consulted on how to do that job better. You can guess the answer.

Understanding the system may not, as the team aver, have presented the majority with difficulties, but the sizeable minority that are struggling should not be dismissed.

The sole difference between the old system and the new one for us is that I no longer have to take my bottles to the local recycling hopper. So, it takes all those extra men and lorry miles to recycle my bottles. And it is only cheaper to the taxpayer because the new company is charging the councils less than the old one to do it. Whether they can sustain that is something we will find out in time. The company's record elsewhere does not inspire this taxpayer with confidence.

As I drive around the district now, all I seem to see are bins of varying colours all along the pavements, as so many householders simply don't have room to accommodate them anywhere else.

For the avoidance of any doubt, the workers who have to operate this system have my complete and unhesitating support. I hope their employers will give them all the opportunity to give proper feedback— anonymously, so that job security is not an issue.

22nd November 2013

Fifty years ago this weekend the first episode of *Doctor Who* was broadcast. You may have noticed that there has been a certain amount of broadcast time and column inches devoted to that over the last few weeks.

Clearly this was an event that has had an impact on my life, and I little thought when I was watching that very first episode in the flat I shared with several other law students in London back then (I was destined for a different career) that William Hartnell's crotchety, impatient character, petulantly grasping his lapels, would be one that I was destined to assume two decades later. It was my intention at that time to right wrongs in a less dramatic way.

Objective hindsight gives a different view of those years than I had at the time. For me, 1983 to 1986 was perhaps the best, most enjoyable time of my career. I was part of something that, even in those more turbulent days in the history of the programme, was held in great affection by the majority of the viewing public. Without a screen test or audition, I had been offered the role by the producer and felt enormously empowered by that. Immersed in the day to day business of making the programme, I was at the time unaware that behind the scenes there were problems and that the BBC management of the day were by no means as inordinately proud of the show as they demonstrably are now. Indeed, they seemed intent on killing it off.

Timing is everything, as everyone knows. I got the best job on television at perhaps the worst time.

The end result is that my era is sadly viewed with less favour than others and, of course, that hurts. As Shylock memorably said, 'If you prick us, do we not bleed?' And the current interest in the programme invites commentators to draw up lists, around the bottom of which the poor old Sixth Doctor languishes unloved, it seems.

All I can say is that I did my best with the hand that I was dealt and wish that we had had the support, budgets and pride that is lavished on the programme now. I am consoled by one thing, though. I look at all the other actors who have played the part and am proud that I was considered to be good enough to join that illustrious group.

29th November 2013

It's perhaps hard to believe that an expression that once carried implications that everyone understood to be true and could relate to should now be virtually meaningless. I recall 'That's not cricket' as being a very clear indication that the highest standards were not being adhered to. Cricket used to be seen as a game that was played by teams who respected each other and who shared a common belief in minimum standards of polite behaviour.

It would now appear that cricketers who play for opposing national teams can only be seen to relate to each other amicably once they have retired from the game for several years.

The sad evidence is that the fresh-faced, almost innocent-looking captain of the Australian team, Michael Clarke, has been fined for using an obscenity when warning, the English fast bowler to expect a broken arm as he came in to bat. Clarke defended his words, saying that it was just banter. But I thought banter was supposed to be witty rather than blunt declarations of aggressive intent.

I have heard of exchanges between cricketers back in the 80s, when both parties would be hard-pressed not to laugh. Nothing funny, however, about threats of physical violence accompanied by foul language that can be picked up by the microphones. Sportsmen do have a responsibility that comes with their high profile not to show an example to young followers of their sport that might make them think that it is acceptable to behave like that. We hear stories constantly about local football teams having to deal with young players who have seen the aggression and dissent on football pitches displayed by professional players that goes unpunished. They emulate their heroes. It's a no-brainer.

No referee has ever changed his mind on the pitch, so why do football players persist in getting in their faces so aggressively. Interestingly, the potentially roughest game of all—rugby—has far fewer incidents of players arguing with referees, and the sport is much the better for it.

Those responsible for the management and control of all sports would be greatly admired by the public at large if they were to take on this problem with the same single-mindedness as players do in their attempts to intimidate referees. Let a sporting gesture mean what it used to mean rather than be the use of a varying number of fingers raised to the traditions of those sports.

5th December 2013

The Organisation for Economic Cooperation and Development has produced its PISA report, which indicates that, according to their tests on 15-year-old students, education in the UK has not improved since its last report in 2009.

It is perhaps a little presumptuous of us to expect our young people to be of a higher standard than the students of the eighteen countries above us, including the two countries that top the table—South Korea and Japan, all of whom presumably are striving to do their best for their young people too.

Having been involved in education for over twenty years as a school governor, I have no doubt that the standard of teaching and the training of teachers is better than it was when I was at school. My classics teacher, whom I met again recently, told me he was invited to come and teach my year group by our headmaster when they met in the street in Manchester after the former had finished national service. He had no training whatsoever and confessed that he winged it, using the fear of corporal punishment as his main weapon of choice for failure to make the grade in tests. It worked on me. He was a teaching machine rather than a creative teacher; but fear is a great spur.

I have encountered scores of inspirational teachers at several schools in our area. I freely admit that Bucks schools are lucky in many ways. Whatever one may think ideologically about selection, why mess with something that demonstrably works?

No, there is no lack of excellent teachers. There are two main factors that hold us back. Cultural and political reasons play a bigger part than a failure of good teaching. Compare the reaction of many parents today with that of the vast majority of parents of my childhood when a pupil was disruptive (and much fewer were back then). I venture to suggest that almost every parent then, of all socio-economic groups, would support the school and apply further sanctions to the child. Not so now. There are far fewer stay-at-home mums, many more single-parent families, a much more materialistic society and endless opportunities for the young to be distracted and unsupervised.

Add to that incessant political tinkering with education by successive governments, instead of letting the many brilliant professionals create the agenda, and you have a recipe for a continuing mid-table status (if we're lucky).

12th December 2013

Over a year ago, my daughter's car had its exhaust assembly summarily detached when the edge of the tarmac lane at the end of which we live had been, subsided sufficiently to make the crown of the road meet the underside of her car. Other cars subsequently came to similar grief. Bucks County Council was informed on several occasions. Months passed.

We who live here now all know about the danger and keep to one side or the other of the hazard, although undoubtedly strangers with low-s--lung cars must also have come to grief. Imagine our joy then a few weeks ago when white paint— that harbinger of impending road works—encircled the now heavily scraped surface that has resulted from regular contact of sump with tarmac. Even more reassuringly, a yellow highways sign was attached to posts at each end of the lane, warning residents of its closure on a specific day last month, when repairs would be effected. We eagerly waited, prepared to endure temporary inconvenience for the expected improvement.

That day came and passed. The sign remained. So did

the subsidence and its mocking halo of white paint, which serves now as a reminder of our shattered dreams. Nothing happened for weeks. Then suddenly, action—the sign has gone. More time effecting repairs and less time putting up and then removing utterly pointless signs that give false hope would seem to be high on the agenda for Bucks County Council New Year resolutions, I would suggest.

Continuing the road traffic theme, I am surprised there are still drivers who do not understand when to turn on their rear fog lights. I am currently commuting from Basingstoke, where I am appearing in panto, and there have been mist patches along the M4 this week on several nights. None of them were dense enough to provoke the barrage of red light that around one in eight drivers insists on inflicting on us. To clarify, the Highway Code states 'You MUST NOT use front or rear fog lights unless visibility is seriously reduced, as they dazzle road users and can obscure your brake lights.'

They suggest 100 metres as the visibility marker to trigger use of the fog light. Last night I could see cars half a mile ahead, once I got past the glaring dazzle of the ill-informed, who seem hell bent on making things worse for those behind them.

19th December 2013

I feel lucky this year because Basingstoke, where I am pantoing, is altogether more Christmas-friendly for me than past years, and I will be home early enough to join in the Christmas Eve festivities that have apparently evolved due to the enthusiasm of my daughters during years of enforced absence. In fact, the schedule this year is the friendliest I have had for years, as the evening shows are all at 6 p.m. Clearly, Basingstoke folk are not keen on being out late, any more than I am.

This year is my thirty-third pantomime. When I set out to be an actor, I did not see panto as playing such a part in my career. How much I would have missed over the last four decades had I not been offered the role of Dick Whittington in Cork in 1979. It was a sharp learning curve. Because I was in a popular TV series, *The Brothers*, the theatre thought I would be a draw, so imported this novice.

I had to learn fast, as the comic who played the dame had a Cork accent so strong that I could understand only his every fifth word. He took the unmerciful mickey out of me for two months, to the delight of the audience. As the eponymous hero, it was not appropriate for me try to take on this master of comedy on his own patch, nor would I have had much luck had I tried to. But I learned a lot about the role and importance of each character in a traditional panto.

The story has to be told in a way that children can believe. They must identify with the plight of the hero and heroine and they must have every reason to hate the baddie. If you ask any young girl whom she liked best in a panto, she will almost without fail name the fairy or the princess. They need to identify and care. Boys are different—they tend to favour the Silly Billy characters—and the would-be tougher boys will name the villain.

And even though adults love the comedy of the dame and the comedians, we must remember that panto is for families and particularly for children. If what may well be their first experience of theatre is something that excites and delights them, they may in later years revisit theatres to sample some of the other wonderful things that live theatre can offer.

26th December 2013

My wife has had a lifetime to get used to the fact that her birthday falls on Christmas Day.

She is quite relaxed about something that some might find a tad annoying, especially if you are the only member of the household who is capable of presenting anything remotely resembling a Christmas dinner. So she spends a significant amount of her birthday slaving away in the kitchen and invariably producing a superb feast for me and our four daughters, who still return to the fold for the festive day. Mind you, only one of them has actually moved out into a home of her own, so it's not much of a return to the fold. In that respect, it's less of a fold and more of a luxury hotel.

Every year I accept that it may be the last time that we six spend that exclusive time together; so far, they seem to want to hang on to the tradition. Certainly, I have no wish to compel the unwilling to spend a reluctant day en famille.

I have seen many examples elsewhere over the years of how painful and unlovely that can be. I freely admit that my desire for family exclusivity is partly based on the fact that I am invariably only free on the actual day itself—being a regular panto performer and therefore obliged to twinkle-twinkle on stage somewhere on both Christmas Eve and Boxing Day – usually a theatre's most popular shows.

At Baker Towers we divide the day in two. The morning is my wife's birthday and the rest of the day is Christmas. So birthday presents in the morning and the Christmas exchange of gifts is in the afternoon/evening. Although, my daughters, all of whom are in their twenties, insist on leaving mince pies and refreshments for Santa, who therefore is still obliged to treat them as little children and provide a stocking full of goodies for early morning excitement and jollity.

My stories of a childhood where I thought myself lucky if I got an apple studded with cloves (which I dislike intensely), and a piece of wood and a whittling knife to make myself a toy, invariably fall upon deaf ears.

But as I have to reluctantly acknowledge that I have more Christmases behind me than ahead—each one becomes even more precious. Do all have a peaceful and happy one yourselves.

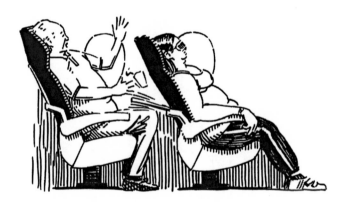

2014

2ⁿᵈ January 2014

The events of the last couple of weeks have thrown up what seems to be a perennial but avoidable problem yet again. Whether it's an airport, a power company, the rail network or almost any public service or utility, in the age of instant and worldwide communication, no one can find out what's going on when things go wrong.

It surely cannot be beyond the wit or budget of these vast organisations to set up a system whereby a dedicated team—and it wouldn't have to be a large one—is mobilised when there are power outages, railway line closures or significant flight departure delays.

No one has ever reasonably complained about the frontline services on these occasions. The power engineers, the track repairers, tree removers and flight despatchers all do a fantastic job in the most hazardous situations to restore our services. Nor should we expect them to stop what they're doing to phone every household or individual who is left in the dark—literally and figuratively.

But the salaries of a small team of incident coordinators (who might have other responsibilities during times when things are hunky dory), would not be a significant drain on their resources.

It would be their job to liaise with the teams on the front line and inform the public of developments. The worst example of the failure to see this as a priority occurs whenever there are hundreds stranded at international airports or railway stations. The abiding image is one of frustrated would-be travellers who have no information for hours; and although the case may be that for some of that time there is no concrete information available, even that lack of information could be managed better.

Of course, in the case of rail travel, the fragmentation of service providers doesn't help any more than the number of airlines, but the airport and track authorities really should be able to institute a system whereby the sharp-end employees, who are as uninformed as the travellers, are not the only point of contact for the frustrated passenger.

We can have instant email conversations between New Zealand and the UK; we can Skype each other and watch news unfold as it happens anywhere in the world. Big organisations should be able to communicate with their customers better.

Let their New Year's Resolution be 'It's good to talk!'

Mine? Oh, lose weight—as usual! Sigh.

9th January 2014

Hats off to Chris Phillips and his intrepid team of volunteers for successfully providing Wycombe with a broadcast radio station for four weeks over Christmas. After the demise in 2009 of Mix 107, which had evolved from Swan FM and its earlier AM existence as 1170, Wycombe has not had a dedicated radio station that serves the whole community in the way that those stations had tried to do.

There is Awaaz 107.4, which serves the local Asian community, and BBC 3 Counties, which transmits over a much wider area than Wycombe, but it would be excellent to have a single point of reference for both the receiving and transmitting of really local news and information, and for those few weeks Wycombe Sound provided that for us.

I was asked to come in and chat to the listeners during its last week and was impressed by the commitment of the volunteers, who had identified a need and done all the hard work in setting up and operating the station over the short Christmas period. Another four-week stint is due, apparently in July.

It really is a no-brainer. The only stumbling block to providing a regular service is, of course, finance. And the finances will hopefully arrive when local business and institutions realise that there is a market for a local station. The only local station that I have access to currently is Marlow FM, which I cannot receive at home but always tune in to as I drive through or around Marlow, particularly when there are weather or road issues that I need an update on.

A permanent Wycombe-based and Wycombe-serving radio station would be a godsend.

It appears that an application to Ofcom will be made towards the end of this year when the new round of applications is being considered. I would urge readers to support this initiative and reward both the hard work and imagination of the Wycombe Community Radio Company in reviving something that most people would agree should never have been allowed to disappear from the airwaves. The benefits could be considerable, whether it be from giving local politicians and local government the opportunity to be heard by the public on a more regular basis, and even more importantly, from advertising job opportunities and community needs and initiatives.

The best of luck to Chris Phillips and his team.

16th January 2014

I was much taken by the recent news story of the young man called Jonny Benjamin, who had intended to end his life on Waterloo Bridge six years ago this week, but was talked out of it by a passing stranger. Jonny was just 20 years old and a victim of schizoaffective disorder, which had resulted in him reaching the decision to climb over the railings on the bridge and jump into the murky waters of the Thames. The stranger, whose name he never knew, told him that he had been a victim of depression himself but had come out the other side and suggested they should go and have a coffee and a chat.

The normality of this image penetrated his pain, it seems, and he relented. His life has turned around; he now works for a mental health charity and is an active campaigner in the cause of helping others whose plight he now so clearly understands.

Jonny is now attempting to find his Good Samaritan to thank him, saying, 'His act of kindness changed my outlook on life and I have thought about him ever since. I want to find this man so I can thank him for what he did. If it wasn't for him, I probably wouldn't be here today.'

I hope he finds him, if only because I suspect it would be rather uplifting for that person to know that those few moments in his life had had such a profound effect on another human being. It has certainly made me think that one should never miss the opportunity to make sure that those who have helped us along the way should know that we are aware and grateful.

I once wrote to the English teacher whom I had revered at school and who, I told him, had inspired me with a love for our language that has never left me. His response was gratitude and surprise, as he insisted that he had only taught me for two terms out of the twenty-one I spent at my school in Manchester. I suppose it indicated even more strongly the power of his effect on me,, as I have remembered him much more than the other teachers, who had the dubious honour of instructing the junior me for longer than that with less lasting effect.

So thank you, anonymous stranger, for reading these inconsequential ramblings.

23rd January 2014

I am staggered at the amount of money that people appear to be prepared (or obliged) to spend on weddings these days. I struggle to believe that this is the best possible use of tens of thousands of pounds at a time when a young couple are starting out on their lives together, when the housing market is so terrifyingly expensive, when jobs are no longer 'for life' and when the economic climate remains unpredictable at best and dire at worst.

An acquaintance, recently widowed, is being pressured by a young about-to-be married couple to spend more than the £30,000 already committed to the event later in the year, which is to be attended by around 200 guests. She herself reflected that her own wedding several decades ago cost around £350. My wedding cost even less than that, as we decided to get married without announcing the fact to another soul and have never for one second regretted that decision. We had a fantastic day with each other without worrying about guest lists, menus, flowers, entertainment, what to wear and speeches. Our mothers, both widowed and impecunious, were relieved and grateful to us. Only my brother voiced his disapproval, and we had never agreed about much anyway.

It strikes me that the only real beneficiaries of these lavish, money-guzzling follies are those who work in the mammoth wedding industry that seems to have sprung up recently. The abundance of wedding fairs is evidence of the competition that seems to have burgeoned to have a bigger, better, more lavish wedding than anyone else.

I have four (as yet unmarried) daughters. I sincerely hope that they will all find partners that are right for them and make them happy. If I have any funds available when that time arrives, I will happily be as generous as I can without endangering my wife's and my financial future. But it will be nothing like the figures currently being spent and will be applied to enabling their home together, not entertaining two hundred people, at least half of whom would rather be somewhere else.

There is also that awful nagging feeling that girls are considered as a burden that needs to be disposed of at any cost, with echoes of the dowries of yesteryear. I shall miss all my girls and have no intention of throwing money away when they need it the most.

31ˢᵗ January 2014

Last week I attended the opening of the Jackie Palmer Stage School's new premises in Bridge Street in High Wycombe. There were several reasons I enjoyed the evening.

The official opening of the excellent new facility was performed by their ex-student James Corden, whose gently self-effacing speech, for me, hit the nail absolutely on the head about what the study of drama, dance and singing is all about. He spoke very movingly about how he had been transformed as a young boy by his time at the school.

Even though he has subsequently become a very successful actor and entertainer, the most important thing for him then was finding something that he could do and sharing exploration of that with other likeminded-folk. This is, of course, not the only area that offers that. I am aware of that. Sport, for instance, offers precisely the same opportunity, without necessarily leading to a career in football or cricket. It is the participation in the activity that has intrinsic worth.

It was delightful to see the choir of young students performing with such freedom and joy, every one of them smiling and showing every sign of relishing their various roles. The confidence that the study of the performing arts brings is sufficient return on the investment of time and energy, because it is a quality that can be transferred into every aspect of modern life.

Confidence is so important. I am not talking about arrogance, about thinking you're better than everyone else— or worse, saying that you are. I am talking about that quiet confidence that says you are no more or less worthy than those around you and that your voice is worthy of being heard. I know that ethos is shared by the staff at Jackie Palmer, which is why it has been successful over the years and enabled the school to finally acquire its own premises.

The worth of drama and performance studies is something, too, that I hope schools do not forget. Drama as a syllabus subject is not a luxury. It is almost uniquely a subject that can impact and enable other subjects to be explored in a different and more subjective way. Literature, Geography and History are obvious examples. Again, it is not about training young actors. It is about enabling the exploration of what it is to be a human being—and isn't that what education ought to be about?

7th February 2014

The very public sacking of cricketer Kevin Pietersen this week and the similar departure of football manager Michael Laudrup from Swansea and the rather odd, yo-yo pseudo-departure of Leeds manager Brian McDermott all raise interesting issues about attitude to success and failure in sport, and indeed all areas of life these days.

Billionaire owners and selectors share characteristics, it seems. They all want success and they want it now, if not sooner. In pursuit of that, some are prepared to pay millions of pounds to get rid of unsuccessful managers. But the fact that the opposing team's owners are similarly motivated seems sometimes to escape them. At least Wycombe Wanderers are giving our popular local football manager—Gareth Ainsworth—the chance to do what he can with the limited funds available, despite the recent frustrating absence of success.

In the cricket, England's comprehensive loss didn't just happen in a vacuum. There was another team playing against them and it was a team packed with testosterone and aggression that really wanted to win and arguably deserved to win. To a keen cricket fan who stayed up into the wee small hours to witness this depressing humiliation, it seems to combine spite, envy and folly to scapegoat the highest scoring batsman on the apparent basis that he is charismatic and ruffles feathers. Our best sportsmen have frequently included mavericks who irritate those charged with running their sport. Handling the wayward genius is an art that escapes them, it seems. Better to cast them aside and cherish the steady, non-controversial players who toe the party line, even if they never set the airwaves alight.

I have frequently in my profession had to work with actors or directors whose methods and behaviour is (shall we be kind and say), challenging. If the end result is great, then we willingly knuckle down and endure the irritation. Of course, when the performance is even worse than the behaviour, they don't last long. I heard the story of an actor whose fame turned him into a monster, who sacked the caterers because they left a label an apple that he bit into. It seems he had forgotten that he, as the producer, had hired them and would have to bear the cost.

But most 'difficult' people will respond if approached sensibly. More often than not, they are difficult because they have high expectations from everyone, including themselves.

14th February 2014

If the human race needs a wake-up call, then it is regularly being delivered to us in many areas of the world. Suddenly, a smaller alarm bell is ringing in the UK and it only serves to highlight how lucky we have been for many years to live in a part of our blue planet that has not been prey to the storms, floods, famines or earthquakes that regularly blight large chunks of the world.

But the Earth, Nature, Gaia—call it what you will— only needs to flex its muscles very slightly for our toehold on this planet to become very precarious. During the planet's existence there have already been at least four cataclysmic 'back to square one' events that have required life to reassert itself every time. Most of us are aware that if the planet's history were to be represented by, say, a monopoly board, the time that we have been strutting our stuff on the planet would be represented by the thickness of the line that separates Mayfair from 'Go'. And in that comparatively short time, we have made a very significant and possibly irreversible impact.

Now we are seeing the effects of the planet's power in the south-west and south-east of England, a country that until now has never endured the depredations of nature to the same extent as what we choose the call The Third World. There have been floods before, but certainly not of this impact or duration. The Prime Minster has very properly suggested that the government spend whatever it takes to help the afflicted— and hopefully to take robust action that perhaps could have been taken before—but now is frankly not the time to play the blame game, but to act.

It will be expensive just to restore the pre-storm status quo. It will be even more expensive to take the proactive measures that reduce the risk of further flooding. The money that is needed is our money. It comes from our taxes. Maybe we should consider the possibility of a one-year only increase in income tax to help the thousands of people for whom insurance will no longer be an option in the future, and all the businesses whose livelihoods have been terminally affected?

Maybe too builders who build on flood plains should be

compelled to provide a lifetime flood insurance for those who buy their houses? Or to build on stilts?

28th February 2014

Charlotte Dawson, an Australian TV star, has been found dead at the age of 47. Her death has been linked to internet bullying. She was an anti-bullying activist who had been targeted online by what are called 'cyber trolls', a label that makes them sound more interesting than they actually are. In reality they are the worst kind of vicious bullies, ones who do it from a distance and hide behind false identities.

Any brief research on the subject will reveal scores of recent cases in the newspapers when vulnerable young people receive torrents of hateful abuse from their schoolmates, who mindlessly collude on websites to persecute the weakest and least able to defend themselves. Even the most grounded and supported young person would wilt eventually under such relentless persecution. As an adult, I can just shake my head and pity the morons when I receive, as I do occasionally, hateful comments. Then I block them.

But whether you're 14 or 47, if you're in a bad place already, this kind of attack can tip you over the edge. At least the bullying of pre-internet days was usually directed in person to the victim and therefore visible to others, who could do something about it. Now, the bullies are even more cowardly and skulk behind the anonymity of a computer screen as they conduct their hateful persecution.

The volume of this corrosive phenomenon is aided by the social network websites that we all use and which can be hugely beneficial in countless areas of our lives. Campaigns for things worth campaigning for can be focussed, and conducted swiftly using, say, Twitter and Facebook. The denouncing of corruption, corporate greed, political duplicity and the mistreatment of children, old people and animals are all the benefits of the instant communication offered by these web giants.

Who can deny that the benefits are legion? But, as

always, the malevolent and the stupid seize the opportunities offered by instruments designed to help mankind in order to perpetrate evil. These are the same people who, when they see sandbags being brought in to flooded areas to help their less fortunate neighbours, steal them and sell them, or who break into a flooded shop in Old Amersham and steal their stock. Having a bad time, eh? Let's make it worse!

Twitter and Facebook are worth billions now. They must be able to be more proactive in weeding out the persecutors and the poisonous.

7th March 2014

Can't airport checks be done any quicker?

I have been travelling a lot recently and am amazed at the stoicism of the majority of us sheep who allow ourselves to be herded and corralled to the extent that currently seems necessary to ensure our individual and national safety.

I am writing this in New Zealand. A quick calculation has revealed that in order to get to Dunedin, I have spent more combined time queuing to be scanned, interrogated, vetted and patted down than I spent on three of the four flights it took me to get here in 36 zombiefying hours.

Only the 13-hour leg across Australia trumped the security lines. You would be tempted to think that they really would rather you hadn't come there to spend your money. As you totter, brain-dead, into immigration halls in the USA, Australia or New Zealand (my most recent experiences), you will invariably behold a roped snake of leaden-footed, exhausted travellers shuffling through seven or eight parallel lines of the comatose to present themselves at one of the couple of desks available for non-residents. It is tempting to believe that they constructed a facility with dozens of desks to underline the fact that they're not going to open them all for the likes of you.

They know when the planes are coming in and how many people will be on them, people whose first impression of their country might be the treatment they receive on arrival. Two hours spent inching forward in despair is not the way to show how much they value the dollars we are about to spend in their country.

I sincerely hope that our own border security system offers a better service to those entering the UK. As residents, of course, we don't see how our visitors are treated. I just get the 'Oh, you've come back, have you? Ah well, never mind, on your way!' And all that technology that was supposed to speed things up, fingerprint and eye scanners, digital passport readers, has inevitably had the opposite effect. Despite their protestations to the contrary, all those innovations are designed to make 'their' lives easier, not ours. We know that in order to safeguard our safety and security, all the checks are essential. They could just be done much more quickly and more efficiently.

I suppose the simple answer is that we should all stay at home.

14ᵗʰ March 2014

I wrote last week about the frustration of border controls and security checks when travelling by air. My gripe was mainly with the undermanning of these processes at many airports, at a time when air travel seems to be growing, rather than any suggestion that rigorous safety procedures are not necessary. It must be done; but it could be done better.

The disappearance of the Malaysian aeroplane last week serves to focus our minds, however, on the need for the endless stringent checks that we tend to have to endure these days. Until last Friday, the total disappearance of a plane would have been, for me, the stuff of action films and lurid fiction, not the real world. However, as I write this, it is five days since Malaysia Airlines Flight 370, a Boeing 777 with 227 passengers on board, simply disappeared off the coast of Vietnam, without trace.

I was astonished to learn that the transponders that identify planes to radar beacons can be turned off by the pilot and that, it appears, is what may have happened, as the plane disappeared from the radar screens at around the same time as the last radio message was received from the cockpit. We can only imagine the agony being felt by the waiting hundreds of relatives who still know no more than they did when they were first told that their family member or friend would not be landing in Beijing as planned.

I have travelled on three planes since Friday, on my thirty-six hour return journey from New Zealand, and I must say that as a frequent flier and one who usually subscribes to the 'It's safer than driving on a motorway' maxim, I was less sanguine about the process than I have been in the past, and I know I paid more attention to the safety demonstration and accompanying video than has been my custom previously. It is also true that I tolerated being comprehensively frisked in Dubai more stoically when the metal edge of my wallet triggered the alarm as I passed through the scanner.

It is in the context of all this effective and comprehensive security that someone may have still managed to cause harm to a plane full of people, whose fate is still a mystery to us.

It is hard to imagine an outcome that is not tragic. We can only hope.

21st March 2014

When I was a lad, my mother would give me a shopping list to drop off at the grocery shop on my way to school, and then later in the day, if it was a small list, she would pop in and collect it. If it was the weekly shop, he would deliver it. This was, of course, a long time ago.

Readers of my own age will not be as surprised as younger readers to learn that our bread and milk was delivered then daily by horse and cart. For that reason, I suppose, I still associate that lovely sweet smell of horse's breath with freshly baked bread.

Shopping has evolved since then. I often do our weekly shop online, and I am sad to say that I haven't shopped for food in other than a supermarket for far too long. The power of the supermarkets drove prices down to the point that individual traders were no longer able to compete, and now they have been eliminated from the market, the big players only have to compete with each other.

How long before that ceases to be to our advantage, I wonder? One of the unlooked-for results of shopping online is a rather irritating phenomenon that is gradually becoming more prevalent. When did your local bookshop proprietor contact you a few days after you bought your *Doctor Who* annual to ask you if you were satisfied with your purchase and to evaluate the quality of the wrapping and delivery into your hand?

Or when did your fishmonger pop round to ask if your scallops were up to snuff?

Whenever I buy anything online, I am now subsequently asked to fill in an ever-growing list of questions about the delivery and nature of the product I have bought. I buy online for speed, convenience and value. The speed and convenience are being gradually eroded by the time taken answering or, in my case now, deleting the endless stream of customer satisfaction questionnaires that follow any purchase. I would let them know if there was a problem. Take my silence as satisfaction, please.

All these surveys and tick-box forms are getting to be a total pain. And it's just so they can say that nine out of ten dentists recommend it. Not that that necessarily works. I always worry about that one dentist who knows something the others don't.

28th March 2014

There was a programme on Channel 5 this week that highlights an unlooked-for result of our national terror of being accused of being a paedophile.

Back in the Sixties, when I was studying law at a college in Bayswater, I was spending an afternoon with my law books in Hyde Park. I saw a little girl distressed and crying and asked what the matter was. She told me that she had lost her mummy. I took her by the hand and said I would help her.

After some minutes of searching without success, I spotted a policeman and went over with my little friend to enrol his assistance. He took charge and I can only assume that he eventually reunited her with her mother. I had no qualms back then in thinking that was the right and only thing to do. Certainly, the possibility of being accused of abduction and worse never crossed my mind as a valid reason not to help the child.

This week's programme, *Little Girl Lost*, showed us child actresses aged seven and five standing alone and forlorn near Victoria Station as over six hundred adults passed by, many giving each child as wide a berth as possible, before one woman in her seventies finally checked on the well-being of the five-year-old. The reason for the six hundred non-Samaritans couldn't be clearer. For some it may have been a selfish desire not to get involved in the hassle of stopping what they were doing to help, but I suspect that most people today would be reluctant to engage with a young child in case it might be misinterpreted. And that is a terrible indictment of our society.

In my lifetime, incidents of child abduction and murder by strangers have not changed from around six or seven a year. That it happens at all is sickening and vile, but the threat is clearly diminishing as the population has grown considerably during that time. But we are all bombarded with defensive rules and regulations that result in a kind of mass paralysis of the decent human behaviour those rules are trying to safeguard.

I would do the same today as I did fifty years ago. I might try to enlist the help of a female passer-by quickly to protect myself (sadly,) but that would only be after I had tried to reassure and secure the safety of the child.

4th April 2014

It was with great sadness that I learned this week of the death of Kate O'Mara.

I first met her on stage. Literally. Barely out of drama school,

I was working in theatre-in-education for the Yvonne Arnaud Theatre in Guildford. We were touring Surrey, performing *Shakespeare—Cabbages and Kings*—you get the picture, I'm sure. To earn a few extra pennies, we all understudied whatever play was on that week at the theatre. One Saturday lunchtime, when the members of a local youth club had been rendered insensible by our mangling of the Bard, I was seized by the stage manager and propelled into his car as he told me. 'You're on!'

We had not seen the play, *The Holly and the Ivy*, nor met the cast. But I had learned the lines, thank goodness. I was thrust into an itchy army costume and introduced to a couple of anxious-looking cast members and, like the worst cliché from the movies, I was thrust into the wings.

Onstage were two elderly ladies and Kate O'Mara. I recall entering, not knowing which aunt was which and addressing my line to the wrong one. Later, I was offered a cup of coffee and took it, prompting the elderly actress to mutter, 'The other one doesn't take it'—meaning the actor currently having his hand bandaged at the hospital after gashing himself that morning. I may have known the lines, but my moves were, to say the least, arbitrary. For them it was a long afternoon.

I next encountered Kate when she came into *The Brothers* to lock horns with my character, the hated Paul Merroney, in that brilliant 70s Sunday night must-see series. Then a decade later we met again in *Doctor Who* when she played, superbly, a renegade Time Lady—The Rani.

She was a consummate professional and bravely set up her own company to tour Shakespeare, risking her own money to do what she did best—perform. She was one of the last of a dying breed of actors who justify being referred to as 'troupers'. Acting and theatre were not for her a way of earning money, but a way of expressing who she was. The last time I saw her was just a few weeks ago at a *Doctor Who* convention when, though frail, she was as warmly theatrical and flamboyant as ever. The theatre is poorer for her loss.

11th April 2014

While sorting through the half a small tree's worth of marketing bumf that cascades into our letter box every week, my wife spotted something in a catalogue that she actually liked. So I suppose that means that this deluge of advertising does work, although the hit rate must surely be insufficient to justify such profligate use of our dwindling resources. Anyway …

She phoned the successful advertiser to order said desirable goods. Details were taken, including our address, whereupon the voice indicated that we were already on their database. This should have been an advantage, she fondly imagined, but that thought was soon dispelled when she was asked if she was the account holder.

It appears that the last order was made by me some years previously. The next question was whether she 'had the account holder's permission' to order something. 'I don't need it,' she replied, explaining that she was intending to pay for it on her own credit card and it had nothing to do with me. I wasn't there to 'give my permission' she added, and she was not in the habit of asking my permission before spending a few pounds of her own on an article of clothing. But the possibility of two people sharing an address and being independently able to conduct a small financial transaction did not accord with the instructions on the screen in front of the distant employee.

I have encountered similar problems in the past and my reaction has depended on how much I actually want the item in question. I have, on occasion, simply hung up and redialled, assuming the persona of my wife and speaking in my normal voice, saying my name was 'Marion Baker'. After all, John Wayne's real name was Marion Morrison. No one yet has said that I did not sound like someone of that name.

All of which highlights the absurdity of what the 'computer says', sometimes. How we all long for common sense to nudge its way back into our daily lives and how surprised we all are (sadly) when the person on the other end of the phone helps us to find a way round a problem, rather than place it between you like the Berlin wall.

She told the probably uncaring employee that she would therefore not be purchasing that day and would never trouble that company again by offering them her money.

18th April 2014

Next week, the annual Wycombe Arts Festival kicks off its 50th anniversary programme in St Andrew's Church in Hatters Lane, with the talented young wind performers from Wycombe Music Centre presenting an evening of chamber music. Sadly, I cannot be there, as I shall be en route to Antwerp, where I am working that weekend, but I know that, like many of the events of the Festival, it will continue the tradition of offering opportunities to young performers from the area to show the breadth and depth of talent that we have in abundance in Wycombe.

A sizeable proportion of the events on offer serve to prove yet again that our excellent local schools are encouraging creative and artistic talent in the young people of the area. But there are also artists, speakers and performers from further afield.

John Beaumont and his team of volunteers have once again gathered together a wonderful selection of talent to compile a truly rich and eclectic mix of events. There really is something for everyone. I am delighted to have the opportunity of joining the talented young choir from the Jackie Palmer Stage School as narrator when they perform Roald Dahl's *Little Red Riding Hood* at St Lawrence's Church, West Wycombe on the evening of 31st May.

I shall also be in the audience on 21st May, the first night of WYSPAS' production of *Godspell*, which has been one of my favourite musicals ever since 1971 when I first saw it in London.

Whether your interests embrace local history, music in any of its forms, drama, crafts, poetry or dance, there is something for you. There is even a demonstration of flour milling at the Pan Mill on The Rye (water permitting!). So I urge you all to help celebrate this anniversary in style by delving into the brochure and seeing what event grabs your imagination.

In an age when the practicalities of earning a living can dominate our lives to the exclusion of everything else, this festival serves to remind us that it is the music, drama, literature and art that we create and share that separates us from the animal world from which we have evolved.

That is why I am a passionate advocate for the arts having a place in education at a time when there are political and commercial pressures to reduce the time spent in schools on the arts and drama.

25th April 2014

Last weekend my iPhone was purloined while I was shopping in one of our busy supermarkets. It was fully charged and turned on, but promptly vanished off the useful computer programme with a map that tells you where your phone is when it's lost. Clearly, the miscreant knew of that possibility and had turned it off. I waited as long as I dared before sending out the autodestruct command.

I thought my phone was covered for loss or theft as part of my bank's gold card package, but apparently I had 'the wrong gold card package, I'm afraid, sir'. With a year left on my phone contract, it would be hideously expensive to replace what I had, so I tried to download from iCloud all the data and apps (are you losing the will to live yet?) to my old iPhone 3, which I discarded a couple of years ago. Uh-oh! Can't do that—sorry.

The operating system on your old phone is different. That is after four or more hours wrestling with iTunes and then iCloud and finally phoning for help. I am fairly computer-savvy for a geriatric, and have a reasonable grasp of the processes involved in getting most of the bells I require to ring to do so appropriately on my phone and desktop, but the circular frustration finally takes its toll when you are told that you need to authorise something and then, when you try to do so, are told that it is already authorised—over and over again.

I wish I were wealthy or uncontrolled enough to vent

my spleen by jumping up and down on the offending machines and imagining them to be the bullet-ridden corpse of whomsoever is now unlocking my phone somewhere and flogging it to an unsuspecting punter in the pub. But I suppose if I were that person, I could just as easily spend the few hundred quid required to replace my phone and save myself hours of frustration.

We are so dependent now on these bits of kit that a mere few decades ago were the province only of the privileged. Now every ear you see in the street has clamped to it a supercomputer more powerful than those that took Armstrong and Aldrin to the moon.

We've moved on from those inelegant half-bricks with big floppy aerials that we thought were the 'thing' back in the day.

2nd May 2014

I travel a fair amount and my passport was due to run out next month, so I sent off my passport after my last trip abroad with a four-week window before travelling to Antwerp last weekend. Why we still need passports within Europe defeats me, but …

My old clipped passport was returned with a week to spare, but of the new one no sign, so I rang the passport helpline. I rang repeatedly over three days to ask where my new one was on the assembly line. They couldn't tell me. On Thursday, two days before my trip, I was told it was at Peterborough Passport Office. Could I use the old clipped but still valid one? No. Could I go to Peterborough to collect it? They gave me an appointment in Peterborough at 8.30 a.m. the following day.

In Peterborough on Friday I was told it had been sent out by courier on Thursday and would arrive 'next Monday or Tuesday'. I was booked on the Eurostar the following day. At first they wouldn't tell me the details of the courier, but I eventually got far enough up the decision-making chain to get that information and the reference number. I contacted the couriers and eventually the payment of an extra fee 'guaranteed' me delivery before 1 p.m. on Saturday. My train was booked for 4.10 p.m. It would work. Except, of course, the passport did not arrive by 1 p.m., or 2 p.m., or indeed 3 p.m. I missed the train. My umpteenth phone call to the couriers, after repeated assurances it would be there any minute, moved up the decision-making chain once more, and I was told I could go to Colnbrook near the airport and pick it up at 4.30 p.m. The driver was new to the area and couldn't find my house—despite having my phone number for that very reason. I collected it and headed for St Pancras and the expensively rebooked Eurostar. A mobile crane was blocking the entrance to the station car park I had booked and the detour took 25 minutes. I arrived at the station barrier breathless and stressed at 6.55 for the 7.04 train to be told I was too late. Something in my demeanour made him check on the radio. They let me in. I ran, hauling out my new passport as I wheezed through the platform checkpoint—they barely so much as glanced at it.

9th May 2014

I missed the television broadcast of *Jamaica Inn* but, after the media furore about the sound and inaudibility of the actors, my professional curiosity was piqued. I downloaded it to watch for myself.

Despite my actor-solidarity predisposition, I have to admit that I struggled to understand more of the dialogue than one might reasonably expect. The style was very dark, ominous and intimate, and the story dealt with smugglers who risked their lives in pursuit of their contraband. If caught, they might hang. This led to an understandable tendency amongst the characters to speak in hushed tones so that others couldn't hear. Sadly, on many occasions that meant us too.

But it is unfair to lay the blame entirely at the feet of the actors, if at all. I have played scenes on film where the other actors and I could barely hear each other on set but were still asked by the director to give it less volume. On seeing the film, I could hear everything perfectly.

In the weeks of post-production on film and television

projects, there are several layers of sound added to what has already been recorded. Atmosphere, background noises, special effects and music. Getting the balance right between all those different tracks is the job of the editorial team and the director.

The composer of the music, for instance, may not always believe that the dialogue is more important than his composition, although all the added sound should, in theory, enhance rather than obscure the story. Also, they have all read and heard the script many times over and have it in front of them while they are doing the edit.

It is all too easy to forget that we, the willing audience, have variable hearing and are hearing it for the first time through TV speakers in busy homes, not a state-of-the-art dubbing studio. This time they did get it wrong, which is a great shame, because it was beautifully imagined, designed and acted and, had the sound been better, would have been rightly considered a definitive adaptation of Daphne du Maurier's novel.

Don't blame the actors, though. On set we are totally at the mercy of sound recordists and directors, and afterwards on all the elements of the editing process.

On stage, if you can't hear an actor, it is entirely their fault. On film, not necessarily so.

16th May 2014

There is a line to be drawn between being able to write or say whatever you like in a free society and the other extreme. Race and religion are understandably subjects that we treat more sensitively today than a generation ago. The incident that nearly derailed *Top Gear*'s Jeremy Clarkson serves to highlight this.

The children's playground rhyme that Clarkson apparently 'nearly said' was off camera and not broadcast, but was considered a serious enough breach to provoke a furious response from many quarters.

The rhyme is one that in all innocence was used by my

generation as children to determine who would bat first in cricket, with no intent to offend or knowledge of the possible offence. But now we know differently. We all know that the asterisked-out word can and does offend, so we rightly avoid its use.

When national chains of fast food providers stop selling bacon because it might offend Muslims, I think it is perhaps a step too far. I am offended by manufacturers who slightly change the order of letters of the most common swear word to emblazon the initials of their company over clothing; but I have to accept that others don't react the same way. Those who dislike bacon for whatever reason are free to refrain from buying or consuming it. In a multicultural society it is up to those of us who are susceptible to being offended to avoid unnecessary occasions to be offended. I prefer not to eat Halal food and would appreciate knowing, when buying meat, whether it is. Giving us all undeclared Halal food to avoid offending those who do want it is not the answer.

It is, however, unacceptable to gratuitously offend without justification. The excellent series *Prey* concluded on ITV this week. It contained some superb performances, most notably that of Rosie Cavaliero, who played the harassed, dogged investigator of the murder of the central character John Sim's family. So why did Philip Hensher, a drama critic on BBC Radio 4, deem it acceptable to refer to Ms Cavaliero as a 'fat actress'? In fact, untrue, but irrelevant and vile anyway. I've been on the receiving end of this kind of gratuitous offence myself. 'Colin Baker, who has put on weight since he played Doctor Who ...' Were I playing the undead Count Dracula, it might be relevant enough to mention. I wasn't. I was playing Van Helsing.

23rd May 2014

It is not just as a father of daughters, as a lover of sport or as a passionate believer in justice that I am disappointed by the reaction of the Premier League to the content of the emails written by Richard Scudamore. I am struggling to think of any other comparable position that would not be deemed untenable within that industry or organisation after the tone and content of Scudamore's utterances.

If, for instance, it had been the chairman of the BBC? The fact that they were not intended for a wider audience than the recipient is irrelevant. He has been intemperate or arrogant enough to think he can say things via a notoriously leaky medium —the Internet— that are not only entirely contrary to his public utterances about women in football, but also puerile, laddish and not dissimilar to the offensive utterances that damaged the careers of Andy Gray and Richard Keys in 2011.

Because Scudamore has 'done a good job for the Premier league' and is higher up the pecking order in that male-dominated organisation, it seems that his reassurance that he doesn't really think like that is enough. If what he says is true, then it is doubly offensive that he wrote what he wrote. Bear in mind that writing takes a little more effort than it does to make an unfortunate laddish put-down in a pub with like-minded mates. I would like the man running my favourite sport to be bright and sensitive enough to think beyond the need to be seen bantering with a lawyer (for heaven's sake) about the ability and sexual attributes of women in the sport.

I would have had more respect for the man if he had fallen on his sword in the interests of establishing the Premier League as the progressive and inclusive organisation it is allegedly trying to become.

And yes, the ladies involved in the higher level of football have come out in support of Scudamore.

No surprise there. They have had to fight to get to where they have in the male-dominated sport. They don't want to draw attention to themselves in the way they would have to in order to truly hold Scudamore to account. Listening on the radio to some of the apologists for him has served only to confirm that talk is cheap and action often lags a long way behind mission statements.

30th May 2014

As a result of having played the Doctor three decades ago, occasionally opportunities are offered to me that others might rightly envy. For instance, I can't imagine that many people would pass up on the offer of a guided tour of NASA Mission Control Centre in Houston.

So when this was offered to me while I was there last week, I leaped at the chance. I was attending a science fiction fan event as a guest with Paul McGann, who played the Eighth Doctor. We were treated to a privileged 'backstage' tour guided by an actual, for-real astronaut. Michael Fincke served two tours aboard the International Space Station as a flight engineer and commander.

Fluent in Japanese and Russian, he logged just under 382 days in space, placing him first among American astronauts for the most time in space. He completed nine spacewalks with a total EVA time of 48 hours and 37 minutes, placing him 6th on the all-time list of spacewalkers. I mention these facts because it makes it doubly impressive that he was prepared to take the time to wholeheartedly guide us round the modules and landing craft, the control rooms and training areas at NASA.

It was a huge privilege and very humbling for we who pretend feats of derring-do to meet a real modern hero, and one so self-deprecating and charming. We spent three magical hours, which included sitting at the desk of the Mission Controller in the old 'analogue' control room used for the moon missions in the 60s and in the pilot seat of a module. You don't have to be a techie or a geek to realise that was a 'Wow' moment.

It was heartening to learn that while those in political power in the Kremlin and the White House may be glaring somewhat balefully at each other at the moment, the astronauts and cosmonauts remain good friends and both scientific communities are fully committed to their joint ventures. Apparently, looking down at our big (but small) planet from space focuses the mind and serves to demonstrate the unimportance of borders. We were also told about the exciting Orion project later this year, which may eventually take men to Mars.

I was left with an abiding relief that those clever, brave, resourceful and dedicated people are still reaching for the stars—and offering a glimmer of hope for the long-term future of humanity—if humanity ever deserves a future.

6ᵗʰ June 2014

There are millions of bright, educated, good people worldwide who fervently believe completely different things, worship completely different gods and follow the rules of completely different religions. Some of these religions have followers who interpret the rules that are written in their sacred books or have been decreed by their prophets in a variety of ways.

The majority are tolerant of others who believe different things. But all belief systems have their extremists and zealots who choose to interpret texts written in millennia past in ways that are intolerant, absolutist and reflect a belief in a vindictive and vengeful deity rather than a loving and forgiving one.

We have seen an example of this recently in Sudan, where a young Christian woman languishes with her babies in prison, sentenced to death for apostasy, having, as a Christian, refused to convert to Islam. She is also condemned to receive a hundred lashes for adultery, as her legal marriage to an American Christian was annulled by the same Sudanese court.

It is when incidents like this happen, incidents that to most of us scream injustice, madness and intolerance, that the sane and the good who belong to the religion that is being so hideously contorted by the Sudanese Islamic Court system must stand up and loudly condemn the inhumanity of the treatment of this young mother.

This is one example of hideous injustices meted out to people and to women in particular, in many areas of the world where religion is allowed to dominate governance of countries.

Like the rest of us, I do not know for certain what happens after this brief time we spend on our planet. Like the rest of us I have my own theory. I am, however, as certain as I can be about anything that I am not going to meet up with an all-powerful being who not only approves of, but demands, this young lady's cruel and unspeakable treatment.

It may be Islam that is being the focus of this kind of extremism today; but throughout history all religions have been hijacked at some time by the cruel, the empire builders and the zealots who can only be stopped or neutralised by the rest of their number refusing to remain silent. And love and compassion always achieves so much more.

As Edmund Burke said: 'All tyranny needs to gain a foothold is for people of good conscience to remain silent.'

13th June 2014

Listening to Victoria Derbyshire on Radio 5 Live in 2011, I heard a lady called Rachel talking about her problem with alcoholism. I had always been aware that for thousands of people this is a medical condition and not simply a deliberate act by thoughtless and selfish people. But listening to Rachel, an anaesthetist (who had. for obvious reasons lost her job), underlined that even more. The hopelessness and desperation of this intelligent and tormented woman was such that I can remember exactly where I was when I listened to her slowly peeling away the layers of her addiction and misery.

On the same programme over the three years that followed I heard her several times chronicling for us her journeys in and out of rehab, into and out of the relapses. This week we heard that she had died, having just come out of yet another slide back into the agony of alcoholic addiction. It seems that many others like me were moved by the sadness and waste that inevitably characterises the life of the addict.

We never heard from her husband and daughter, who had to support her and endure her frequent lapses back into the temporary euphoria and prevailing despair the alcoholic experiences. There is finally a numb kind of peace for them, at least, after what must have been a horrendous and helpless time watching someone they loved systematically destroying themselves.

If the 'pull yourself together' brigade—and we have all been guilty of saying that, I suspect, on occasion—ever needed proof that alcoholics needed a lot more help than those three words, then Rachel offered that proof.

I consider myself very lucky in that I do not have an addictive personality. And it is entirely a matter of luck. It may be that I have a controlling personality, because I really dislike not being in control. I never enjoyed those occasions in my youth when I experienced the effects of excess. If I had, it could have been me phoning in. Or you, dear reader.

We are the product of more than our DNA, of course, but genes, combined with early life experiences, can undoubtedly go a long way to removing the ability to function in this pressure cooker of a modern world. It ill becomes those of us who are lucky enough to be able to escape alcoholism (or indeed anorexia or self-harming) to be judgemental.

20th June 2014

I have been asked on many occasions when I will be producing my autobiography. This may surprise those of you who share my feeling that the numbers of those who have earned the right to expect others to care about the minutiae of their lives is considerably less than the number of those who write them.

But even if I were convinced that there were sufficient numbers of people avidly awaiting me to parade my life for inspection to justify my doing so, I have a major problem. I can remember very little about my childhood, teenage years or indeed much of my life. I just have a vague feeling that it was alright and normal, really. Yes I was bullied at school, but so, it seems, was everyone else. So nothing to write home about there. I kept diaries intermittently over the years, but I don't think the time that I got up, what I had for supper and the times of my appointments with the dentist and doctor are of great universal interest.

Yes I have had a high profile career but, I am glad to say, a comparatively low profile life. I once spoke to a very successful actor and comedian, now deceased, who gave me excellent advice on the whole after-dinner speaking and book-w--riting thing. He told me to make most of it up. Tell scurrilous, racy and funny stories about dead people who you have known (when they were alive), and no one can argue with you. Certainly no one can sue you. But the fact that I am not naming him in this article is sufficient to establish that I don't have the bottle for that.

And the other impediment is that what I do remember often turns out to be simply wrong.

I had an English teacher whom I have for years regarded as the genius. inspirational teacher who gave me an enduring passion for language. In my mind, he had taught me for five years.

It turns out to have been less than a year. He was still inspirational, but an autobiography is about detail and I don't have a handle on that.

A fiend recently recounted to me a succession of things I got up to when in repertory in Canterbury in the early 70s. I couldn't remember any of them.

Maybe I should get him to ghost my autobiography.

27th June 2014

You would think after years in the acting profession I would have learned to box clever with the press. But I haven't. I was at a media event recently and asked what I thought about the arrival of Peter Capaldi in the TARDIS.

I think it is a brilliant choice and said so, adding mischievously that it was great to have a 'grown-up playing the Doctor again after all those bloody kids.'

I should have been sharp enough to wind forward mentally and see how that could be reported later. I am now reading that 'Colin Baker is at it again: calling Matt Smith and David Tennant "bloody kids" in the role of the beloved Time Lord … "bloody kids"? Sheesh!' Oh dear.

There is a huge difference between deliberately faux outrage about the youth of David and Matt expressed in a filmed interview to entertain the fans and the bald presentation in print months later by someone looking for controversy where it really wasn't. The net result is, of course, that one refuses to do any interviews for fear of a subsequent mangling out of context by those who seek confrontation where there is none.

I have total control of my words in this column, so am taking the opportunity to confirm what I have said a thousand times —that all the Doctors that have graced our screens since the show's triumphal return have been superb and excitingly different to each other. That is the joy of *Doctor Who*, of course. The lead character can be seen in an almost infinite number of ways as long as his core values remain the same.

Will the same people who printed my alleged criticism publish this forthright denial? I doubt it. Such is the nature of the sensationalist journalist/blogger who selectively edits for spurious headlines.

Jon Pertwee and Patrick Troughton used to attack each other with water pistols at conventions. Sylvester McCoy and I constantly snipe at each other playfully at fan gatherings to entertain the troops, but I see him frequently and we are comfortable about that. David and Matt I see much less often, and I would hate them to think I held them in other than the highest esteem (if they care about what I think—and why should they?).

No wonder footballers are drilled to be evasive with the press and talk in clichés about it being 'about the team'.

11th July 2014

It may be that future editions of dictionaries will contain extra definitions of the words 'consultation' and 'wide'. Judging from Bucks County Council's recent attempt to save money on school transport, 'consultation' seems to mean you ask the bloke at the desk to your right what he thinks; if you then turn to the one on your left, then you are consulting 'widely'. No need to bother anyone else. Why slow the process down?

Three local secondary schools discovered, without any advance warning at all (let alone consultation), with only days to the end of the school year, that their school bus service was to be radically changed next term. Eighteen double-deckers would replace the existing coach services, and routes and schedules would be changed. As a result, some journey times would increase to up to an hour or more (each way). Many pupils would be obliged to leave home much earlier than before and be home much later. That would really help their attention span during their school day and their ability to continue their studies at home later. Parents pay a significant amount for their children to travel to school, so it seems odd that this unilateral and ill-thought-out initiative could possibly save £5 million over four years, BCC allege. The three heads concerned made it absolutely clear immediately that the proposals were completely unworkable, and highlighted their serious concerns about pupil safety.

As a result of the heads' understandable anxiety and timely intervention, Deputy BCC Leader Mike Appleyard has finally met with them and, as a result, seeing the sense of their objections, has delayed any changes until 2015, so that proper consultation can now take place. Why must it always be like this? Do they think we won't notice and they might get away with it? That several thousand parents won't mind their children spending two hours on a bus every day to travel a total of six to ten miles? And did they think they could load all those buses simultaneously outside the schools during peak travel hours?

And to those who will undoubtedly harrumph that children should all walk to school—the world has changed. Traffic is a hundred times worse than when I walked to school, and scheduled bus services are now comparatively non-existent. Bucks schools offer excellent education. The least we can do is provide sensible (and of course affordable) means of getting our children to them.

18th July 2014

I know that no one ever promised me a rose garden, but after years of encountering a variety of examples of the mindless gratuitous behaviour of that strange minority who enjoy seeing the shoulders of others slump, I still cannot begin to comprehend them.

Viewed in the context of the history of mankind to date and of the lives that millions of others live in the world today, it is impossible to deny that we live in the kindest and calmest of times in one of the freest parts of the planet. Yet vandals, thugs and spoilers still abound.

The reason for this observation stems from a very minor incident in the grand scheme of things. I am on Twitter. It is a very useful way of disseminating information to those who are interested—and because of my profession and slight fame, there are a few who are interested.

I tweeted yesterday of my delight in discovering the brilliant TV series *Breaking Bad*. I had just finished the first series and said I couldn't wait to see what happened next. Wrong! Red rag to a certain kind of bull, it seems. Total stranger (now blocked) tweets me several facts about characters, saying 'that's what happens next.' He was the only one among the many others who envied me the impending discovery of the story to come, having watched themselves and shared my eager anticipation.

It seems the more we have as a species, the less some of us appreciate the fact that we are so lucky to have the breadth of experience and quality of life available that most of us enjoy. And certainly someone who has access to a computer and the Internet is not by any measure that makes sense 'deprived'. And the life experiences that are offered to excuse the anti-social behaviour of some people apply equally to those who would never willingly hurt another person for fun.

Yes, I know this incident is minor to the point of being trivial, but it is an indicator of an increasing desire by some young males (mainly) to spoil, to disrupt and sneer. The Internet offers them the opportunity to do so without raising their heads above the parapet.

The trolling of the vulnerable in schools is the most repellent example of this. At least the old style school bully did it face to face and ran the risk of detection and retribution.

25th July 2014

Is it just because I am a grumpy old(ish) man that the number of things that drive me bonkers is increasing day by day?

My wife says so; but she only thinks that because she doesn't venture out into the wide world as frequently or as far as I do. A domestic life ministering (magnificently, I hasten to add) to the five adults who live in our home and the couple of dozen other assorted quadrupeds who live in and around it offers less opportunity to be Appalled of High Wycombe on a daily basis.

Take today. Three drivers in quick succession felt no need to indicate to me, immediately behind them, that they were about to turn right.

Yet another service provider presented me with a series of phone options (humorously purporting to be helplines) that either led nowhere, didn't fit my requirements or instructed me to access their website. As the service provider concerned was BT and my internet was down, this was more than a tad irritating.

My less-than-a-year-old computer has had, it transpires, a USB failure. The manufacturers will sort it out under the guarantee and would collect it. Did I have the original packaging?

Now, there may be people out there with mansions and tied cottages who could stash all the original packaging materials for their repairable items in some uninhabited mundungus room in the west wing, but I am not one of them.

I wonder if anyone reading this is? I was instructed in that case that I must package it as securely as I could but they couldn't take responsibility for any damage, etc. etc.

Half an acre of bubble wrap and cardboard later, and the courier whisks my computer away for 'five to ten days'. What will I do?

Then I turn on the radio and hear people talking about 'innocent victims' of all the horrible things that are happening around the world at the moment.

Why does a victim have to earn the right to be pitied and cared for by presenting their innocence credentials? Who would a guilty victim be in an aeroplane, or suburb of Gaza, or in Iraq?

Very few of the slaughtered are guilty of anything other than the fact that they have the misfortune to live where they do when they do.

Forget all the other stuff. We should all be very grumpy about that.

1ˢᵗ August 2014

It used to be the cheaper wines that had screw-top bottles, and wine snobs would make assumptions about the content of the bottle were they to be offered one. Now, presumably, the efficacy of the screw-top has improved and they are no longer considered inferior.

It appears that the days of corked wine (in the bad sense of that word) are soon to be over. It is estimated that up to 10% of bottles with traditional corks have wine within them adversely affected by oxidisation caused by the cork.

This set me to thinking about other complete reversals of attitudes to the way we do things.

I remember very clearly how we all greeted wind farms with enthusiasm initially, but now the 'anti' lobby is growing, based on aesthetics and bird deaths, mainly. Personally, I rather like these great modern giants striding across hilltops, and the domestic cat kills a lot more birds than any wind farm ever will.

In my lifetime, what we know about smoking has moved us from being a society that considered it a rather cool, modern and stylish activity to being unacceptable worldwide.

Coffee, eggs, milk and butter have all see-sawed over the last few decades on the good for you/bad for you scale. Currently, they are all having something of a second chance, although the see-saw is moving up and down more quickly than it used to. No sooner do we start enjoying any of them again than another vested interest will fund research that says they're killing us. Maybe moderation really is the answer.

The latest trend is to say that all those vitamin supplements we take may be doing more harm than good. The case being that they exist to replace deficiencies, not to add to an otherwise sensible diet which should contain enough for most of us.

Even the suggestion that we should drink eight cups of water a day is now being called into question. One study has suggested that over-hydration is more dangerous than dehydration.

They now say that your body will tell you what you want— so trust it.

Those hand dryers that we believe are more hygienic than disposable towels are in fact just the opposite, as they are usually drawing in bacteria-laden air from the toilet area they are situated in and blowing it all over our hands. You can't win, can you?

8th August 2014

I'm not one for regrets, and high up among the many things I don't regret is not having a big slap-up wedding. My wife agrees. Thirty-two years ago we spent no time agonising over the decision to just go and get married and tell people afterwards. Most friends expressed their complete understanding (nay gratitude); our respective widowed mothers were delighted and relieved. My late brother was the only one who was vaguely curmudgeonly about it, but he disapproved of everything I ever did, so that was no surprise.

We married at a registry office in Oxford with the cleaners as our witnesses. They were delighted and delightful. Our dog was a third less official witness. We went for a magnificent lunch together, came home and went to celebrate a friend's birthday over dinner in the evening. We then went on honeymoon the following day to Burnley, where I was filming *Juliet Bravo*. Romantic, eh?

We have a few photos, not a hugely expensive book full of pictures of people whose names we might now struggle to remember. The pretty dress in which my wife looked stunning still hangs in the wardrobe and still looks perfect on her. Would that I could say the same of my white suit. Fashion has been less kind to men over the years.

I mention this because we have just been to a wedding, and another is imminent. The combined cost of these weddings would be a more than adequate deposit for a house. Both couples are young and starting out in their lives together and need money much more than they need a showpiece wedding. How society has evolved to require such vast expenditure on food, clothes, drink, music and flowers at a time when the money would be much more productively used, I cannot understand. It may be a distorted development of the dowry system, I suppose.

At the wedding we have just attended, at not one point did my wife and I turn to each other and say, 'I wish we had done this.'

I have a business development idea for professional photographers, who are suffering harder times now anyone can take a decent photo eventually in the digital age. The computer-generated wedding album. One quick session of headshots for the main participants.

Then add in the clothes, churches, ruined abbeys and banqueting halls. Much cheaper and no more confetti problems for churches.

15th August 2014

As a sports fan, I am a regular listener as I drive to BBC Radio 5 Live, which is also a rolling news station. I have recently begun to see a pattern emerging in the way that interviews are conducted. In a world where the attention span of audiences is apparently deemed to be that of a shoal of goldfish, broadcasters are desperate to keep our attention so that we don't start channel hopping.

The way they have chosen to do this is to not dwell too long on any subject, which results in cramming more topics into a programme than can be easily managed. Today I heard five head teachers and two educational activists being told that they had just a minute each to make their point about league tables, etc. as the programme was about to end. One can only imagine their irritation, as they had probably spent some ten minutes or so talking to a researcher (who would invariably pass on incomplete information to the presenter, resulting in the latter getting their names wrong).

Then they had held on for another ten or fifteen minutes listening to the programme on their phone only to be given short shrift when they suddenly found themselves on air. Frustrating for them and even more frustrating for listeners who had been awaiting the trailed discussion and might reasonably have hoped for a little more information than they ultimately got. Add into the mixture the aggressive interviewing style (verging on sneering) that is becoming more common these days, and the end result is that I succumb to the temptation of inserting a CD and listening to a recording of *Paul Temple* or *Dick Barton*, made in the days when the BBC knew the value of a good thriller serial.

I am often asked to go onto rolling news programmes on radio stations all over the country, to comment on the latest *Doctor Who* appointment, regeneration, anniversary or new series.

I have learned the hard way that it is easier to say 'No' for all the reasons given above, but also because I don't have anything new or enlightening to say, and all these programmes are now after the quick sound bite rather anything resembling a meaningful chat. If there is a controversial question to be asked, I will be asked it, and I now prefer to avoid fending off interrogatory minefields that have repercussions for months afterwards.

22nd August 2014

I am, like many males, a fan of gadgets, and find it difficult to resist any new piece of kit that I can convince myself might make my life easier or more enjoyable.

And that is no mean feat—the convincing bit. Because all the evidence is, that on a day-to-day basis, most of the stuff I already own frequently has the opposite effect on my life.

I suppose the one main exception is the difference between the time I would have spent typing this article on my old portable Olivetti and then posting it to the *Bucks Free Press* in its Tippexed and smudged glory. I found the carbon copies of all the theatre reviews that I wrote for the *Croydon Advertiser* in the 1970s the other day, which were ample evidence of that. The computer as word processor has certainly been a boon in my life.

But the use by large organisations of computerised systems which were trumpeted as being for the benefit of us customers frequently fail to live up to the hype, and benefit them more than us, principally by making it nigh on impossible to ever speak to someone with any power to help you. Sometimes the IT solution nearly works.

For instance, the computerised check-in for outpatients at Wycombe Hospital works very well indeed. You input your date of birth and up pops your appointment (or a choice, I imagine, should your birthday coincide with another patient). Then you are directed to the designated waiting point. Brilliant.

When, however, you leave and have to make another appointment, it's a different matter. This week, I watched the receptionist going through more key operations than I do in writing this article. I suggested that her job might be made easier with an appointment book rather than whatever hoops she must be going through on the other side of the screen. Her response was a smile of recognition and a nod of the head. Of course, that's no big problem, but illustrates my point.

And I so regret abandoning my old system of keeping addresses in a succession of books and trusting the computer. When I moved from Windows XP to Windows 7 and lost Outlook Express as a result, the transfer of all my mail and addresses to the insanely complicated Outlook jettisoned everything from 2006 to 2012. If you knew me, then sorry— and goodbye.

5th September 2014

I have never been good with heights. I share with many the (mercifully resistible) urge to end the feeling of terror and anxiety by leaping into the void when I am near cliff edges and high buildings. Strangely, I can deal with aeroplanes without problems. For some reason I can't quite fathom, sitting in a window seat 30,000 feet over the Atlantic doesn't induce the same visceral terror as, say, I experienced on a visit to Durham Cathedral years ago when a clergyman friend played a joke on me.

He was a canon at the cathedral and he and a fellow man of the cloth offered me a behind-the-scenes guided tour. The crypt and undercroft were fascinating. I demurred at going up into the roof until they assured me it was all interior and safe. Indeed, seeing the curved and contorted tree trunks that arched apparently randomly within the roof was fascinating. How the building had stayed up for millennia was astonishing.

But then they led me through a door on to a narrow parapet inside the highest elevation. The ledge had one narrow rail at thigh level and the high altar was a dot below me. That, I truly believe, was the scariest moment I have ever lived through, as I inched my way slowly away from my worst nightmare. My friend, and for some reason he is still my friend, laughed.

I mention all this only because of an experience I had today. I am staying in a hotel in Atlanta, Georgia, this week and my room is on the 45th floor and has windows down to the floor. The interior of the hotel is open and balconied to its full height, and for that reason was used as a location in *The Hunger Games*. An acrophobic's nightmare. The view is spectacular, but I keep away from the edges even though the windows don't open.

Imagine my reaction when I notice four ropes dangling outside my window and a pair of feet waving into view from above. With sucker pads reminiscent of *Mission Impossible*, the window cleaner—yes, the window cleaner—descended into view and lathered and wiped my windows—on the 45th floor!

The ropes continued to sway and shudder as he continued on down with his flashing chamois and blade.

I hope he is very well-paid. Unknown warrior, I salute you.

12th September 2014

A community-minded bunch of citizens in Normanton, Derbyshire got together some years ago to pick up litter in the streets of their town, in the perceived absence of any significant desire to do so by their local authority. The latter, perhaps feeling a little embarrassed, offered them some litter-picking implements to assist them in their public-spirited endeavours, which they gratefully accepted.

Now they have been told that they are not allowed to use them after all, until they have been trained in the arcane art of operating what are basically long-handled tongs. The great god Health and Safety has decreed that, should one of the human pickers injure themselves while using the tongs, there could be legal ramifications.

Once again, the combination of ludicrous regulations and ambulance-chasing lawyers is sufficient to paralyse an endeavour that common sense (remember that?) would decree to be fairly basic and hardly worthy of provoking forensic scrutiny to eliminate the 0.00001% chance of injury. As one of the worthy citizens pointed out, when told that the paralysis was caused by the fact that the council concerned had supplied the litter picker-uppers, the council also supplied all the population with wheelie bins everyone operates on a weekly basis without any training at all. Surely there are more likely to be injuries dragging a bulky and laden bin down to the end of the drives, roads and lanes of Derbyshire than walking along with a pair of four foot tweezers.

What worries me is that for every citizen who views the ritual dance with the same astonishment as I do, there will be a public sector employee who has been so inculcated with the defensive operational mentality as to see nothing wrong with this tale. 'Better safe than sorry.'

It is up to the legislature and judiciary to crowbar some much-needed common sense back into our lives again. To acknowledge that not all accidents carry fault or blame.

It is, I am delighted to observe, happening with insurance companies, who are much more ready to fight the spurious whiplash claims that accompany countless minor shunts on our roads. Paying out to save the expense of litigation in the past has resulted in claims escalating (being seen as a nice little earner), costing them millions, and they're finally starting to tackle the problem. Let's hope the pendulum swings back soon.

19th September 2014

My maternal grandfather was born and raised in Glasgow. His genial and affectionate personality was a major influence in my early years, as he skipped around, aged 80, in his slippers, bamboozling this five-year-old with his nimble-footed football skills. He had had a trial for Chelsea, but given that footballers' incomes over a hundred years ago bore no comparison with today's massive salaries, he opted for the safer life of being a printer in Fleet Street.

Being a Scot ran through him like the lettering in Blackpool rock, but it was a quiet pride. I do wonder what he would have made of the vote on Scottish independence, the results of which will be known as you read this. I spent the most of the first two decades of my life in Lancashire and have an abiding affection for the North, which is certainly greater than my attachment to London, where I was born and spent my first 18 months. I mention this only because if Lancashire were to seek independence from the rest of the UK, I would regard that as being just as perplexing as the desire of a lot of Scots to detach themselves from the United Kingdom.

I can only quote the only astronaut I have ever met, Mike Fincke, who told me that one of the many abiding impressions he brought back from hundreds of days spent on the space station was the absurdity of border disputes and wars over boundaries. You only have to glance at what is happening between Russia and Ukraine, and Israel and the Gaza strip, and scores of other parts of the world, to come to the conclusion that coming together must be better than allowing wedges to be driven for ideological or economic reasons.

A glance at any world map will reveal two little islands nestling close to the western edge of Europe. Surely it defies logic that those two comparatively tiny land masses should contain three different countries and four different administrations.

The European mainland is vast and subdivision was inevitable, but many countries would now like to work towards a completely unified Europe which, all historical nationalism aside, is a much more logical way of conducting affairs. We are very lucky in the UK. We can be English and British, or Scottish and British—in whichever order we like. I think my grandpa Jock would agree.

26th September 2014

Back in July 1995, I wrote a letter to the *Bucks Free Press*, my local newspaper. I haven't a clue what the subject was, but it must have been something about which I felt quite strongly at the time, as I have never troubled any newspaper's readers' page since.

But whatever I wrote was sufficient to induce the editor, Steve Cohen, to ask me if I would care to contribute a weekly column. I never decline an opportunity to do something different and challenging, unless it involves vast physical prowess or pain, so I plucked my quill from its stand and started out on a journey that reaches a milestone with this particular offering.

It is with a sense of pride, (definitely with a small 'p'), that I write my 1000th consecutive column. And the consecutive bit has, for some reason, been important to me all these 19 years. None of your 'Colin Baker is away; his column will return in a fortnight.' In more recent years, I have found internet cafes all over the world.

Back in the last century, when I started, I even had to use the postal service to send hard copies, to ensure my unbroken line of burblings. There was, quite recently, nearly a devastating break in the chain when I was late, the BFP offices were closed and I knew the paper would be going to press imminently without my copy. Steve Cohen has, after two decades as editor, moved on to loftier climes, but I had his number and hoped he could help. He could and did, and my precious copy got into the works just in the nick of time.

For that I am in his debt, which I can say without worry, as the likelihood of his still reading my column is as small as his team Tottenham Hotspur's chance of winning anything this year.

The response I hope to get from strangers who recognise me as this noble weekly's columnist is 'I enjoy your column even though I don't agree with everything you say.' That is how it should be. I am simply offering an opinion. My opinion. I don't think what I say should carry more weight than what anyone else says.

Having reached this milestone, I am now casting my eyes on next August, when I will complete 20 years. Unless Peter Capaldi takes my place, of course.

1st October 2014

Back in July the head teacher of John Hampden School, Stephen Noakes, told this newspaper that he would be very surprised if Bucks County Council's plans to make radical changes to the delivery of the school transport service in the Wycombe area went ahead. He and the heads of neighbouring schools went so far as to describe the plans as 'farcical and dangerous', whilst expressing astonishment that the changes had been scheduled without any consultation with the affected institutions or parents. Cllr Mike Appleyard (the Cabinet Member for Education) met with the heads several times as a result of their concern, and whilst affirming that Phase One of the planned changes would still go ahead in September, there would be further consultation about subsequent changes being made to save £5m from the County Council budget.

And what happened?

As predicted by the schools, the return to school for the new academic year was chaotic. School staff were taken away from their teaching duties to help children who were arriving up to twenty minutes late, some for their first day at secondary school, because unrealistic schedules for rush-hour travel rendered the timetable impossible for the poor drivers, who have to bear the brunt of the frustration and anger of parents.

And these parents had their annual charges raised from £390 to £570 this year, a 50% cost increase for an inferior, ill-thought-out service, resulting in much longer journeys for many. Small wonder some parents are looking elsewhere for their children's travel.

BCC are at pains to point out that they only have a statutory obligation to provide school transport for students between the ages of 5 and 16 who live more than three miles away from their school. However, anyone who drives regularly around the area will know the huge difference in the volume of rush-hour travel that happens when the schools return in September. If more cars were to be introduced into the mix by parents who, for whatever reason, decide to deliver their children themselves, the result will be gridlock squared.

Yes, it is a difficult job to balance local authority budgets at present, but it cannot be achieved to anyone's satisfaction without extensive and real consultation and complete openness. Employing a company as a buffer between the Council and the bus companies to organise it all may not be the most sensible or even economical solution.

8th October 2014

When Wycombe District Council vetoed Steve Hayes' plans to create a stadium/sports complex in Wycombe to accommodate both of the teams he then owned—Wycombe Wanderers and Wasps, I suppose it was inevitable that the ground share arrangement between the clubs would be less secure. When the teams became separately owned, the decree absolute became even more likely, given that Adams Park could not accommodate the crowds that Wasps could attract.

However, it is undoubtedly true that the presence of Wasps in Wycombe has been of huge assistance in enabling

Wanderers to survive the last few nail-biting years of financial and league insecurity. The net benefit to Wanderers has never been publicised—but there clearly was a fairly substantial annual amount in the coffers, without which we may have followed the ever-growing list of clubs that have gone into administration, had massive point deductions and sunk without trace through the conference and out the other side.

Mercifully, the departure of Wasps in December coincides with a renaissance of form and ambition for Wanderers. If anything shows the wisdom of sticking with a manager and allowing him to develop a team—then Wanderers' necessary retention of Gareth Ainsworth, despite the team tiptoeing to the edge of the precipice at the end of last season, is a great example. As he gets better and better at the job, let's hope we can retain him as he and the team bounce from one end of the division last year to the top this year. The finances may tremble at the departure of Wasps, but if the crowds come back to see their local team battling with pride—successfully—it may not be so bad after all. And the new chairman, Andrew Howard, seems encouragingly upbeat about the opportunity offered.

I feel sorry for the Wasps fans who now have to face a trek to the Midlands if they want to follow their team, turning all games into away matches. Many of them will be South Bucks Rugby fans, who started to support the team twelve years ago when they came out from London. Others will have been travelling from London to continue their support.

MK Dons eventually weathered the storm when they left Wimbledon, so Wasps have a strong enough brand to do the same.

Let's hope both teams flourish apart. At least the Adams Park pitch will have a better chance of surviving the season!

15th October 2014

The recent events in the Rugby League match between St Helens and Wigan raise very important issues about when the police should get involved when trouble kicks off in sporting events. Because Lance Hohaia, the victim, has declined to prosecute, it may well be that a piece of sickening violence witnessed by thousands will not be the subject of criminal charges.

Garry Schofield, former Great Britain captain said, 'I know people are saying if Flower did that in a pub car park or outside a nightclub he'd be arrested, but that's the point—it wasn't.'

So walking across to a man you have already rendered unconscious with a blow in the heat of the moment and then deliberately punching him again in the eye socket is less deserving of prosecution than a similar offence committed by drunks in a brawl? Far from it. It is worse.

In fact, when anyone in the public eye commits an offence, they usually receive harsher sentences in order to discourage the rest of us. And the fact that the victim hasn't complained shouldn't affect the decision of the police to prosecute. Imagine the opportunities afforded to the violent and criminal to discourage their victims from seeking justice by suggesting further visitations should they do so? Clearly a Rugby League player isn't going to lose face by whingeing about a small thing like being punched while unconscious—something the rest of us would consider unspeakably barbaric.

In fact, the only quotes I have seen so far suggesting that the sport should be allowed to discipline its own players without involving the legal system are from other rugby players. That's a bit like allowing other burglars to decide whether one of their number should be arrested for breaking and entering.

The six-month ban Flower received is no more than a slap on the wrist, I got a six-month driving ban several years ago for doing 40 mph in a 30 mph limit, when it was totted up. No complaint about that, but it serves as a comparison. The thousands that witnessed the event and the millions who are now waiting to see how it is treated need to see that such savage malevolence is punished with appropriate severity.

In a sport where the handbags don't have rocks in them, good news at Adams Park. Wanderers are top of the League! Long may it stay the case. COYB.

22nd October 2014

November the 5th approaches, and with it the thousands of firework parties held across the land to celebrate a failed plot to blow up the mother of parliaments over four hundred years ago.

I freely admit to thoroughly enjoying trotting round the garden excitedly with sparklers and watching Catherine wheels and rockets when I was young. But the choice then was comparatively limited and the volume and number of explosions were both considerably less.

However, nowadays the night's calm and darkness is ripped apart by ear-splitting noise and exotic flashes for up to two weeks, as private parties are often scheduled to fit the availability of those attending and the weather. The bangs are bigger. The flashes are brighter. And for those with animals in particular, it is gradually becoming an unmanageable nightmare.

The papers are full of tragic stories of death and injury to wildlife and pets, all of which could be avoided. Animal owners have to rush around calming livestock, horses, cats and dogs with some (if not complete) hope of success, but given the expansion of the window of celebration and the variety and scale of whiz-bangs, it has now become pretty difficult, to the point that in an age when health and safety dominates every other activity, I am amazed that fireworks are still available to all, rather than just to those organising public displays and over which there can be some measure of control.

The inherent danger of fireworks was highlighted this week with the deaths of at least seventeen workers in India when their factory exploded.

Every year our horses thrash around in their stables and hurt themselves; the dogs, understandably but dangerously, try to run away from the noise (and us!), the cats run in as if the devil is on their heels and our elderly goats break out of their stable. It is a week we dread.

If an outright ban on private firework parties is not possible, then wildlife and all of our pets could be partially protected by a ban on loud fireworks, at least. I support the Ban the Bang campaign wholeheartedly. As a country that is famed for its love of animals, I am surprised that the uncontrolled sale and use of fireworks continues to be an issue.

And please all check your bonfires before lighting. To hedgehogs and small animals, they look like palaces built for them to hibernate in.

29th October 2014

In every area of public life we are enduring reductions in services.

Emergency hospital care, maintenance of our roads, education, policing, care of the infirm and elderly—add your own service to the list—are all subject to swingeing cuts and downgrading of service. You only have to read Mike Appleyard's recent comments to learn why this is happening, if you didn't know already.

He is under fire as the councillor responsible for providing the buses that should get our children to school. For years it has worked well and reasonably efficiently. This school year started chaotically, with travel times for young people increased exponentially whilst delivering them to their schools late. Parents have rightly been making representations to Mr Appleyard about this.

His response in this paper was to thank them for their input and then spend the rest of his time telling us how much money he has had cut from his budget. Understandably. You can't make even a half-decent workaday purse out of the particular sow's ear that central government has doled out to councils this year. Every public service is being compelled to try to provide the same service for less money. Naturally, this is impossible, so once all the obvious savings have been made in past years, the pip is now beginning to squeak more and more insistently.

If we demand the same level of service from all these public services, we have to pay for them. In order to get elected, politicians all know that they stand a better chance if they can convince us that they really, really want to cut taxes. Saying 'What you want, citizens, costs money, and if you let us have a bit more, then we can do a lot more' won't attract votes.

Unless the politicians across the board are prepared to forego voting advantage and agree on the need to increase taxes to provide what the electors clearly want but are not minded to pay for, then we are doomed to less health care, less care for the aged, Third-World transport systems and a police force that has two officers on duty when a major event kicks off in one of our towns. It is getting to be that bad, and we should be demanding better and telling them we are prepared to pay for it. And perhaps seriously considering removing one level of local government provision? Or cancelling HS2!

5ᵗʰ November 2014

Anyone who has been a part of any popular sporting or entertainment activity will acknowledge that most fans are just that—decent folk who, for some reason, are sufficiently impressed by what we do as to want to let us know that. However, within that mix there are the occasional incidents when the fan fails to grasp that we are, in fact, human beings, different only from them in terms of the job we do.

A female colleague told me recently that one fan asked for her autograph and then spent ten minutes telling her why her performance in a recent television programme had not been very good. Apparently, she dissected it scene by scene, line by line, before smiling, thanking her for the autograph and disappearing into the crowd.

Most employees in less high-profile jobs are free of the constant danger of being told how rubbish you are, how they preferred most of your predecessors, how much weight you've put on and how your blond curly hair is no more. To be honest, I can't really complain, because the majority of fans I meet at conventions are enthusiastic, friendly and happy to meet you.

But every now and then, as happened to me this last

weekend in America, there will be the young man who comes up to me, looks at the photograph on the wall behind me—of me as *Doctor Who*—and says 'What time will Mr Baker be here?' What can one say? Do you shatter his youthful illusions and tell the awful truth? That the dribbling dotard standing before him is what happens to Time Lords thirty years after their TARDIS has been taken away? Or do you do what I did—forlornly mutter, 'Soon ... He'll be here soon.'

Later that day I was asked for an autograph by a lady who was a little too eager to say that it was for her father. She told me that he was a great fan of 'old Sixie', as I refer to myself (being the sixth incarnation of Doctor Who). Before I could express my thanks and admiration of his good sense, she added, 'I never liked your Doctor that much—I liked Jon Pertwee'. I resisted (just) the urge to compare her in like manner to the other fans standing around slack-jawed at this slight to their idol. But hey, it goes with the territory; i;f you don't want alien attacks, then stay out of the TARDIS.

14th November 2014

Because I am usually rather quick to criticise large organisations that let us down, I feel I should put on record that there are occasions when some deserve praise rather than brickbats.

One such incident occurred this week. For years I had used the same local supermarket for deliveries of groceries and staple goods. Then three times on the trot they let me down by botched deliveries and non-deliveries. On the last occasion, after several telephone conversations when I was promised a rescheduled delivery after the driver had claimed I was out when I wasn't, I finally gave up when I received neither an explanation nor an apology after days of frustration. I told them never to darken my door again, and although my wife still uses them for their cheap petrol, I have resolutely taken my custom elsewhere.

I have been trying other delivery services, and this week a supermarket delivered a large order, and on unpacking I discovered there were eight items missing. Thinking the bag was probably in the driver's van, I phoned the 0800 helpline. The pleasant Welshman at the other end rang the driver, who couldn't find the missing items, and the conclusion was drawn that the packers had failed to pack them. They were very apologetic, credited me with the cost of the items and offered to send them out again later.

Twenty minutes later, I found the items under what I thought was, only a bag of vegetables and had taken to the appropriate store place. Oops. My bad!

I rang the store back and apologised profusely, saying that I hoped that no one had been castigated for what was entirely my fault. I told them to debit me back the money. My second customer services Welshman said that my call back to admit the blame was so rare that I could keep the £9.50. I demurred, knowing that the supermarket giant concerned had had bad financial results lately, but he insisted that my honesty should be rewarded.

Of course, that store now has a more than satisfied customer who will use their service again.

A sad reflection on life generally though that an honest customer was sufficiently rare as to merit genuine surprise on the part of the telephone helpline operator. It may have been more hassle than it was worth to recharge the few pounds, but my guilt will ensure my loyalty.

21st November 2014

The new manifestation of the flat-earther mentality seems to be the global-warming denier.

I'm not sure how much evidence is needed before something drastic is done about carbon emissions. The Intergovernmental Panel on Climate Change has warned that action needs to be taken now to reduce emissions by 40 to 70% by 2050 if the world is to avoid irreversible damage to our ecosystems. By 2100, we are told, global temperatures are likely to rise by between 2 degrees and 5 degrees centigrade.

Whilst the effect on the UK might be less catastrophic than on other areas of the world, the whole world will suffer the effects of reduced crop yields and the acidification of the oceans. Food insecurity on such a scale would undoubtedly lead to mass migration and new wars to gain control of water and food supplies.

The IPCC have added, however, that investment now in energy from renewable sources would have a huge impact still on halting the otherwise inevitable slide into economic and social chaos.

UK Secretary General Ban Ki-Moon has said, 'Science has spoken. There is no ambiguity in the message. Leaders must act. Time is not on our side.'

If ever there was a challenge to politicians to find a way of circumventing the ritual party political dance, this it. Voters generally tend to vote for the party that will, in their opinion, cost them less in the short term. Politicians want to get elected, and know this. Telling it how it really is doesn't often work to the advantage of those who tell it.

And 2100 impacts on neither us nor our children, and only a few of those alive now will be affected. But we have to somehow tap into the same mentality that deems it worthwhile to secure the existence of the human race thousands of years from now by investing in space exploration today, despite the legion of naysayers. The worldwide meltdown of life as we know it is much more imminent, and we must act now to instruct our politicians of all parties to cooperate as they have never done before in taking action.

Wind farms, river bore barrages, solar power—all have their champions and detractors, but better to have the horizon dominated by windmills, the rivers and countryside invaded in some places by new technology, than have our descendants curse this generation for our selfish folly in doing too little too late.

28th November 2014

I would like to challenge the use of the word 'dream' to signify something wildly beyond the speaker's hope or expectation. It was 'his dream job' or it was a 'dream holiday, or wedding or house. You name it. I would really like to know what percentage of dreams are uplifting or pleasant.

I cannot recall ever having that kind of dream since my youth, when I regularly dreamed that I could fly. It often involved sliding down the banisters at home and, as I reached what one might term the tipping point, I lifted myself from somewhere round the base of my spine and floated high above the grasping hands of those trying to haul me back to earth. Pretty basic psychological stuff there, I'm sure—trying to escape from something—which most teenagers and young people are rightly aiming to do.

I'd love to have those brilliant, optimistic dreams now. I'd love to have dreams that involve having fun, lazing by a sunny lagoon, sipping cocktails, picnicking on the banks of a gentle river in the spring—you name it. The things that the word 'dream' is supposed to signify. What do I get? And I do most fervently hope that I am not alone in this. I get what might loosely be termed 'anxiety dreams' that often involve me standing in the wings of a theatre, begging the people around me to tell me what the play is I am supposed to be doing, or grabbing holding of people and demanding a copy of the script.

Invariably, they're too busy or they laugh and tell me to get on with it, as if I am being tedious. Very often, not only do I not have the right costume on either, but I have absolutely nothing on at all and am running around trying to find my dressing room in exactly the same way as Alice ran after the White Rabbit—with no hope of finding it.

Whereas I used to really hate waking up when I was young and painfully adjusting to the fact that I couldn't actually fly, nowadays I am delighted to surface and find that I am at home and not facing the derision and scorn of a company of actors. I suppose it's all nature's way of making dotards like myself get up in the morning rather than loll around in bed like our juvenile selves.

5th December 2014

Whenever I have written in the past about the perplexing anachronism of fox hunting, I have received more responses than I ever get for anything else I write. And in the past it has tended to be vitriolic and abusive, too. It is somewhat ironic that the supporters of hunting with hounds don't like being harried and cornered themselves, albeit only verbally.

It is common knowledge that many hunts are flouting the law, secure in the knowledge that the police are massively undermanned and unable to commit the numbers needed to take effective action. But hunting a fox with hounds is just as illegal as organising a dog fight, and doubtless those who are currently stealing people's pets to provide victims for this abominable activity will protest that what they do is a long-practised rural tradition too. At least they don't dress up and try to pretend that there is something picturesque and charming about what they do. They skulk, while the hunts still strut their stuff.

If, despite your sensible safeguarding efforts to protect your chickens, a fox predates on them, no one will object if you 'take up arms against a sea of troubles and by opposing end him'. But to invite dozens of your friends to bring a pack of dogs along to have a jolly good time harrying one animal to its miserable and savage death seems to me to be disproportionate in the extreme and lacks both style and decency.

And let's have none of this anthropomorphic guff about the fox being 'evil' because it kills every chicken when it can only eat one. This is because the poor hens can't escape when we've stuck them in sheds that must seem like Charlie's Chocolate Factory to a peckish fox.

The fox is doing what evolution has led him to do—kill to eat. We should do what we have evolved to do—think! Our wildlife is rich, varied and beautiful. Culling may be necessary and even kind in many cases; and hunting for the pot is defensible.

We are carnivores, after all. But ritual slaughter that turns killing into fun cannot have any place in a society that has pretensions to being civilised. The majority of voters deemed fox hunting with hounds to be worthy of control and legislation. It's a great pity that there appears to be a reluctance to enforce it on the part of the authorities.

12th December 2014

It is very interesting that in the Street Survey feature in last week's edition of this newspaper, all five of those asked about their views on the subject were supportive of the process of selection for secondary education at 11 years.

It may be that the choice of interviewees might not satisfy the rigorous criteria laid down by MORI or Gallup, but usually the *Bucks Free* polls present a wider spectrum of opinion than were seen on this occasion. This would seem to indicate that the majority of residents are broadly supportive of the current system of grammar schools and upper schools in Bucks.

I am a great believer in the message (if not the grammar) of the adage 'If it ain't broke, don't fix it'. We are lucky in our county that we have excellent schools of both types, each with different challenges and each doing a really good job. I believe I am perhaps in a position to judge better than some, because two of my daughters attended a local grammar school and two a local upper school. I genuinely believe that all four of them did better at the school they attended than they would have done had they attended the other school.

The pressure that is allegedly put on children during the 11+ selection process is entirely attributable to the expectation and desires of others, whether that be parents who, entirely wrongly, think of non-selection for grammar school as a 'failure' of some kind, or some primary schools who are painfully aware how their perceived failure to squeeze children through to grammar schools will be seen by prospective parents.

Some might consider me a bad or perhaps unambitious parent, I suspect, because I wanted my girls to be educated in an environment that best suited them when they were at that age.

Streaming happens in every school all the time. All the Bucks system does is provide wider opportunities for managing that streaming.

I would take issue, therefore, with the publication of tables in this paper last week, headed 'The 11 Plus Pass Rate', because the implication is inevitably that those who did not pass failed.

And that is not the case. I don't blame the *Bucks Free*, because that is the way the majority think of the selection process, but perhaps in the future we could talk about The Secondary School Selection Process? Please?

19th December 2014

This will be the first year in many that I have not been knee deep in twice-daily panto by now. I decided to take a year out so that I could find out what a family Christmas is like on the days before and after the big day itself. I may end up regretting that new found ability; time alone will tell.

One benefit, I blithely thought, would be the opportunity to get my Christmas cards written earlier than is usually the case, when I end up frenziedly scribbling between shows in a dressing room somewhere.

I would have them all done in November, I resolved, stamped and ready to pop in the letter box around about now with a relaxed and slightly smug smile upon my face. Then November came and went with complete disdain for the plans of mice and men, and I've just got round to that annual task, which always makes me feel slightly guilty for a variety of reasons. The trees tumbling so that I can send a picture that someone else will only glance at for three seconds. The people whom I haven't contacted since last year when we each promised that this year we would meet up, we really would … (At least that's their bad as well as mine.) My inability to remember all the names of the recipients or their children.

But I have done the cards now, and then I encountered the biggest hurdle of all. I took the envelopes with the names on the front and went to look up the addresses.

I changed computers this year. When I reluctantly got rid of my lovely old XP computer, I copied all the data to a separate hard disk to install on my new computer. But the programme that contained all my street addresses is incompatible with anything I can get now. I rarely use snail mail any more for letter writing, so have only just discovered that years of building an address book on Lotus Organizer has been useless, as the data won't transfer to Outlook, Google Mail or any other similar programme I can find. Don't you just love technology?

So I would like to take this opportunity to ask you, dear reader, to think of this as my Christmas card to you this year. I hope you have a delightful time. Jingle Bells.

We really must meet up next year!

26th December 2014

Like everything else, Christmas is evolving.

Since AD 350, when Pope Julius decreed that 25th December was the birth-date of Jesus, the public and private celebration of that birthday has changed frequently, culminating, in modern terms, with the spin that Queen Victoria added to the mix with her introduction of Christmas trees in 1848, the same year as the Christmas cracker was invented by Tom Smith. The whole Victorian panoply of yuletide decoration and menu has remained basically the same since then.

Even those who are rarely seen in churches other than for funerals or weddings might still feel Christmas is not complete without attendance at midnight mass or a candlelit carol service. What is embedded, however, can be summed up as food, drink and presents. We routinely eat and imbibe ourselves into an amiable stupor—although the stupor is not always so amiable in some families?

And we spend money we can't afford buying a lot of things that only exist because of Christmas and the need to buy something for people that we can't think of anything to buy for. Stocking fillers. Or put another way—glittery tat that the recipient will not be able to remember six months later.

What has changed massively, however is where we go to buy the assorted stuff we press upon others. The switch to online shopping means that what Bing Crosby would be dreaming of today would be a white van Christmas, as the various delivery companies grind to a halt as their workload increases exponentially. I have already had several failed deliveries that were promised for specific times, without any explanation or apology. I suspect they are so inundated that they don't even have the time to let us know that they're not coming. Maybe next year I'll revert to personal shopping, if there are any shops left after we desert them en masse for the seeming ease of armchair shopping.

Another rather sad evolution is the cancellation of the great Christmas Day swim in Brighton—a favourite regular item in the news on the big day since 1860. The reason? Brighton Council are concerned that the general public, fuelled by advocaat and cheap sherry, will try to emulate the experienced swimmers of the local swimming club and get into difficulties.

Understandable, but sad.

So I won't be able to join you on the beach this year, guys.

2015

2nd January 2015

As I contemplated this New Year's article, I foolishly looked back over nineteen years of similar columns and find that what I wished for remains depressingly similar.

To illustrate that point, I unashamedly reprint my personal wish list for 1998.

1. A transport system that makes it more desirable to travel by public transport; in other words, one that is cheaper, quicker and at least as convenient as using one's own car. Currently, I have no alternative but to use my car for all but a tiny percentage of the journeys I make. Caning the motorist incessantly without offering a viable alternative is pointless.

2. The proper funding of education. No one wants to pay more taxes; but I believe the majority would support an increase in taxation, if it delivered smaller classes and better facilities. The consequent benefits to the country, within a generation, could be dramatic and reduce the number of young people who feel disengaged from society and, as a consequence, turn to drugs and crime.

3. A fresh look at the whole question of drugs and the political courage to set up a commission to examine whether criminalisation of the user rather than just the supplier is really the answer to reducing drug abuse and dependency. Is the present system working?

4. Preparation for parenthood and the responsibilities of citizenship as an integral part of school life. However useful Algebra and Geography may be, the world of parenthood, mortgages and employment is one that everyone has to live in.

They might learn, for instance, that to tell children not to do something several times and fail to follow through appropriately, in the event of continuing disobedience, results in not just wilful, but confused and unhappy children. I am talking about discipline; but discipline with love and support.

Nothing much has changed, though now I would add to that list a properly funded health service available to all and a supported and adequate police force.

This year I would also love it if, as a nation, we really made 'them' earn our vote in May and if we all forced them to be honest with us and we turned up en masse at the polls. I can dream.

I cannot in fairness exclude myself from this long list of disappointment. I am still overweight and grumpy. I also still wear crocs and shorts all year round to the confusion of right-minded people.

9th January 2015

Dr Challoner's Grammar School have recently told parents that they will be opening up their 6th form to girls from December 2016. This letter presumably indicates that the ongoing consultation period announced in their recent press release is seen by them as a formality. It was ever thus with alleged consultation periods, so no surprise there.

Clearly, schools are in competition with each other to attract pupils and with them the accompanying funding that enables schools to operate effectively, particularly at a time when the education budget is squeaking in tune with all nationally-funded activities. But the reasons for this initiative offered by DCGS would lead one to suspect that the benefit of adding the promised 23-ish girls to the 200+ boys that will be entering Year 12 in 2016 would accrue mainly to the boys and the school's budget. The school has already stated that the single sex education model is preferable for students aged 11 to 16, but says it feels that girls should be allowed access to the 'excellent education' that the boys enjoy in the 6th Form. Perhaps a little disingenuous? Only 23 of them? Might it not be rather the case that those few girls give DCGS the opportunity to save subject provision in areas where girls might boost numbers, thereby making that provision viable?

The argument that the plan prepares 6th form boys for life at university is not compelling either. The world in which I went to an all-boys school is long gone. The existing close cooperation with Doctor Challoner's High School is likely to prepare them more reliably than a couple of dozen female sixth formers. And whilst one can see that the so-called civilising presence of girls in an all-male school might be of advantage to the boys, thereby civilised, one wonders whether the educational and pastoral needs of the girls rate highly in this initiative.

For some years now the Grammar Schools have operated a broadly consensual and unified approach to admissions. One can only imagine that Dr Challoner's High School might view this foray into poaching their potential sixth form as less than desirable. The end result could be harmful to the existing cooperation between our excellent secondary schools in this corner of Buckinghamshire.

I sincerely hope that this does not presage detrimental boat-rocking amongst schools, the majority of whom see the hard-earned status quo that has evolved over decades as worth preserving.

16th January 2015

The Mayor of Wycombe, Councillor Khalil Ahmed, echoed the feelings of the overwhelming majority of Muslims in this country in condemning the savagery of the fanatics in Paris last week. It is tragic beyond comprehension that Islam, which preaches peace, tolerance and love, should be hijacked by a tiny minority who embrace none of those virtues. Islam is not the only religion that has been misinterpreted by the obsessed and deluded to justify depraved and insane acts. The Catholic religion, for instance, has been distorted in similar ways over the centuries.

I echo Cllr Ahmed's hope that the people of Wycombe and the wider world will acknowledge the disconnect and resist any temptation to demonise Islam as a result of the behaviour of these purveyors of terror and death, or indeed the rabid fanaticism of the Islamic State.

Quite rightly, Catholics in the UK were not demonised when the IRA attacked civilians in the UK. That is because it was clear that the majority of Catholics were opposed to and appalled by the atrocities committed by those claiming adherence to that faith—although the Church at the time, I believe, could have done much more to disassociate itself from their actions. And the more that Imams worldwide make it clear that slaughter of 'infidels' is no longer acceptable in a multicultural and tolerant world, the sooner all religions and peoples can coexist in harmony.

Similarly, the population of Norway was not asked to apologise for the actions of the white supremacist psychopath Anders Breivik.

But I also hope that the hard-won right to free speech that exists in most of Europe and the free world is not eroded by recent events.

'I do not agree with what you have to say, but I'll defend to the death your right to say it' is an excellent starting point. Clearly, the right to libel and defame must be curtailed by law, but the right to express an opinion—however much it may offend—must always be protected.

The use of satire and the cartoon to challenge the political, religious and social status quo of the day has been a powerful and peaceful form of agitation for change for millennia—from Horace, Da Vinci, Hogarth and Voltaire on to *Punch* and *Private Eye*.

And anyway, surely our gods and prophets are made of sterner stuff than we are—by definition, perhaps?

23rd January 2015

It is hard to imagine a luckier generation than mine.

I was born just before the last world war came to an end and therefore have no memory of it.

Yes, during the first decade of my life rationing was in force and we used to have to take our coupons along to buy the limited amounts available of meat, sugar, sweets, bread, milk, potatoes— you name it. It was 1954 when rationing finally ended and food became more and more plentiful and varied. The arts began to thrive again; television came along and enchanted us all; health care really was available to all and we all took it for granted that we were safe walking around the streets.

At least, that is my memory. The standard of living was a probably generally a lot lower in many ways than today, but so were expectations. I don't think I am viewing my childhood through rose-tinted spectacles when I say it was a simpler world and it felt a less dangerous one. The policeman was very visible on his beat and we knew him and he knew us. We had a family doctor who also knew us and remembered our medical history when we went to see him—maybe on a Saturday or in the evening. I don't remember hospital waiting lists being an issue. Buses ran regularly and went pretty much wherever anyone might reasonably want to go. Children walked to primary school not because they were health conscious and needed the exercise, but because most children went to their nearest school.

Despite all the advances in medicine, technology, transport and science during my lifetime that might reasonably have been expected to make all our lives easier, safer and more comfortable, the world the next generation has inherited seems to be heading in a direction that they will struggle to control.

Religious intolerance is reaching mediaeval proportions, natural resources are being squandered, the health service is being eroded, doctors and policeman no longer have the true community presence we enjoyed in the past and transport is all about long distances, not going to town for shopping or visiting neighbouring villages.

Events like those in Paris and Africa suggest that our children are entering a dangerous time in our history. I wish there was more that I could do about it than hope their generation can weather the storm and put things right again.

30th January 2015

There was a story in the papers this week about a man on a train who, as he disembarked, slipped a note with five pounds in it to a young mother whom he had noticed on the train with her young son. The note read, 'Have a drink on me. You are a credit to your generation, polite and teaching the little boy good manners.'

The fact that this is newsworthy says a lot about our expectations of both young mothers and gentlemen on trains. We read so much about man's inhumanity to man, cruelty and disasters in the papers and it is important, of course, that such things are reported so that we can do whatever we can to stop them or improve the lot of the worst affected.

But wouldn't it be nice if we read more about the acts of kindness, big and little, that help us to view our fellow man with less nervousness, fear and suspicion that many of us do at present.

For instance, perhaps *The Bucks Free Press* could dedicate a page (or even half a page initially) for people to express their gratitude to all the kind strangers who hand in lost property, help someone who has dropped their shopping all over the pavement or come out without their purse or can't find their child in a supermarket. A regular forum for 'thank-yous' and acknowledgements of the good that certainly exists in most of us might serve to highlight for the many doubters that there is good in humanity.

Knowledge that there are some good people out there might just make someone think twice before breaking into a Telecom exchange and stripping out all the copper wire, depriving an area of the town of telephones and internet. That happened this week in Desborough, apparently.

I may be fantasising in suggesting that the celebration of the good in us might deflect those who care for nothing but themselves from committing crime, but it must be worth a try.

Maybe too, we'll no longer be so surprised when the Good Samaritan does stop to help us when we are in difficulty. It is another symptom of our age that the expectation of the basic decency of mankind has so diminished over the last decades to the point when that gentleman on the train's actions are so memorable as to be worthy of publication.

6th February 2015

Shadow Culture Minister Chris Bryant recently expressing delight that Eddie Redmayne had won a Golden Globe, added that we can't just have a culture dominated by Redmayne and James Blunt 'and their ilk'. Blunt has now entered into a public spat with Bryant, accusing him, basically, of posh-bashing. Leaving their squabble aside, it is undeniably much, much harder for those without personal funding to have access to the kind of training that I was privileged to have.

If you were good enough to convince the interview panel at a drama school that you were more worthy of a place than the other several hundred hopeful applicants, grants were readily available to pay fees and subsistence. I was lucky. Today I wouldn't have had a chance, I suspect. My father was a permanent invalid and my mother cared for him. There were no funds to help me. As it was, I had to get several part-time jobs to afford to survive, but not to the extent that would pertain today.

With student loans terrifying young people, even if they can get them, and arts funding dwindling steadily into a black hole, it is becoming increasingly difficult for young people of talent to enjoy a career in the arts unless they have financial backing or connections. And when they move into the workplace, salaries are very low, except for the very successful few.

Eddie Redmayne, Damian Lewis, Dominic West and Benedict Cumberbatch (Eton and Harrow, all) are all superb and rightly acclaimed actors, but increasingly, the people who are able to pursue a career in acting are those that can afford to, and they will therefore tend to come from more affluent backgrounds. Added to that, public schools have superb drama facilities, denied to most state schools.

Drama schools typically charge between £35 and £85 for auditions. Given that most would-be performers apply to half a dozen or more schools, they have to invest several hundred pounds to be seen; and few are accepted first time round. Nowadays, thousands apply for around 30 places per school per annum.

Drama used to be an area where real talent could always find a way through. But as the artistic director of The Globe, Patrick Dromgoole says, 'It's becoming harder and harder for children and young actors without means to get into drama school. I think that's an enormous shame.'

I can only agree.

13th February 2015

When I go to my local fish and chip shop and buy a takeaway for the family, they have never (so far) come round to my house the following day to ask whether the newspaper in which it was wrapped was up to the task, whether I got the contents home undamaged and fit to be eaten, or whether the batter was crunchy and the chips of a decent size and temperature. When I buy a shirt in person from Marks and Spencer— no, sorry, I mean Alexander McQueen or Givenchy—well whoever I buy a blinking shirt from, no one subsequently pesters me to ask whether I found the fit, the packaging, the stitching or the detail to my satisfaction. Nor do they ask me to rate out of ten the style, presentation or the display in the shop, or the unctuousness or otherwise of the sales assistant.

I would like to put on record my gratitude to all those retailers and service providers that resist the urge to pester me endlessly about their goods and services.

On the other hand, like increasing numbers of my fellow citizens, I am enjoying the ability to make purchases at leisure on the Internet. There is a some guilt involved, I confess, as there are shops that I would miss if the swing to internet trading drove them out of business, so I try to ensure that I make on-site purchases whenever possible. But I make a lot of online purchases, and am bombarded with irritating emails asking me to give feedback about the goods, their delivery and packaging. As I write, this one has just popped up on my computer, asking me to rate my delivery of a phone charger on a scale of 1 to 5. I ordered it. It came. What more is there to say?

But there are a dozen and more requests to know whether I

am happy, very happy, not happy, not happy at all or neutral! Well, Mr Box-Ticking Programme Writer, I was happier before I had to read and delete your annoying email than I was after I had wasted a few more precious minutes getting rid of it and the scores of feedback requests that daily clutter up my inbox.

I'll let you know if I'm unhappy, don't worry, so stop spending millions on statistic-gathering and use the savings to cut your prices.

20th February 2015

Whenever one of my children came home and spoke of an incident they had endured that day in or outside school that went beyond casual or minor injustice or harassment, I instantly felt the need to do something about it. To expose the wrongdoing; to right the wrong. That is possibly due in part to my having spent five years in my twenties working in the legal profession, which often only righted wrongs for those who could afford to hire the services of the expensive knights in shining armour of the legal profession.

Even as a child, I struggled to shrug off injustice as part of life's many brickbats, and as a result got into endless trouble. My children eventually stopped telling me stuff because they knew I would feel compelled to 'do something about it', and we all know how embarrassing that can be, for heaven's sake.

So I am predisposed by nature as well as experience to support the notion of whistleblowers. The culture of members of any profession covering for and assimilating the wrongdoings or incompetence of co-workers may seem appealing in principle—solidarity, 'all for one and one for all', and all that. But in practice, hospitals, police stations, pharmaceutical companies, public authorities and private companies alike all benefit ultimately if they are seen to listen to and act upon those uncomfortable revelations from within.

The demonising of those whose conscience compels them to bring into the light things that others would prefer to conceal serves only to confirm what many fear—that no one really cares about anything much outside their own well-being and a quiet life. 'The only thing necessary for the triumph of evil is for good men to do nothing' may not have been the exact words written by Edmund Burke as often quoted, but they have never been truer than today in a world of adversarial politics and mega-corporation world dominance.

Can it really be true that no one suspected what Savile and Glitter were doing? Of course not, but no one was prepared to risk their careers by exposing the repellent creatures for what they were.

I am not suggesting we all report our friends for speeding, illegal parking or minor infringements, but when hospital patients, the vulnerable, children or old people are being maltreated or ill-served, we should all speak up without hesitation.

27th February 2015

The reason that we have such winding and erratic roads is that (those built by the Romans excepted) they evolved from the routes taken by people with very specific needs about where they needed to go, following the detours they had to make to avoid obstacles, whether man-made or natural. Most roads in America don't suffer from that historically-evolved randomness, because they were able to start from scratch in a modern transport environment. Hence the efficient, if less quaint, grid system in New York, say, as opposed to the ancient labyrinthine meanderings in London.

Local footpaths evolved in this way too. Pedestrians (and most people were on foot when the paths appeared) found the shortest practical way to walk for their provisions, to attend church or school, to take their cattle to market. The original purposes of many footpaths have long been forgotten. Certainly, very few are actually essential to daily commerce or human interaction any more.

So we have a network of footpaths understandably beloved by those of a rambling disposition, by walkers with dogs or those in search of a post-prandial family country stroll. The right to roam is important and cherished, and rightly so, but many footpaths evolved in places where their existence is not only anachronistic or bizarre, but unhelpful. Ask any farmer how he views the footpath that marches proudly across the centre of a meadow in which his sheep are lambing, and you will see what I mean. It strikes me that a little flexibility might help. As the law stands, farmers and rural homeowners have no legal right even to request that rights of way be altered. The Deregulation Bill, which will receive its third reading in the House of Lords next week, may, if enacted, allow a little more flexibility, and not before time.

We have dogs at Baker Towers. We take them for walks in the farmland and woods around our home, and greatly appreciate the ability to walk in the local countryside. But in many cases, small changes of route could make life much easier for farmers, and indeed some private homeowners, whose land is often bisected by a footpath that was necessary two hundred years ago but difficult to justify in its present position today.

There is no reason why common sense should not prevail without endangering the precious right to roam enjoyed by us all.

3rd March 2015

I can't be the only person who thinks that some television adverts are decidedly odd. Very often they have, for me, the opposite effect to that presumably intended. Knowing how these things get put together makes me even more perplexed. Nothing makes it to the screen without a whole bunch of people thinking that it should. In times long gone, an established and respected director could make programmes or films purely on the strength of his own reputation, without any editorial interference, but nowadays everything that makes the screen in any form has been presented repeatedly before the forensic gaze of countless layers of producers, departmental heads and controllers. When none of them object strenuously, the programme or film is made.

This process is no different for advertisements. In fact, you have to add into the mix what is referred to rather ominously as 'the client'. This means that the company for whom the advert is being made has a phalanx of suits sitting in at every stage in the process. They're spending the money, so they rightly and understandably want to have input. And measured by the second, many advertisements cost much more than the average movie.

That being the case, I cannot help but wonder why so many people clearly thought that a CGI-generated Audrey Hepburn getting off a bus, stealing the driver's hat and climbing into a young man's drophead coupé was the best way to encourage sales of the chocolate bar she then eats in the back of the car. And why does every car advert show pretty ordinary cars leaping over helicopters or outrunning collapsing buildings? Neither of those qualities are ones that most of us are looking for in the cars that we are obliged to drive on our congested, potholed and speed-restricted roads.

I marvel, too, that a whole bunch of people clearly got enthusiastic about the idea of a man in high heels and denim hot pants strutting his disturbing stuff to advertise yet another insurance comparison site. This despite the demented tenor, whose irritation value was so high that the advertiser had to resort to blowing him up on screen to restore credibility.

And then there's the bearded man in drag on the online betting advert, the ghastly Wonga wrinkly puppets and making living and vulnerable characters out of cheese straws or chocolates. Who thought that was a good idea?

10th March 2015

Someone once said, 'No good deed goes unpunished.' Philanthropy is often the target of suspicion, usually based on the detractor's certainty that the person is only doing good for some hidden motive, or so that people will like them. Leaving aside the obvious riposte 'What's wrong with that?' in the latter case, it is also not always true that everyone is necessarily always putting their own interests first.

Another widely-held misconception is that millionaires are obsessed only with money. The very few millionaires I have met or know enough about to form an opinion seem to me to be motivated only by the desire to make an idea work, to make something better, to create something different or exciting. Most of the super-rich could have stopped pretty darn quickly and bathed in asses' milk for the rest of their lives had money been the sole motivation. Take the case of Richard Branson. Had he only wanted to make money, his Virgin Records empire would have been enough. Wind forward through planes, trains and rockets and you see a man motivated by the passion to achieve and to create, not to amass wealth.

I am also a conspiracy sceptic. All the evidence would suggest that very few conspiracies succeed, and the reason is obvious. The people required, say, to convince a world hungry for sensation that men had landed on the moon, if that were not the case, would number in the hundreds. And none of them have since whispered to a loved one that it was all filmed in a studio in Burbank? None of the hundreds of NASA employees have broken ranks? No file has fallen into the wrong hands?

Come on …

It is for these reasons and more that I am perplexed that some fans of Wycombe Wanderers really believe that long-term Wycombe resident and fan Ivor Beeks and the club's new chairman Andrew Howard have some secret agenda for devoting hours of their time without financial reward to a club that has no prospect, even in the eyes of the most optimistic, obsessed fan, of producing a financial reward. Andrew Howard has stated that only five of the seventy-two league clubs are profitable, but that he relishes a challenge like that and wants to do his best for our little club. For heaven's sake, let's welcome him with open arms, applaud him and get behind the effort.

17th March 2015

I'm not a great one for joining things, but if there were an organisation whose sole aim was to put an end to the annual rigmarole of renewing car and house insurance, providers of telephones, gas, electricity, the Internet and oil, then I would be a founder member.

When there was little or no choice, I'm not sure that we were actually paying that much more for these services; and if you value your time at all, those frustrating hours spent poring over deliberately opaque figures and comparisons designed to obfuscate, not help, would negate any alleged savings anyway.

It is a constant battle between a lazy acceptance of what is already there and the readiness to dive recklessly into the cleverly-spun blandishments that entice and bamboozle us away from the status quo. I suppose that is why comparison sites entered the fray, nominally to help but also to make a further pound or three out of us. But how else can you make sense of the bewildering array of tariffs, unit prices, standing charges, weekend rates, Wednesday afternoon rates, toss-a-coin-in-the-air rates and contract lock-ins? In the spectrum of those who have to deal or not deal with this annual conundrum, I suppose I am probably better equipped than some to eventually make some sense out of the maze they lay down for us to stumble through, but there comes a point when you are tempted to do the equivalent of shutting your eyes and sticking a pin in the list.

And often the end result is that you yo-yo between, say, home insurers who give better rates to new customers. Where lies the economic sense in that? All that administrative work generated to perform a ritual circular dance every year.

I am contemplating, after decades with the same phone and internet provider, trying to find one whose bill I can understand and whose tariff doesn't require a Masters in Comparative Balderdash. My default position is conservative (with a small C). (I have remained with the same bank all my life, as they haven't put a foot wrong yet.) But a seventeen-page document that purports to explain my usage and charging for phone calls and emails, and fails spectacularly on both counts, is sufficient trigger to give them the bullet. And after innumerable hours talking to low-paid helpline operators in distant lands, the writing on the wall is legible, at least.

24th March 2015

All drivers have experienced the frustration of finding our paths blocked or restricted as we rush headlong to yet another aspect of our oh-so-important lives. It could be a tractor, a bus, a delivery van, a dustcart or a caravan. What they all (apart from the last) have in common is that they are vehicles being driven for the benefit of all by drivers who are worthy of our respect and gratitude rather than the abuse which is regularly heaped on them as they go about their business.

I mention this mainly because of witnessing the behaviour of a driver of a car that was behind a dustcart servicing the bins, along a local main road that was coned off for repairs and had traffic control lights at either end. The refuse wagon was moving at a pace that enabled the hard-working loaders to run (not stroll or amble) alongside, emptying and replacing the scores of bins placed by the kerb. A sane observer would acknowledge that they were doing all that was humanly possible to discharge their duties as swiftly as possible and minimise inconvenience.

Mr Apoplectic, however, bellowed abuse at the driver and suggested, in all seriousness, that in his weird world, they should have parked the wagon at the end of the roadworks and walked up and down with the bins, so that he could save a few minutes on his journey, which was clearly much more important. The same oafish twerp would probably be the first to complain if his bins weren't emptied on time. I was astonished and impressed by the calm manner in which the dustcart driver tried to explain (in a situation where anyone with more than one brain cell would need no explanation) that he had no option but to do what he was doing and his loaders were going as fast as they could.

There are too many Mr Apoplectics out there, sadly. I overtook one recently who was driving at 40 mph on a 60 mph-road. As I passed, I could see he was on the phone. Moments later, he accelerated up behind me with headlights full-on and tailgated me until I pulled over and let him by. Doubtless, he then felt better.

So let's all try to be kinder to people who do jobs that benefit all of us, even though we are occasionally inconvenienced by them doing it.

3rd April 2015

I was in America last weekend, and while there was afflicted with an earache that demanded more attention than a couple of painkillers and a lie-down. My hosts took me to a local drop-in medical shop, where a 'nurse practitioner' diagnosed acute sinusitis and a middle ear infection. She prescribed antibiotics and presented me with a bill for $135.

At the pharmacy I was charged $270 for ten antibiotic pills. As I was returning home the following day, my friend suggested that I bought only three for $81 dollars and went to my own doctor to get the rest of the course. The air journey home was, as you might imagine, challenging.

If anything were needed for me to trumpet the unparalleled glory of our National Health Service, this comparatively minor incident certainly confirmed it. I hear horror stories of uninsured visitors being charged tens of thousands of dollars when, in one case, going into labour three months early. I do have travel insurance, but with an excess that makes it unlikely that I will bother to claim.

The experience has confirmed for me that we must man the barricades to protect our NHS in the UK. I see abundant signs of its erosion. Accident and emergency services are being closed everywhere and nurses and doctors are becoming ever harder to recruit within the UK.

It is only a few decades since appointments with GPs were, more often than not, for the same day, when the length of hospital waiting lists did not need to be the subject of targets, when surgery receptionists saw their job as more about helping the patient than protecting the busy doctors, many of whom spend more time satisfying a bureaucratic hunger for forms, targets and statistics than helping patients. This is why many good and caring doctors are leaving the profession.

This is perhaps why the doctor to whom I spoke on the phone left me feeling more an irritant than patient, as he told me that he didn't need to examine me, the American antibiotics were wrong and a prescription would be ready later.

Why things are changing so disastrously, it is not entirely easy to understand. Yes, there are many more of us and drugs are expensive, but the many more of us pay more taxes, too. Maybe the expensive NHS trusts that replaced a largely autonomous medical profession have not helped.

10th April 2015

I have been travelling around the UK for decades for work and have witnessed the steady erosion of individuality in high streets from Truro to Aberdeen. One by one, traders with family businesses have been forced out by the spending power of the bigger companies, to the extent that now every high street has exactly the same mix of outlets and is indistinguishable, one from the other. The butchers, fishmongers, haberdashers, bakers and hardware shops have all been displaced either by supermarkets or chain stores. And it is, of course, our fault. We all shop where the goods are cheaper—very sensibly, most would suggest. But then we have to accept the inevitable consequence. But when the big boys have flushed the minnows out, they can then price as they choose, as they only have to compete with each other and not the more expensive, but arguably more appealing, sole trader who has been in the town for years.

Our local towns have evolved to such an extent that in one generation the high street has far fewer traditional family businesses still operating. In the four decades that I have lived in the area, I have seen both Wycombe and Marlow town centres evolve so that the majority of shops no longer actually sell goods, food shops are all owned by large chains and little other than branded service providers remain. Banks, estate agents, hairdressers, restaurants, phone shops and bars dominate. The reason is principally the cost of renting premises from the investment property companies that now own large swathes of British high streets.

In years gone by, shopkeepers could pay the rent and still

make a profit. Today, the rise in rents has outstripped the rise in income from sales. The end result is that this week Marlow has now lost Jolliffes from Chapel Street and Turners from the High Street, forced out after five and two decades respectively; the former will now trade from Wooburn Green and the latter from Station Road.

Residents are understandably concerned, but I suspect we all know deep down that the trend will never be reversed, any more than yellow lines on the road will vanish, or bobbies will reappear on the beat along your street and know your name, or a teacher can take children out to pick dandelions without completing innumerable Health and Safety forms and risk assessments.

They call it progress.

17th April 2015

No one could fail to be impressed by the way that Wycombe Wanderers have managed to achieve so much in the last year, both on and off the field. With one of the smallest squads in the whole league, manager Gareth Ainsworth has somehow contrived to confound all the pundits, and with three games to go this season, the Blues are still in the automatic promotion spots. I am sure many other Wanderers fans will remember the annual pre-season TV pundit's panel prediction last August of who would be promoted or relegated in each division. Given the last minute nail-biting escape from the drop last May, the majority named Wanderers as prime candidates for the drop.

The combination of Ainsworth's clear genius for putting together a team that will go the extra mile for him and each other, some very skilful loan acquisitions and a great goalie have kept the team in the automatic promotion spots for the majority of the season, and with the chequered flag in sight we are still there, thanks to the nail-biting victory against Exeter on Tuesday night that broke the midweek-match jinx and a club points record. Whatever happens now, the season will have been a resounding success. To go from down and out to promotion candidates on a budget that wouldn't pay a

Premiership player's tax bill is miraculous. And heaven only knows how the physio and fitness team have managed to get a full squad of players out on the pitch every week.

And off the field, the current trust and its chairman have really achieved the impossible and kept the club afloat in the most challenging of financial circumstances. Many other clubs in similar situations have crumbled, and tumbled down the leagues into oblivion.

Obviously, the finances are now crucial, and so the fan-owned club is going out to the community it has served so well to try to get the necessary investment that will keep the club going. In the week that a Blues fan raised three thousand pounds for the club by jumping out of an aeroplane, it launched its Enterprise Investment Scheme, set up to fulfil the club's ambitions of 'survival, security and then success.' It hopes to raise from small investors £2m over five years, thereby increasing the community ownership of the club and securing its future.

Check out the Club's website for more information.

24ᵗʰ April 2015

We, the British public, surprise ourselves constantly by defying the odds and knowing best. However much politicians may suggest that we can't be trusted to vote on things like capital punishment (apparently, we'd bring back hanging, drawing and quartering, if we got the chance), we constantly find ways of proving that prejudice misguided. But it can often take far too long to dislodge the paternalistic Nanny State attitude of those who rule us. There is certainly a widely-held belief that on certain emotive issues, there would be a majority in favour of all sorts of controversial issues that we are only allowed a vote on when the likely outcome is expected to coincide with the ruling party's view.

But we, the great unwashed, have responded by moving slowly into a position where the uneasy coalition will become the governmental norm rather than the exception. As the major parties coalesce into a vote-seeking middle ground and principle becomes obscured by pragmatism, the need for a reformed voting system becomes steadily more apparent.

The present system offers not really even a 'general' election. It is a lot of local elections, six hundred and fifty of them, to be precise. And if you live in one of those five hundred and odd constituencies in which likelihood of a change of MP exists only when the previous incumbent retires or goes off to do something else, your electoral X contributes as much to deciding the occupancy of 10 Downing Street as my dog did to the design of the Great Hadron Collider. At the last election, the Conservatives would have had a working majority had only a very few thousand people voted differently in the key marginals.

This is why a system of voting that removes the need to vote tactically must eventually emerge if we are to remain truly democratic. The First Past the Post method has been serviceable until recently, but arguably no longer produces the fairest reflection of what the voters actually want. There are several contenders to replace it.

The Alternative Vote System, Proportional Representation and a complicated but interesting system, the Condorcet Method. If we are to re-engage the disengaged and generate an interest in politics in the young, something radical needs to be done. I would suggest that working to find a way in which our votes really do ALL count might be a sensible and enfranchising first step.

1st May 2015

I was appalled to hear this week of the possible demise of Out of the Dark, the local charity that has been doing remarkable work in offering disadvantaged and alienated young people the opportunity to turn their lives round by restoring old and unloved furniture.

The organisation's title came from the notion of bringing both the young people and the furniture out of the shadows where they were languishing and into the light. And the work they did was excellent and imaginative. Jade and Jay Blades, the co-founders, met at Bucks New University, where she was studying textiles, and they discovered a shared passion for design and also for making a difference for many of the troubled and thitherto unmanageable youth of our town. And I know from first-hand experience how successful their venture was.

Young people who had failed to survive in the community and the workplace and who, in many cases, came from disadvantaged homes responded to Jay's inspirational way of identifying with and channelling their energy and anger into constructive activity. By showing that taking something unloved and giving it a new life (and therefore value) could, at the same time, give them money in their pockets, Jay, who commanded the respect of even the most intransigent, showed he was as shrewd as he was talented. Some truly striking and contemporary pieces of furniture emerged. It was never an easy ride, but by offering to the young men in particular a male role model they could respect and relate to, when they had previously had none, Jay achieved miracles.

What a crying shame, therefore, that our town has allowed this venture to fail. A cancelled large order at the wrong time of year and a failed grant bid has forced the charity to declare itself insolvent. I urge the Council, or indeed any funding body or any wealthy potential patron with the resources, to have a look at the work this remarkable couple have done in a very difficult community area and financial climate and try to find a way to let them continue to trade and do what they do so well. In a town that was built around the furniture industry, it would be doubly tragic to lose them.

Had I known about this when I was chairing the hustings at Bucks New University this week, I would have certainly asked the parliamentary candidates to offer their help.

8th May 2015

Between my writing this and you reading it, the nation will have made its decision about how the country will be governed for the next five years, or not. And although it may well be that many millions will have yet again declined to take part in the democratic ritual dance that some argue gives us little real choice, even that inactivity says something about how the abstainers view the whole process. Many, like me, would love to live in a marginal constituency where we could honestly believe that agonising over the finer points of the manifestos and going to the hustings before casting a vote actually meant something.

My challenge to the politicians for the next five years would be to find a way to energise the population to see the democratic process as something worth engaging in. In a sense, UKIP has introduced an element of drama into this election, as indeed have the SNP. Who would have thought a few short years ago that a leader whose party exists only in one of the four countries of the United Kingdom, and is in essence a separatist party, and who isn't even standing in the election would share a platform with the other party leaders? It may well be that, when this is published that same party leader will be providing the means for another party to form some kind of government. It is the sort of scenario that would lend itself to the kind of satire written by Jonathan Swift in *Gulliver's Travels*.

I chaired the hustings at Bucks New University and was therefore able to meet and talk to the candidates who attended, all of whom were men committed to their cause and articulate in sharing their views with the audience, which seemed, sadly, to be comprised of a significant number of party activists rather than genuine, uncommitted and enquiring voters. I noted that the forthrightness of the candidates was in inverse proportion to their likelihood of being elected. After all, if you have every reason to think that you are the Wycombe MP elect, you have to be a little more circumspect about what you promise.

We will no doubt now be watching the unfolding of scenarios that they all denied they would enact a few short days ago. Will it be that canny Scots lady or the Lib Dems that are being wined and dined, I wonder?

15th May 2015

Back in the mists of time, on my first visit to New Zealand, I was walking across a square in Auckland when a voice called out my name. It was the son of a local farmer. I had seen his parents a few days earlier and they had told me that their son was on a backpack trip round the world and they hadn't heard from him for a while. I immediately rang them on my phone and passed it to him. The world is getting steadily smaller.

As a student, I was on a boat with some friends in the Mediterranean when the father of a friend spotted my appendix scar and asked where I had had it removed. It turned out he was the surgeon at Rochdale Infirmary who performed the operation. He said the scar looked like one of his. In the 70s, when I was on a diet and had alerted all my friends to help and encourage me to stay on the straight and narrow, I gave way to temptation and bought some illicit chocolate on a solo trip to the Ring of Kerry. The shopkeeper turned out be a cousin of the stage doorman at the theatre I was working in, and on my arrival there I was greeted with his soft Irish lilt enquiring, in front of my colleagues, if I had enjoyed my Mars bar?

So this week I was having Sunday lunch to celebrate my youngest daughter's birthday in The Boot—the community-owned pub in Bledlow Ridge. A voice uttered my name and I turned, expecting to see a middle-aged *Doctor Who* fan who had recognised me despite the ravages of time, but saw instead the unmistakeable features of Ian Ogilvy—who once played The Saint so memorably and, more to the point, whom I had persuaded one convivial evening in 1985 to join me in jumping out of a plane with the Red Devils the following day. I had not met him before, but we had spent a pleasant evening with mutual friends, and he had been intrigued by the opportunity to train with and jump with Britain's finest to help them raise funds for a new plane. So we spent two exhilarating days together and had never encountered each other since. He now lives in Los Angeles and was over on a flying visit and ended up in the same pub.

22nd May 2015

I have never been a great fan of tipping as a means of raising the income of those who serve us in hotels and restaurants. I admit this partly because I don't want to appear tight-isted on the one hand or flash on the other, and it can be quite tricky to judge the tipping point sometimes. I would much rather that waitresses, bar staff, porters, hairdressers and taxi drivers were paid a proper wage in the first place and did not have to rely upon the random generosity of strangers to reward their hard work.

There is something in the whole process that strikes me as being as being no less divisive and anachronistic than, say, hunting wild animals for pleasure and then posing proudly with the forlorn remains of a rhinoceros or grizzly bear. It simply doesn't compute in the 21st Century. And at the end of a pleasant evening with friends, wouldn't it be so much easier to simply divide the first number that is placed in front of you instead of having to do complicated maths in order to boost the zero-hours employee's meagre hourly rate to something less shameful? Add the cost of rewarding staff properly to the pricing of the food or service, and you avoid the reduction of the relationship between waitress and customer to one where the latter has the unilateral right to judge whether their relationship has been conducted in a satisfactory manner. If we are to keep this anachronistic formula for funding workers in service industries, it should at least be reciprocal. When groups of drunken males shake their inconsequential plumage in front of each other by being rude or aggressive towards waitresses or bar staff, then there should be a an equal and opposite right for the victim to say, 'Sorry, gentlemen, that's another ten percent on the bill.' An elegant use of Newton's Third Law in the service industry.

On a recent visit to Sweden, I was delighted to discover that they had a much more modern attitude to tipping. Staff there are paid properly; the consumer knows what the final reckoning is likely to be, and there are no tricky decisions to be made when fellow diners chip in too little and you have to compensate for their stinginess. Maybe it's time they won the

Eurovision Song Contest again, though I love our entry this time.

29th May 2015

I suspect there will be many column inches in this week's edition of this paper in praise of Wycombe Wanderers' mighty effort last weekend, and I am going to add to them. I was working in Germany and could only watch the match on my iPad. My wife was at Wembley. The drama that unfolded would have been tremendously exciting to an uninvolved spectator, but for the fans of both teams was almost unendurable.

A year ago, Wanderers survived in the league by the few atoms at the end of our fingernails. The jubilation was, of course, massive. Had we been relegated, given the resources of the club, it may well have been just the beginning of a catalogue of disasters that might have resulted in many years in the wilderness.

But, against all the odds, we survived, and our sensible ambition was limited to consolidating our position in League 2. Had mid-table security been predicted, many of us would have been more than satisfied. But a combination of careful administration, and Gareth Ainsworth's superb management of a small squad of men with big hearts and the will to work for Wycombe, meant that we spent all bar the first eight weeks of the season in the top three. And we began to dream the impossible dream. Nearly relegated, to promoted within one season.

It was not to be, and I have only just recovered from the tension of pacing a hotel room in Dusseldorf with my stomach dancing round my ears (not a pretty image, I know) as first the one goal, lead disappeared with seconds to go and then the unbearable agony of the swing of fortunes in the penalty shoot-out. Ecstasy if you win and misery if you don't.

But as the dust settles, there is not one member of that team that should do other than hold his head high. A penalty not scored does not eradicate the two hours of total commitment and courage that preceded it. Those players should all know they have nothing to apologise for, and as fans we owe it to them to make sure they keep on remembering that when the new season starts with new hope. Gareth rightly won the League Two Manager award, and I only hope we can keep him with us for many successful seasons ahead.

On a separate note—anyone notice I correctly predicted the Eurovision winner last week?

5th June 2015

Aren't politicians extraordinary? The Transport Secretary, Patrick McLoughlin, described the result of the recent general election as a 'massive vote of confidence' for the HS2 project, which in a couple of years will be inflicting an ugly gash through some of the most unspoilt countryside in the region.

Does he actually think that this gross distortion of the truth will sugar the pill that our county is going to have to swallow when the diggers move in and tranquillity moves out? If they had lost the election, would Mr. McLoughlin, in opposition, have lamented the loss of his project after the British people had turfed his lot out because they couldn't accept HS2? The truth, of course, is that no one other than those adversely affected by this unnecessary vanity project allowed HS2 to colour their voting deliberations for more than a second or two. I would go so far as to hazard a guess that if you polled all Conservative voters, not one of them would lay claim to voting as they did because of HS2. Even the successfully re-elected Conservative MP's whose constituencies straddle the route of the proposed folly are against it, partly for reasons of self-preservation, it could be argued, but possibly because they know and care about their constituents and the area.

It is simply the kind of utterance that politicians will always make when shoring up a particularly unpopular piece of government policy. And it therefore smacks of desperation. For some reason known only to them, the present lot seem to attach huge importance to the notion of businessmen being able to get from London to Birmingham (and presumably vice versa) slightly quicker than they can now. And they think that the fifty billion pounds spent achieving that is good value for money at a time when our road infrastructure is in national disrepair and accessibility to public transport in rural areas is being eroded to the point of non-existence.

Earlier this year, the House of Lords expressed its opinion that the costs had been hugely underestimated and queried the validity of the cost/benefit analysis of the project. It seems no one outside the Cabinet really wants this monstrously expensive white elephant. Furthermore, if it were (we can dream) kicked into touch, we would also be spared the endless reference to 'Haitch' S2, as far too many broadcasters and commentators insist on calling the project.

12ᵗʰ June 2015

I am not defeatist by nature and have tilted at a few windmills in my time, but the leviathan that is the Conservative vanity/ insanity project of HS2 is one where none but the sunniest of optimists can foresee a happy outcome for anyone. We'll all have to pay squillions to allow men in suits to have an extra ten minutes or so to do what many of them could probably do on the Internet. Passengers will hardly notice the difference. The taxpayers will, though, especially those surrounding the proposed route, and the rest of us as the roads amass potholes faster than FIFA officials can pocket a gold watch.

Another juggernaut that we seem unable to deflect from its destructive path is the hay made by dodgy claimants. I was told a tale this week by a dentist friend of mine from Manchester. It appears that nearly a decade ago a man came to him with a broken tooth-straightening wire. On hearing that the wire had been broken for years and the teeth had not resumed their previous disarray, he advised him to monitor the situation and seek help if his teeth moved. The man did not join his patient list, but nonetheless reappeared a decade later with teeth pointing in different directions and demanded that my friend sort him out free gratis as he had given him bad advice. When he threatened to sue, my friend contacted his professional body's legal department for support. They advised him to pay up, as he had not written on patient's case note card that he had given specific advice to the man as to when and how often he should have them checked, merely writing words to the effect of 'I told him to wait and see.'

Trying to save a stranger money by not doing unnecessary work has resulted in him now being advised to pay for a man with the mind of a suer to have expensive remedial treatment done, when any right-minded judge in a sane judicial system must surely kick the opportunist, fanged fiend into touch.

The cost of lawyers, however, and the possible damage to his practice's reputation has led him to bite the gold-plated bullet and resolve to write copious defensive notes on all future patient records.

Is this the world we want? No, but it's the one we've got and it isn't going to change, I fear.

19th June 2015

I have never been able to understand why any human being can knowingly and deliberately inflict pain on another creature or delight in his, her or its suffering. This stems from no religious or moral belief, but from the simplest of base points—the gift we humans have of imagination. Do as you would be done by. It couldn't be more obvious. And if we, the dominant species, in our superior wisdom decide that the life of another creature must be ended, how can we do other than ensure that is done in the least cruel way possible? That imperative becomes more than problematical in times of war, as we have repeatedly experienced, sadly.

What is happening at present in the Middle East at the hands of those who have hijacked and hideously distorted the Islamic faith is almost beyond comprehension, and so much so that the instinctive desire is to build a high wall round the region and hope it will all go away. But how can the world refuse to give refuge to those savagely mistreated and abused families trying to run headlong from that carnage? Imagination again. We must use ours and act accordingly, however much we may be tempted to raise the drawbridge and sit it out. If only we could remove the innocent from harm's way until sanity returns after the hatred and bile has abated or their internecine ferocity has done its cruel job.

How does it happen? How does the terrified look in another's eyes fail to stem the tide?

But when you see pictures of the trophy hunters who hail from allegedly civilised countries standing proudly by the carcass of a newly shot giraffe or lion, having spent a fortune in poverty-stricken lands for the privilege of taking the life from such beautiful creatures, you get another glimpse into the darker corners of the human soul. If a cull is deemed necessary for whatever reason, do we really want to allow that job to be done by those who revel in killing and post pictures on the Internet, gurning triumphantly, as if they've just won a Nobel prize? And if the fox really must be controlled, do we really want to turn it into a sport, so that killing for fun becomes woven into the fabric of genteel society and an event to celebrate? I had hoped that we might be moving away from all that.

26th June 2015

One can only feel for Barack Obama, as once again he attempts to change the mindset of hundreds of thousands of Americans who cling tenaciously to the notion that having a gun makes you and those around you safer than not having a gun. The whole 'right to carry arms' thing was contained in the Second Amendment to the American constitution for very understandable reasons back in 1791, in the aftermath of civil and international war. Fear of possible future oppression and the need to defend the recently created and hard-won State against invasion made the right to own and bear arms a sensible precaution in those more violent days. But even the most purblind of militaristic apologists would have to concede that their great democracy has evolved considerably since those days when the need to break away from England, and then to decide whether slavery was acceptable, meant great loss of life and liberty.

However, nothing seems to shake the resolve of a powerful section of American society to ignore the cost to its citizens of this anachronistic right. President Obama points out that for every ten thousand people in the USA, there are over ten gun-related deaths, slightly more than South Africa, which has similar adherence to the gun culture, but massively more than every other 'developed' country. For the majority of European countries, that figure would between one and three in ten thousand. In the UK it is one in four hundred thousand.

The National Rifle Association has an alleged four and a half million members. And, (surprise surprise), the gun manufacturers are regular donors of millions of dollars to that organisation.

Obama states that 11,000 Americans were killed by gun violence in 2013. They were killed by people with easy access to weaponry that only an army should have the need to bear. It may well be that most USA career politicians who have the ability to look around more than the narrow parameters of their states and the State would support tighter control. But were they to say so, you can bet your sweet bazooka that the voters would kick them into oblivion at the next election.

Hats off to Obama and all those who are still trying to ensure that decent people praying to their god can do so without fear of being the victim of a racist with a gun.

3rd July 2015

I learned something about hotels last week. Apparently, they adopt the same tactics as some airlines do, and overbook regularly. And while one can understand that a no-show, resulting in an empty seat in an aeroplane, would offer the opportunity to allow someone else to sit there, routinely overbooking and taking payment for seats that may not in the event be available strikes me as a bit of a liberty when booking restrictions are so inflexible.

I was invited to the Students' Union in Hull last Saturday to help them raise funds for a local charity, and I also collected for Stokenchurch Dog Rescue by requesting donations for selfies. The event organisers booked me into a Village Hotel and paid in advance for bed, breakfast and even Internet. We all like to keep connected these days, don't we? On my way across to Hull I visited some friends for the evening, so didn't arrive at my hotel until midnight, to be greeted by a sheepish young night porter, who had to tell me that the hotel was full. Tiredness and being a stranger in a strange land led me to enquire somewhat tetchily of the poor lad how such a thing could possibly happen.

It appeared that there was a wedding party there and there had been a 'confusion over bookings'. I imagine that that meant one of the party had a drink too many and decided that it might be better not to drive home. It turned out that said porter was a *Doctor Who* fan and was mortified that it was me who had been bumped to squeeze extra revenue from a room now twice paid for. His paroxysms of regret would have been more pacifying had I not been tired and very irritated. He phoned around and found me another hotel six miles away, so I lugged my bag back to the further reaches of their full car park and drove off grumpily into the hinterland of Hull.

The night porter at the haven I reached at 12.30 a.m. confided that hotels overbook routinely, and, yes, even when rooms are paid for in advance.

Shame on them, I say. Unless they make it a condition on booking that unless you arrive by a certain time you forfeit the room, and then reimburse the traveller, they have no right to bump a customer and get double payment.

10th July 2015

The tendency of human beings to have an instinctive desire to accentuate the negative and eliminate the positive, rather than the other way round as recommended in the song, is not an attractive one. It exists throughout nature, but our ability to think, to rationalise and to imagine should steer us away from the stranger danger reflex a little more than it all too often does in practice.

I was told a story this week about a group of friends walking in North Wales who stopped at a pub whilst on their trip and noticed that those already in there instantly switched from speaking English to speaking loudly in Welsh as they entered.

One of the group that contained my friend was a Welsh speaker, and he was able to share with his fellow walkers the many uncomplimentary anti-English things being said that were provoking Celtic mirth between the regulars. On the way out, the Welsh speaker expressed in their language his gratitude to them for their running commentary and wished them Good Day. This provoked the worried question 'Can they all speak Welsh?' I should add they are all strapping lads. 'Yes,' he replied, 'but unlike you, we're friendly.' Lesson learned? Who knows?

Another friend went into a Welsh Tourist Office to ask for help when she couldn't get a taxi to come and take her to her hotel four miles away after phoning many different firms. 'It's your English accent,' she was told. 'We'll call for one for you.' One came immediately. Presumably, she kept quiet in the back. I wonder if she tipped?

A Finnish-speaking friend recently had a similar experience on a tube journey in London, when two young female Finns were making derogatory remarks about all their fellow passengers, including my friend, and giggling irritatingly. As she left the carriage, she said in that most difficult of languages, Finnish, 'You really should be more careful, you know. You never know who you're with.' I am pleased to say the girls went bright red and were mortified.

Whilst these are possibly minor events in the grand scheme of things as evidence of our propensity to marginalise or shun 'the other', these incidents do serve to remind us all that we should all try to be a little kinder to strangers. If these seemingly minor slights remain unchallenged, grudges can grow into tribal hatred before you know it.

17ᵗʰ July 2015

Who would have thought that the pugnacious Scottish Nationalist leader would have mustered her troops from north of Hadrian's Wall to defeat the Government's attempt to bring hunting with hounds back. Whatever her motives—a good deed well done.

It defies belief that, at this point in the slow struggle of humanity towards civilisation from a past characterised by barbarism and cruelty, Cameron could shoot himself so spectacularly in the foot immediately after acquiring a majority. Most of us are slowly realising that we share this planet with more than our immediate family and neighbours and are trying to adjust our lives accordingly, but he chose to celebrate his majority by restoring a so-called sport that enables those who enjoy hunting a small animal with a pack of hounds while wearing fancy dress to indulge their grotesque hobby.

The fox is part of our rural and now urban scene. Because he is a predator, he needs to hunt and scavenge to live. He only slaughters chickens en masse because we have corralled the poor birds for our benefit and they can't get away. To characterise him as a fiend from Beelzebub's lower regions for this reason is not only laughably anthropomorphic but stupid.

We have chickens at Baker Towers and they have a secure compound. We look after them. If a fox gets them, it's our fault, not his. He is just being a fox. If a sheep farmer loses lambs to a fox, it is quite understandable that he should do something about it. But to invite his landlord and the local gentry in dozens to trample his crops, kill a few cats on the way and celebrate as if they've defeated the spawn of Satan when their pack of hounds tears any old fox to pieces is like hanging, drawing and quartering a shoplifter. Ridiculous, disproportionate and cruel. What was acceptable three generations ago is no longer acceptable. Hunting foxes, deer, or any animal with hounds belongs in the dustbin of history along with bear-baiting, dog fighting, witch-dunking and the slave trade.

We should be better than that by now. If a fox is a real problem, then one trained professional marksman should be enough to deal with it. And that would be a lot cheaper than the thousands spent by those indulging their desire to ruin a good ride with a bit of torture and slaughter.

24th July 2015

We would all love it if we could go back to the days when you could ring the doctor's receptionist and she knew your name and offered you an appointment to see your doctor the following day. 'Morning or evening? How long do you need?' Times have changed and, however beguiling the nostalgic memories we all have of a National Health Service that really worked and rarely let us down, we have to face the unpalatable fact that unless we vote for politicians who offer us the choice of a better health provision funded by commensurate tax increases, those halcyon days will never return.

A doctor told me recently that, when she qualified, she and her colleagues were rarely called upon to treat patients over 90 years old. That is no longer the case. Eighty is no longer considered the ripe old age it was a generation ago, and unwell octogenarians expect to receive the same level of health provision as forty-year-olds. And quite right too, I say, as I head inexorably in that direction. Put simply, people are living longer.

Those brilliant pills that cost a fortune and control our cholesterol, blood pressure and heartbeats mean that we are not keeling over as early as we would otherwise, and our health provision is therefore expected to accompany us for an extra decade or two. Many treatments for cancer are hugely expensive—the pharmaceutical industry is a separate matter—and, of course, we expect all patients with cancer to receive the best care possible. The NHS bill goes up and up and no political party has the guts to say to an electorate that wants everything as well as low taxes, 'You can't have both.'

I feel sorry for the medical profession currently trying to cope with the massive under-provision of doctors in both general practice and hospitals that results in longer and longer waits for appointments and operations. I had to wait over two weeks for an appointment with my GP of choice recently.

And now doctors are being told that they will all have to work at weekends as well. The thought that strikes me is that there aren't enough doctors nationally to cover a five-day service at the moment. Is Mr Cameron going to increase the budget by a third to cover the extra provision, I wonder? Perhaps HS2 is more important.

31ˢᵗ July 2015

Social media truly comes into its own in cases like that of the Minneapolis dentist, Walter Palmer, who reportedly thought that the $50,000 he spent procuring greedy men to lure a magnificent and widely loved lion, Cecil, out of a reserve so that he could wound it with a bow and arrow was money well spent. Palmer has already slaughtered a rhino, a bison, a cheetah and another lion. He is clearly insatiable.

Cecil was ultimately killed 40 hours later, when the injured lion was tracked and shot. Despite wearing a checking collar, as he was a part of a university study project, he was then skinned and decapitated with a view to being an ornament on the dentist's wall, no doubt. Cecil was a huge tourist draw in the Hwange National Park and, even worse, his demise means that the next lion in the pecking order will probably kill all Cecil's cubs to ensure the dominance of the pride's new bloodline. The region may also suffer financially for the loss of its star attraction.

Without the uproar generated worldwide by the news of this grubby and despicable transaction and its aftermath, we would never know that there are people out there whose bloodlust is such that they get their kicks by spending huge amounts of money in impoverished countries to indulge savagery that they masquerade as a sport.

It is one of humanity's less admirable qualities that we are still unable to accept that the hunter instinct, necessary for our survival as a species thousands of years ago, is no longer required in a civilised society. Most of sentient nature only kills for food or survival. Man is the only species with members who think killing for fun is acceptable; who fail to have the imagination that might lead them to want to minimise the suffering of another creature, if its death is truly necessary.

When I wrote my first column for this newspaper exactly twenty years ago today, the news of this shabby and degenerate enterprise would only have been widely promulgated if the broadcast media or national newspapers had deemed it of sufficient import. Today, thanks to the power of Twitter and Facebook, the perpetrators will undoubtedly ultimately bitterly regret their vile enterprise. So despite the trolls and the inconsequential chit-chat, let's be grateful for a world in which the unacceptable is recognised more widely and more speedily.

7th August 2015

A neighbour was taking her dogs for a walk recently when two men in the middle distance called out to her dogs and threw treats for them. She was able to call the dogs back and shouted at the men, who got into a white van and drove off. Another neighbour saw a white van outside her house and then noticed a man leaning over her gate to entice her dogs towards him. She banged on the window angrily and he got in the passenger seat and the van sped off. No one yet has got a registration number, but all the dog owners I know are on high alert.

A man in Beaconsfield answered the door to a stranger asking if he had a towrope, and noticed the man, on leaving, chalk the wall outside his house. He repeated this all the way along the road. All the houses identified with chalk marks were houses that had dogs. Thames Valley Police have now advised dog owners to be especially wary. It would be slightly less appalling (only slightly) if these men were dog lovers and wanted to have them as pets. Of course, the truth is far from benign. These degenerate and vile men are mainly looking for practice dogs for their dogs to tear apart, to ready them to meet and entertain similarly depraved men at dog fights, which apparently still take place in remote places far from the gaze of either the law or the majority of people who find such practices repellent. Other dogs, apparently, are stolen for sale overseas.

For any pet owner, the notion of their dog or cat being used in such a disgustingly cruel way is beyond unthinkable, and

I would urge anyone who sees anyone loitering suspiciously around a property or attempting to lure a dog away from its garden to notify the authorities immediately and make a note of the registration number of any vehicle, white van or otherwise that they see nearby.

At the moment, the penalty to dognappers is not a sufficient deterrent, because a dog is viewed by the law as no different to a laptop or handbag. It is a thing. However, we all know differently. Dogs are living creatures and very precious to most animal owners. The punishment needs to be considerably stiffer than at present if we are to deter these heartless criminals from causing so much pain to animals and humans alike.

14th August 2015

Every time I have flown anywhere in the last few years and have used the flightside shops, I have been asked for my boarding card when buying a newspaper or bottle of water, and every time I have politely asked why. The reaction to the question has varied from mute surprise and a shrug, as if to say, 'Why would I know, any more than I know why I have try to answer questions like that?', to the stare direct stare accompanied by 'It's the law—we have to.'

Other explanations have included 'So we know you are genuine passengers', 'Security check', and the catch-all 'Health and Safety', an answer that seemingly covers every pointless activity these days. I always asked out of genuine interest rather than any suspicion of an ulterior motive, and have only continued asking because I hoped that eventually some light would be shone on the reason I have to put everything down to search yet again for a piece of paper I have already shown at least three times elsewhere.

It is a relief, therefore, to learn that good old corporate greed is at the back of it. If I am travelling to America and buy something VATable, the seller can claim back the VAT that I (not them) have paid. What a shabby racket. I suspect that I will not be alone hereafter in declining to produce my boarding card unless I get the 20% VAT back myself. Apparently it's not illegal for the retailers to keep this money. Really? Well, it should be. They say that their systems couldn't handle the complicated business of differentiating between EU passengers and the others. Well, they're practically doing that already by claiming only the non-EU VAT—so just reprogram the tills in our favour not yours, you mendacious megacorps!

It's bad enough trudging, shoeless and beltless, through eternal loops of tape, holding one's trousers up like a five-year-old who's wet himself, without being conned comprehensively on the other side.

And while I'm on foreign travel, a quick word of appreciation for the excellent Lost Property service at Heathrow, which managed to find and return to me my iPad, which I left on a plane from the States this week. It was one of forty handed in that day, apparently. The system was smooth and efficient—so a word of thanks to Heathrow's staff and BA. Credit where it is due.

21st August 2015

Ex-Sr William Ramsay student, Leigh-Anne Pinnock (of Little Mix fame) and James Corden, who trained at Jackie Palmer's in Wycombe, were reminiscing on his show in America about their home town—High Wycombe. The fact that they were doing so is remarkable, not because Wycombe is not a town worth celebrating, but because it is rare for those who do that well in life to look backwards when the view ahead is so enticing.

I have only lived in Wycombe since 1986, so cannot pretend to have roots here. But those thirty years have made me realise that, just like everywhere else, it is the people that matter, not whether the physical infrastructure is pleasing on the eye, although if you live in somewhere like Broadway (the Cotswold version, not the New York one), that is a bonus.

But I was disappointed to find that most of the comments posted in the BFP website about these two Wycombe notables were derogatory, either about them or the town.

It is a sad fact that universal access to the Internet and the comparative anonymity that it provides the disgruntled and the uncharitable results in so much negativity. It is the criticism we hear about our media all the time, that the bad news fills the airwaves and newsprint at the expense of whatever good news there is available. And of course I am guilty of that myself. We all have a burning desire to complain about stuff that impacts adversely on or lives, and having a weekly column enables me to do that more freely than most.

The access to the BFP website enables those who dislike Wycombe or, say, James Corden to air their views too, with varying politeness.

So maybe I should take a moment to big up our town and its people. This weekend at the Swan the summer youth project will bring us *Singing in the Rain* and we can all see the breadth and depth of talent that exists among the young of our town. Our football team is continuing its run of success under Gareth Ainsworth, with its best ever start to a new season. Our schools have all shown steady improvement over the last year, and exam results confirm that. Local government may be starved of money to make the physical improvements we would like, but Wycombe is not starved of talent or generosity, as the abundance of many well supported charitable events regularly shows.

28th August 2015

As I started to write this article, a message popped onto my computer screen, saying that I needed to validate Windows 10, which I had (foolishly, it seems) installed after an enticing invitation to do so from Microsoft. Why do I never learn? Technophobes, now is your cue to cross the page and read the letters about global warming or the condition of our roads.

I followed the instructions to the letter, and the validation failed. A message instructed me to contact the supplier of the machine and the Windows 7 on it. Two failed attempts by them to help resulted in the decision that it was a Microsoft problem; they gave me the number that began my fraught and frustrating relationship with Ms Quiet in a distant land talking down a long drainpipe. She apparently could hear me fine. I, on the other hand, could hear one word in three, and whilst her vocabulary was excellent, her accent, combined with her inability to speak slowly, contorted her words to my perpetual disadvantage when I was typing things in to her instruction. Eventually, she gained remote control of my computer and then began her two-hour session, fiddling with endless arcane settings and strings of numbers, punctuated by lengthy and worrying pauses. At the end of the two hours, after a ten-minute absence from the screen, I received the message 'Colin im going to end this session coz it need advance troubleshooting and we only support for download install and activate' (sic), and she was gone before I could blink, let alone ask what the problem was. I only wanted her to support the activation, so why couldn't she? What advance troubleshooting did I need?

The desktop was mine again and heaven knows what had been changed and left unfinished.

By that time, of course, I had forgotten what I was originally going to write about, you may be diverted to learn. But as I have introduced the subject, I cannot deny that understanding what is being said to you in crucial situations by people whose English is good but heavily accented is a continuing and increasing problem.

I have recently been too embarrassed to ask a doctor, for the fifteenth time in a short conversation, to repeat what he had said, and hoped that I had heard sufficient to get the gist. That can't be a good idea. But what's to be done?

4th September 2015

I think we all know that whatever is wrong with the National Health Service has little to do with the workers at the point of service—the doctors, the nurses and ancillary staff.

I had occasion this week to visit the Ambulatory Emergency Care Unit at Stoke Mandeville.

I love the word 'ambulatory'; it carries connotations of walks on a summer afternoon with parasols for me, for some reason. Anyway ... I won't bore you with the reasons, but my GP was sufficiently concerned about me to refer me there for investigation of something that may or may not have been serious. In the event, mercifully it wasn't, so you can all look forward to reading my burblings for the immediately foreseeable future, anyway. But I and they didn't know that until a battery of tests and consultations had been conducted over a four or five-hour period.

I think that it is very important that good, caring service is celebrated wherever possible in a climate where its absence is pounced on at every opportunity. I had dealings with half a dozen healthcare professionals while I was there, all of whom were not only friendly, professional and seemingly prepared to go the extra mile, but were also very good at their jobs, insofar as a patient is able to judge that. At every point I was kept in the picture, at every point I was treated not as an object for investigation but as another human being. Everyone introduced themselves by name, and if I had accepted every offer of tea or coffee, I would have floated away on a sea of caffeine. I also saw other patients arriving and being processed, and in every case their individual needs and dignity were respected.

From the junior doctor who painstakingly did most of the legwork and questioning, to the consultant who finally gave me the all-clear after looking at all the lab results, I can only express my thanks and admiration. The ward sister made me laugh and the ward assistant (I may not have his correct title there) certainly confirmed what we should all know by now—that without the many immigrants working in the public sector, our country would be poorer and sicker. This man works at the hospital and in his spare time is a volunteer fireman, because he wants to give something back.

Well worth remembering in the context of the ongoing debate about immigration.

11th September 2015

A lot of things I would never in a thousand years have predicted have in fact happened to me. Mostly good, some exciting, some strange, some even bizarre. One of the totally unexpected things very much on the plus side happened this week. I was offered a doctorate by Bucks New University, which I was delighted to accept from the Vice Chancellor this week at The Wycombe Swan during the University's annual Degree Congregation. As I mentioned in my (hopefully) uplifting address to the students afterwards, the last time I was on that stage I was Herman the Henchman, sporting a very silly black wig in *Jack and the Beanstalk*.

On Monday, I was dressed in a bright red gown and floppy hat that carried some echoes of the colourful costume I was obliged to wear when I played the other Doctor in my life, back in the 80s.

We who work in the theatre and television do not have the monopoly on pomp and finery. The church and academia can give us a good run for our money in the fancy dress department. As all those bright, hopeful, begowned graduates came up and shook the hand of the Vice Chancellor with varying degrees of pride, nonchalance, embarrassment and cool, I found myself pondering on the three years of really hard work that had led to this, their moment of recognition and reward. I, on the other hand, had garnered my accolade as a result of 'showing off', as somebody once described the work of a performer, being given a doctorate because someone there thought that what I had contributed to my profession and the community merited that kind of recognition.

I couldn't help but think that even my father, a self-made man who had regarded the products of universities with considerable suspicion bordering on disdain, might just have been a little proud had he been there to witness my 'being Doctored'. Given that part of my qualifying credentials presumably includes my three-year residency in the TARDIS, I was diverted to conceive that I could actually be addressed as 'Doctor Doctor'. But as I understand that there is actually a medical practitioner of the same name in the area, I shall forego any temptation to put up a name plate on my door.

All in all, I couldn't help but think that it was a far cry from my time in the jungle!

18th September 2015

It doesn't seem long since I wrote about my inability to understand anyone paying three pounds and more for a cup of coffee in a carton when you can make it for yourself for a fraction of the cost. Many of my colleagues in the theatre had succumbed to this marketing racket, and I certainly wasn't going to. I couldn't understand why they all arrived at rehearsals, cup in hand, when there was a tin of catering instant provided by the management for our use. Pretentious, I thought. They have all succumbed to relentless advertising campaigns and peer pressure. You will never see me in one of those overhyped, overpriced outlets.

Wind forward a few years, and I had to meet up with a friend in one of the well-known tax-dodging coffee-chain outlets. It was the only convenient place we could both make at the appointed time. The list of available concoctions was outside my knowledge and experience, so he chose for me.

And of course, as you may well have predicted, I was hooked. I am now a card-carrying coffophile, and recently took out from the back of the cupboard the expensive coffee machine my youngest daughter gave us a few Christmases ago, which to my shame I had forgotten we had.

It is now our most frequently used piece of kitchen equipment, and I have just accepted a delivery of pods of latte macchiato, Americano and Café Crema, which don't last very long.

What all this says about me, about the power of marketing, about changing tastes and aspirations, I will leave for others to decide. But it does confirm what I probably should have realised anyway— that just because it seems to be a fad and newfangled doesn't mean that it is inherently bad or wrong.

Like if you had told me that a programme on television which watches people watching television would ever be made, let alone watched, I would have thought you certifiable.

However, *Gogglebox* is that programme, and my TV is set to record it, because it is a cleverly-made brilliant vox pop delivered by some riveting people. I met the vicar from the programme last week—she with the quiet husband and upside-down sleeping greyhound. It was refreshing for me to be the fan for a change. As you might expect from a lady in orders, she was delightfully tolerant of my gushing.

25th September 2015

It is no surprise to learn that, despite the clear guidance given in the airlines' emergency evacuation procedure briefings given by video or the cabin staff before take-off, more than 50% of passengers bring their hand luggage with them when evacuations actually take place. In Las Vegas recently, when a BA plane caught fire on the runway, triggering an emergency evacuation, a large number of passengers were seen emerging with hand luggage and even suitcases taken from the overhead lockers while other passengers were trying to exit.

Why is it no surprise? Well, I recall being evacuated in the middle of the night from a hotel somewhere, and while a few residents were shivering in their shorts, the majority were warmly dressed and clutching their laptops and handbags as they gathered in the drizzle outside at 3 a.m. It turned out to be a false alarm generated by drunken revellers (begging the question, 'What revelry is enhanced by such moronic behaviour?'), But the default position for most of us is to assume a false alarm unless flames are licking round the door, in which case I doubt quite as many people would delay their exit by searching for their valuables. To be honest, I was one of the 'preserve your modesty' brigade and dressed hastily, grabbing my laptop and wallet.

The aeroplane on the runway situation is complicated by the fact that getting off a plane takes ages at the best of times. and as you are standing there waiting, it would require the willpower of a saint to resist the urge to ensure that at least your money, passport and valuables come with you, knowing full well the interminable hoops that await your attempts to get your life back on track after such a disembarkation. I do not excuse this reckless flaunting of the very good advice, but do understand it.

Air travel is challenging enough anyway. I fly sufficiently often to have taken steps to simplify it as much as I can. I have a non-metal belt, so I don't have to waddle through security holding my empty-pocketed trousers up. All my few necessary possessions are in a small satchel. Everything else I check in. I wear crocs that not all security systems demand I remove to be scanned. I don't trouble the overhead locker and am amazed by those who must enjoy lugging stuff up the narrow aisles and fighting for storage space.

2nd October 2015

I know we are still going through a period of austerity, but it strikes me that whatever your political beliefs, top of the list of sectors that deserve better funding must be the police.

When times are tough, it is not unlikely that crimes involving property theft might rise. We know that, for various reasons, incidents of burglary are down and the likelihood of their not being reported are less, given the need to do so to claim insurance. But theft from shops it appears is rising significantly. The police service is undermanned, and therefore the hours spent investigating shoplifters who are long gone are not top of any police force's list. Indeed Essex police have disbanded their dedicated shoplifting unit.

Advice is being given by some police forces to shopkeepers, advising them to challenge shoplifters themselves rather than call the police every time. I listened to a police inspector on the radio advising a small shopkeeper to politely approach someone whom he had seen stealing his goods and in a non-threatening way ask them, say, if they needed a basket.

The shopkeeper had already acquired scars on his face when confronting a previous thief who had thrown acid at him. Another store owner (a former policeman, incidentally) said that he had instructed his staff not to risk injury and to do nothing on the basis that a significant proportion of habitual shoplifting is to fund drug habits by people whose concern for others, as well as themselves, is minimal.

Some crimes are not even furtive, but deliberate and challenging, and one cannot blame employers for not wanting their staff knifed or scarred for life to protect a couple of pairs of trousers or packs of bacon. The loss of shop workers this way is also a further drain on the benefits system.

Yes, there is a certain amount that shop owners can do to protect their goods but not everything can be behind the counter, or the counters will be up by the front door and the felonious would probably leap over to get what they wanted.

Maybe the big chain store owners could stop writing off billions in 'wastage'—a cost which is passed on to the customer, inevitably—and fund an increase in police numbers nationally to enable those who are trained in dealing with criminals to do their job more effectively, rather than endanger members of the public who are not trained.

9th October 2015

A nightclub in London allegedly refused to admit a party of four girls last week because they were 'too big'—as in fat—and too 'dark'—meaning dark skinned. The girls had been brought to the club by a promoter, one of the many that work for nightclubs in cities, drumming up business for them. They are apparently charged with the task of bringing in good-looking and successful people who will encourage other customers to want to follow them in to the club.

On this occasion, according to the London newspaper *The Voice*, the promoter who brought the girls was reprimanded because if he brought 'black girls' into the club, they had to be of a 'certain calibre'. The implication was that if they weren't Rihanna or Serena Williams, they could forget it. The four girls concerned, who seemed in their photograph to be delightful and attractive young ladies, simply didn't measure up and were denied admission. It was even suggested by someone in authority in the club that they should line up against the wall opposite the club to be inspected as to their suitability. I am delighted to report that they declined this hugely offensive invitation. Despite the club's subsequent protestations that it was busy that night. etc. etc., it is quite clear that a significant number of these allegedly 'desirable' clubs (that no one in their right mind over the age of 25 would wish to spend more than five minutes in) operate a 'beautiful people only' policy on busy nights.

Clearly, other clubs in cities around the country are less choosy. In my theatrical touring days, I saw queues outside clubs late at night that contained visions that would not have appeared out of place in the more fanciful episodes of our favourite sci-fi programmes as extras in alien speakeasies.

What is disturbing about this story isn't just that the girls were treated as objects to be admitted solely because they looked pretty, slim, fashionable or desirable enough, and I'll bet that few men are similarly rejected for reasons other than complete inebriation or aggression. What is appalling is that their colour played any part at all in the decision to deny them entrance.

I hope that every, one of every hue imaginable gives the club that has no vowels in its name (as well as no decency or morals) the very cold shoulder it deserves.

16th October 2015

It is inescapable to anyone capable of joined-up thinking that nearly all religions have been hijacked by the power-crazed and murderous to wreak havoc down the ages. Even religions widely considered to be more inherently peaceful have had their moments.

On the Indian subcontinent, Hindus, Muslims, Sikhs and Christians have all fought each other at various times, and the principal identifier of the combatants has been differences of belief. It is the Muslim world that currently appears to be in turmoil, with extremist groups seemingly intent on wiping out either non-believers—or each other, in the case of the Shia/Sunni conflict.

In a country where the established religion—Christianity, in the shape of the Church of England—plays no real administrative or governing role in our secular society, it is harder to come to grips with the fact that groups of people who worship the same deity but in a slightly different way could each find the other so threatening or offensive, but they do. We only have to glance across the water to Ireland, a beautiful country torn apart for generations by those who wish or do not wish to be part of the UK, and have for that purpose identified themselves as Catholic or Protestant to ensure support and identify their enemies.

We are all slightly afraid to engage with the problem, and it is with some nervousness that I write about it. Journalists who engage the issue in order to try to affect change have my admiration for their courage, given what happened in France recently.

It seems to me that the priests, vicars, rabbis, imams and community leaders worldwide need to have the same courage as the commentators and journalists who incite the fury of the haters. If all of them spoke out loudly and firmly and condemned violence and hatred every day more vigorously, then the tide of those who see a solution to their lives in joining a group intent on killing 'the other' might be stemmed. Clearly, at the moment I am talking about the Islamic State. But they are not the only group who are using belief systems to assert their supremacy. The extreme Christian right in America is gaining support and advocating action unacceptable to anyone advocating tolerance and peaceful coexistence.

Religion as a basis for mass murder should have died out in mediaeval times, but it is resurfacing and is a massive threat to our species.

23rd October 2015

There is no 'best way' to achieve a convincing acting performance. The only reliable indicator is whether those watching it accept you as the character you are playing and believe what you're saying. It is all about that willing suspension of disbelief. However fanciful the writer's ideas, the actor's job is to convince the audience that they are that person, at least for the time that they are being watched. As a rule, the less the performer appears to be doing, the more we are convinced; but perversely, the more a performer does, the more some people are impressed. But more does not always equate with good or believable, unless the character they are playing is intended to be larger than life.

Over my years in the profession I have worked with actors who appear to achieve excellent performances without any discernible effort in rehearsal, the 'learn the lines and don't bump into the furniture' brigade. I have also worked with actors who agonise constantly in rehearsal, who go out and live like a tramp for a week in order to play one, who wear painfully tight shoes in order to walk in a particular way, who allow the character to dominate their lives offstage/screen as well as on. In both cases, if the audience empathise equally with each type of actor, then that is the way that works for them. Stories abound about great actors like Paul Schofield (my particular favourite) and Laurence Olivier who could silence an audience with a look, move them to tears, then turn upstage and wink at a fellow actor.

That does not diminish their talent in any way, and moreover means that they are really in control of what they are doing. Having once been on stage with the other type of actor playing Macbeth, who, when my sword broke, failed to either acknowledge or help remedy that fact but continued to try to kill me, despite the fact I had to win, I feel safer, shall we say, with the inspired technician than the actor totally subsumed by his character.

I was made aware of the difference in styles this week when I was lucky enough to attend Bryn Terfel's 50th birthday concert at the Albert Hall. He strolled onto the stage and effortlessly delivered magic and musical perfection, where others around him seemed, while excellent also, to achieve that excellence with some effort. A wonderful night.

30ᵗʰ October 2015

Oh dear. It's only October and the festive lights are already appearing in Wycombe Town Centre, despite the fact that Christmas is still more than fifty days away. I remember when we used to complain that anything earlier than December was too soon to start the commercial push towards Christmas, but now we are creeping backwards towards the summer at an alarming rate. The Wycombe lights will be switched on on November 19ᵗʰ, apparently—a full five weeks plus before Christmas. Am I alone in thinking that it makes the celebrations less and less special when they consume around a third of the year?

It's a bit like the modern availability of fruit and vegetables all year round instead of only seasonally. When I was a child, strawberries were really special and there would be great excitement, as seasonal vegetables were suddenly available. When everything is on sale all the time, there is less joy to be had in its acquisition and consumption.

The same applies to Christmas. My memory of the build-up in my childhood is of a couple of weeks of excitement leading to two or three days of festive jollities. Now we have months of build-up and weeks of weary fun and faded frolics. The only exception is pantomime, which has reversed the trend, as few pantomimes now exceed four weeks', duration whereas those of my youth would last as many months. This is arguably an inevitable result of the expansion of the availability of home entertainment.

Wycombe Council claims that the early installation of illuminations is a result of the complex and considerable logistics of ensuring the safety of the new lights, which we have apparently spent £30,000 to acquire. One is tempted to consider whether such a large sum, at a time when swingeing cuts are being made in other, arguably more deserving, areas of the local authority budget, might be a little excessive? If the lights serve any purpose, it would be to attract visitors to our town centre, so perhaps the traders who benefit from the increased footfall could contribute to the cost? The town that says that instead of erecting pretty lights they are giving a like sum to a local Christmas charity would probably gain a lot of respect from their council tax payers. And then perhaps we could enjoy Christmas at Christmas, and not before poor old Guy Fawkes has even started to climb up onto his annual funeral pyre.

6th November 2015

This week, my luck ran out. I have travelled by air many times and never had a significant delay, missed connecting flight or lost luggage. A few near calls and small delays, but nothing to write home about. I went to Belfast last weekend, and my BA flight back to Heathrow was (eventually) cancelled because of fog in the UK. Leaving aside the fact that I thought that modern technology enabled planes to all but land themselves, it was the familiar tale of passengers standing for hours in long uninformed queues that I wish to share.

Having checked in and gone to the gate at the appointed hour, passengers were surprised that there were no ground staff there, and all that happened at the time we were supposed to be boarding was that a sign appeared, saying that there would be more information in half an hour. More? That was the first indication that the flight wasn't leaving on time. Other flights had been cancelled, but not that one. Then the cancellation came and everyone had to leave airside, collect their checked-in luggage and go back to departures, where hundreds of people queued at the only two desks open to spend fifteen or so minutes trying to find a replacement flight in the next two or three days that could get them somewhere they wanted to be. I was third in the queue, because I didn't have to collect any checked-in baggage before returning.

I was over half an hour in the queue, nonetheless. I could only pity those at the back, some elderly, some with children, who might still been there at midnight. I was allotted a hotel and managed to get a seat on a 6.45 a.m. plane to Birmingham, where I was picked up at 4.30 a.m. I then got a train, making the mistake of buying a First Class ticket to High Wycombe, thinking naively that I would be more comfortable after my restless, sleep-deprived night and that it was worth the extra tenner or so. The Chiltern train to Wycombe did not have a First Class carriage. The stationmaster told me that it never did. I am an infrequent rail traveller and may continue to be. I'll certainly know my place next time. Not First Class.

I was nonetheless diverted by an announcement at Leamington Spa Station, apologising that the train was four minutes late. British Airways, please note.

13th November 2015

A few months ago, I met an actor called Vic Mignogna at a sci-fi celebration in America. He earns his living as a clever and very successful voice-over artist for Anime films, computer games and cartoons, and we spent three very enjoyable days, mainly engaging in vocal mock rivalry to entertain the fans. It turned out that in addition to his vocal skills, he is the creative and organising genius behind a web-based film series called *Star Trek Continues*, which is essentially an homage to the original series of that 'other' sci-fi cult series. Fan-m--made films like these can only exist because there is sufficient enthusiasm for them to fund their production personally or from Kickstarter donations; the use of the *Star Trek* copyrighted material is only allowed if the production is strictly not for profit. It is, therefore, a true labour of love.

Using his own money and fan-donated funds, he had produced three 'new' episodes of 'old' *Star Trek*, with him playing Captain Kirk, the late James Doohan's son Christopher Doohan playing Scotty and a group of brilliant actors being Spock, Uhura, Sulu, Chekov and Bones. Fan-made versions of popular programmes come in various shapes and sizes, with varying degrees of professionalism and watchability. Others have essayed *Star Trek*, but Vic and his production team and cast have taken it to another level and set a benchmark that it would be nigh-on impossible to better. The level of detail that he has researched in order to deliver millimetre-correct replicas of sets, costumes and the hardest of all to achieve— the look and feel of the show—is phenomenal.

Therefore, when he asked me to play a guest role in the fourth episode at his purpose-built studio in Georgia, I accepted without hesitation and boldly went where no Doctor Who had been before. I spent a wonderful couple of days with them all on the Starship Enterprise, and I even got to sit on the bridge, in Captain James Tiberius Kirk's chair, gazing at the screen on which my appearance, as leader of a beleaguered planet, appears. To be able to say that I have appeared in both *Star Trek* and *Doctor Who* was an irresistible temptation, and I grabbed the opportunity. I am awaiting the call from *Star Wars* now. Third stormtrooper from the left would do, I guess. After all, Jabba the Hutt has already gone.

18th December 2015

The appropriate salutation at the moment should perhaps be 'Muddy Christmas' rather than 'Merry Christmas', because that's what it seems we are in for. (Two prepositions at the end of a sentence—my old English teacher would not approve!)

When walking the dogs at this time of year, we are normally wrapped up warmly in hats and scarves and marching briskly across frosted hard ground, with our breath sending out clouds of warm mist into the crisp and bracing air, speculating on the likelihood of a white Christmas. At the moment we are in T-shirts and slithering around in the mud of a thousand deluges; the roses and daffodils have been conned into unwisely showing their faces in this false and untimely spring; and we are all worried about the 'bugs' that are not being annihilated by the onset of regular frosts—although that may be—I suspect—yet another of those tales recounted by old wives, and indeed, husbands. No sexism in this column. And there are still global warming doubters? Mind you, there is still the occasional flat-earther to be found who thinks the whole 'satellite photos of earth' thing is a monstrous confidence trick and that men never landed on the moon. Shakespeare said, 'There is no darkness but ignorance' and, as ever, he had a point.

But the evidence that man has blighted the sparkling blue

planet that he has been routinely polluting for centuries is overwhelming, and it is therefore wise that we are still trying to ensure that post-apocalyptic generations might have a smidgeon of a chance to depart from the husk of the fertile planet on which we evolved, in search of somewhere else that can sustain life for our species. It is for that reason that I cheer the efforts of all nations to explore the beauty and peril of the vast universe, in which we wander like a mosquito in Africa. And why I heartily applaud Tim Peake and his international colleagues on the Space Station for the courage and curiosity that inspires them to spend six months or more hurtling round the globe, at unimaginable speeds, to further the quest of humanity to survive past the date when Earth becomes uninhabitable, whether that be naturally or as a result of human profligacy. Money is much better spent on missions like this, I would suggest, than on HS2, or cruise missiles. Happy Christmas, everyone.

25th December 2015

How's your Christmas shopping doing? Mine used to be a frenetic burst of activity between matinees and evenings in panto, in whichever town was graced by my heavily made-up presence that year. Now that exhausting seasonal activity is 'behind me', I have the leisure to take my time and do the whole thing on the Internet. White vans have been up and down to Baker Towers, trundling over the drawbridge on an hourly basis, it seems, and I think I am pretty much there. That is, until my last-minute panic that I haven't got enough when I hit the high street on Thursday! And then it's time for the fun and frolics of Christmas.

There was a time in my life when I used to love playing board games. Half a century ago, there were half a dozen of us like-minded aficionados who used to meet up for regular weekends of Scrabble, Monopoly, Charades, even Ludo—you name it—punctuated by breaks for food, drink and even the occasional walk in the fresh air to sharpen up the brain for the next session of dice-rolling or face-pulling. The key to the enjoyment back then was everybody wanting to be there and being similarly competitive. As soon as the festive season propels a mixture of the keen, the not-so-keen and the positively antipathetic into a jolly situation where they feel compelled to participate in games, then the fun factor can be much more problematical. And a mix of the competitive and the mischievously unmotivated can be explosive. Serious game players can fall victim to apoplexy if a rebellious reveller cheats ostentatiously or cheerily seeks spectacular failure. It's no fun beating someone who wants to lose or doesn't care either way.

I must confess that I now shy away from such dangerous mixes of folk and am sorely tempted to suggest Hide and Seek as the first game, and take the opportunity to flee the building and seek solace in a nearby hostelry, with a view to returning hours later to be playfully mysterious about where I had been so successfully hiding.

I restrict myself now to playing a version of online Scrabble with like-minded friends and daughters' tolerant boyfriends, who are prepared to indulge my desire to keep my senescent brain ticking over by placing those every day words like qi, za and xu on triple-letter scores.

2016

1ˢᵗ January 2016

Do people still talk about New Year resolutions? As the years roll by, it becomes depressingly obvious that very rarely do the optimistic plans for the cleaning up of one's act survive beyond the arrival of the daffodils. That would be less true this year, of course, as those yellow-trumpeted harbingers of spring have got it hugely wrong and are currently being buffeted by Hurricane Frank as we anticipate their imminent demise when the first hard frost of the winter finally arrives. Global warming deniers need to learn from the Flat-Earthers that sometimes resistance is not only actually useless, but also unhelpful.

Anyway, I am going to discard weight loss, joining a gym and running a marathon as unrealistic hopes after years of dispiriting failure and opt for something a little more achievable this year. I urge you to join me in resolving to shout even more loudly about the things that really blight our lives on a regular basis. I am talking about the continuing reluctance of the ever-expanding (both in number and size) corporations, organisations and companies who like to run their businesses with minimal interference or input from us, despite their protestations to the contrary. They build nice little questionnaires for us to answer online, carefully constructed to elicit the information they need to maximise profits, but make it more and more difficult to find out how to contact them directly and talk to someone (in this country) who has the power to improve your situation. Of course, many of us give up when the website hides phone numbers, and when you do find out how to call, you have hung on for half an hour, only to find the options offered don't include anything helpful to you, and you end up being cut off after listening to an unhelpful recorded message.

Don't put up with it. Shout. Write. Despite the inconvenience, change your supplier of TV, telephone, oil, etc. and tell them why you're leaving them. You'll be amazed how you can still change things for the better. As I move into a semi-retired phase in my life, I am determined to be more tolerant in personal relationships (sighs of relief from the family, I think—or is that disbelief?), but much less tolerant of bad service, lies, complacency and poor communication from those who are there to serve us but prefer to serve their own interests first.

8ᵗʰ January 2016

There are only three countries in the world with more gun-related deaths per year than the USA: Mexico, Colombia and Brazil. And in terms of the percentage of the population that own guns, America is firmly in the lead. 88.8% of US citizens own a gun. Most of the Americans that I know share my opinion that the availability of weaponry of all types in the US is scary and perplexing. But defenders of wholesale gun ownership in the community assert that they feel safer because they have a gun. The right to bear arms for them is as important as the right to vote or the right to free speech.

The second amendment to the constitution which was passed in 1791—'A well regulated militia being necessary to the security of a free state, the right of the people to keep and bear arms shall not be infringed'—was designed to protect a new nation by keeping its citizens ready for attack from without or within. For some reason beyond the comprehension of most of the democratic world, at least, a majority of US citizens feel their armed forces and law enforcement agencies are not enough and they need their own weapons.

But if those weapons do afford any protection at all, how is it that, according to the United Nations, 9146 people are killed by guns every year there?

The UK, with limited and strictly controlled gun ownership, averages 46. So exactly what protection did all those guns offer those thousands of victims of gun death in America?

President Obama has recognised this and wants to make a very minor adjustment to the enforcement of existing regulations in a valiant attempt to ensure that at least some of the mentally disturbed have less access to guns. But the power of the NRA and the Republican Party is such that even this aspiration is likely to be frustrated. How one begins to dislodge the gun-toting mindset from a large swathe of America is a dilemma. The repeated slaughter of school children and church congregations by the deranged or angry, who shouldn't be allowed a penknife, let alone a gun, doesn't dislodge the 'good old boy' mentality. Donald Trump's promise to undo whatever measures Obama is able to implement (if elected—and we can only hope that doesn't happen) says it all.

We are lucky to live here in the UK.

15th January 2016

The situation of the junior doctors who have been forced to strike over the government's proposed adjustment of their working hours and pay and conditions serves to highlight yet again what seems to be an inexorable dismantling of the healthcare system we have enjoyed until now.

It is little wonder that recruitment to the medical profession is proving troublesome, when potential medics see that a brand new MP (say) with no training whatsoever can earn more than three times the salary of a brand new doctor after seven years' or more hard study.

We have been blessed for so long with a world-beating health service, so it is doubly heart-breaking to see where it seems to be heading. The common perception is that if you are really very seriously ill, the NHS still delivers; let us fervently hope that that is and continues to be the case. But at every other level the evidence is overwhelming that there are mammoth cracks in the system. GPs are stretched to the limit and have to deal with the increasing frustration of patients who have been used to seeing them with a few days notice until recently and now have to wait weeks. Outpatient appointments are similarly extending to an ever-receding point in the future.

And the inefficiencies proliferate, it seems. A patient with Carpal Tunnel Syndrome was recently informed by his specialist that he needed an arm splint, which until recently he would have got from a cupboard and fitted for him on the spot. The patient now had to wait six weeks to visit 'Orthotics', where he was measured around wrist and palm (taking a minute at most) and told that when the appropriate splint arrived 'in a few weeks', he would be notified. Both specialist and orthotics nurse were unable to understand why this new system had been introduced to frustrate them and patients alike. Presumably, someone in an office somewhere needed to tick some health and safety or storage efficiency box.

And we can all protest until we become apoplectic and rushed off to a distant A & E, but nothing seems to change. Aren't the people who make the bureaucratic decisions robots who are sometimes unwell themselves? If they were, they wouldn't make our GPs spend more time doing admin work than with patients, surely. And they might just listen to the medical profession and patients' many and serious concerns.

22nd January 2016

I can remember large chunks of the Greek and Latin that I learned at school, but not the names of most of the boys who sat in the same class as me while I was learning it. I can't even remember the name of the boy whose sole mission in life was to reduce me to my constituent elements; fortunately, his life's work was curtailed when he emigrated at the age of 12. Lucky Australia. It is perhaps because I cannot remember as much as I would like that I have become fascinated with the past in my senior years.

My parents and older brother are deceased and therefore unavailable for interview, so I was intrigued by the possibilities of Friends Reunited when it surfaced on the Internet a decade or so ago. I entered all the details of my schools and homes and waited for contact from like-minded fellow pupils, students and neighbours. Many others clearly felt the same way and uploaded pictures and memories, but all were from later and more recent years, rather than the 50s, when I was at school or 60s, when I was a student.

The news of Friends Reunited's imminent demise prompted

me to log on again this week, and I found that those original seekers after fading memories were still the only ones who had availed themselves of the research possibilities of the site. I downloaded some photographs, as two of my primary schools in Rochdale no longer even exist on their original sites, and realised why the very good idea was apparently not so good after all. The very few people who want to revive memories of their childhood or schooldays are not sufficient to justify the existence of such a website, sadly.

I have been asked on a couple of occasions to consider writing an autobiography. Leaving aside my suspicion that the number of people wanting to read it is probably insufficient to justify writing it, my other problem is that I can't remember enough to make it interesting or even informative. My illustrious and charismatic predecessor in the role of Doctor Who gave me some very good advice once, when we were discussing his autobiography, and I expressed my reservations about following in his literary footsteps. 'Do as I did, old boy. Make up some good stories about dead people. They can't contradict you.' Anymore, alas, than he can now.

29th January 2016

The news that a supermarket giant has been systematically and as a matter of policy paying suppliers late comes as no surprise. When we are a day late, paying our bills, our taxes or our fines, the machine springs into action and the bailiffs descend within weeks. But it turns out that huge corporations with teams of lawyers and accountants, and therefore no excuse, can fail to pay suppliers for months, and in some cases years, simply to make their accounts look better and fool the stock market.

The fact that the farmer who supplied the produce has to borrow money to survive until the supermarket pays up doesn't play much part in their decision-making. If the farmer goes under, someone else will supply them. There are even stories about supermarket giants reducing vast orders by half the day before delivery, leaving the producer with tons of perishable goods that nobody wants.

If I don't pay my phone bill in time, then in very short order I am disconnected and my credit record will be adversely affected. To avoid errors, most of us set up automatic payment. If I can do that, I am sure that a floor full of accountants, lawyers and business directors could institute something similar for their suppliers. I am also sure that a government that wasn't in the pocket of multinational corporations could enable punitive measures, comparable in scale to those meted out to individuals who fail to pay their debts in a timely way.

We might want to try to avoid paying more than we think we should for things, but are prevented from substantial evasion of our responsibilities by law. We should demand comparable rigour from government in tackling the monoliths of supermarkets and powerful monopolies. In my own employment area, the theatre, there are large theatre chains whose policy of paying touring producers three months in arrears has caused huge financial problems to our employers, leaving many of them unwilling or unable to tour. Weekly costs of touring a play or musical are substantial, and few can carry the costs of twelve weeks of shows without getting any of the box office.

Goliath has been having his own way for far too long, and all the Davids out there have been powerless to do anything about it. We just need a weapon. We need protection from corporate greed, please, Mr Cameron. Can you do something about it?

5th February 2016

A memory I share with millions is laughing out loud while listening to Terry Wogan on Radio 2. I survived many hours of the slow crawl down the A40 into London back in the 80s in part because he made it so enjoyable to be listening to the radio. Glancing to drivers in adjacent lanes, you would know that they too were infected by his self-deprecating and style of irreverence and gentle wit. Why else would they be laughing at the same time as you while sitting in a traffic jam? So thank you, Sir Terry, for all those hours of peerless broadcasting joy.

I was fortunate enough to meet him several times. In 1984 I was a guest on his TV show and, like many before and after me, I succumbed to the twinkle, and while I suspected that he didn't know much about me or *Doctor Who*, this was amply compensated for by his charm, warmth and evident goodwill to all men. I am sure if he was a boss, he could have sacked you and you'd leave thinking he'd done you a favour. I appeared a few times on *Children in Need* in the 80s too, and was always astonished by his ability to sail smoothly(ish) through the hours of live broadcast when many, even experienced, broadcasters would have cracked under the pressure.

The last time I met him was when we were both guests of *The One Show* for the last ever live broadcast from Television Centre in White City. It was a sombre occasion for many of us, including Sir Terry, who shared my sadness and perplexity that this wonderful and iconic centre of decades of excellence and talent should be sacrificed in the name of political correctness to appease a predatory government by expanding into the regions.

We agreed ruefully that decades from now someone will have the brilliant new idea of bringing all the studios to a central location in London.

It must have been quite a burden to carry, being the person that everybody believed was their friend and wanted to spend time with. He appeared to carry the responsibility effortlessly when on show and at work, but it is clear that his family must have been the rock that enabled him to do that. If we all miss him so much, we can only imagine how they must be feeling.

12th February 2016

For over ten years I was a member and latterly Chairman of a CCTV scrutiny panel in Wycombe. Our remit was to ensure it was efficient and complied with all relevant legislation. At least I can assure the public that the dozen-strong panel never failed to be impressed with the commitment and scrupulousness of the control room operators. Their professionalism and attention to detail was always commendable, as was their knowledge of the area. The state of the art system, which cost around £200,000 in 2010, was manned 24/7 and the cameras were constantly monitored, when the Lay Panel voluntarily disbanded last year. The reason we disbanded ties in with the recent concerns expressed by Councillor Brian Pearce last week.

In addition to our scrutiny brief, the Panel was charged with advising Wycombe District Council on how to use CCTV more 'efficiently and effectively'. To enable this, there was a commitment to keep us informed of matters that were not legally confidential (like certain police operations). We were, however, excluded from even the initial consultations on the possibility of relocating the control room operation to other centres in Bucks, and began to realise that, in some respects at least, we were a box-ticking exercise rather than a serious advisory body. I, as Chairman, received a polite acknowledgement of our unanimous decision to disband, expressing 'disappointment', but not addressing any of our strong concerns. Members who had served a decade and more received no individual thanks or acknowledgment.

The reluctance to include us in the process may well have been because the officers were well aware that our lengthy experience had convinced us that Wycombe should be monitored in and by Wycombe, with the added persuasive factor that ours was a proven, recently installed system and was run by a more directly accountable body—a local council. 'Why consult a group that you already know is convinced that watching Wycombe from Slough, Aylesbury or Milton Keynes is a retrograde step?' Tens of thousands have been spent already over four years 'consulting' on the future of our locally run CCTV system, with no discernible progress—money which would have kept the control room running smoothly for years.

It is only six years since councillors stood proudly in the new control room. I hope Councillor Pearce is not the only one who still can see its potential future importance.

19th February 2016

When I wrote last week expressing concern about the future of Wycombe's hitherto excellent CCTV monitoring service, I did not realise how soon I would be proved right. The headline on last week's front page, 'Counting the Cost', referred to the £160,000 lost by the town car parks as a result of theft and the repairs required as a result of those 49 attacks on the newly-installed payment machines. It is manifestly regrettable that the monitored PTZ (pan, tilt and zoom) cameras, which used to be in our car parks to ensure driver and vehicle safety, were removed as part of the cost-cutting exercise last spring.

The cameras that remain are all fixed and, as I recall, not monitored actively. Given the isolated and lonely nature of our car parks, especially at night, I am very surprised that these cuts seemed a good idea to someone. The problem, as always with CCTV, is that there is a tendency at administrative level to see lack of crime as a reason to remove the cameras, rather than a very clear demonstration that they are doing their job of deterring, which is, of course, in a box-ticking bureaucratic environment, impossible to quantify in cash terms. Because there is a lot of disinformation and unnecessary suspicion about Big Brother watching us, CCTV is a difficult service to sell.

The Lay Panel which I chaired for several years was constantly advising the Council to trumpet the many successes and advantages of a well-run and effective monitoring system that really does save lives and really does deter crime. Some panellists joined as sceptics, fearing the potential for abuse, and ended up committed proponents of the benefits to a law-abiding community.

We were unhappy about the cessation of active monitoring in the car parks. Our fears appear to have been proved right. Restore the cameras now, and make people feel safe using the car parks at all times of day and enable law enforcement to be on the spot immediately if there are further attacks on Council equipment.

We are paying the price.

When I go to see the half-term Youth Project—*Into The*

Woods—at the Town Hall next week (if I can get a ticket!), I want to feel safe as I return to my car along with the families and friends of the talented young folk in the show.

26th February 2016

'Choice' seems such a beguiling word. It brings with it messages of freedom and opportunity. It carries undertones of a society where the individual is empowered to see how things are and make decisions based on clear and readily available information. We used to live in a simpler world with fewer choices. A world in which you got your gas, your electricity, your water, your television and radio from one place that was easy to access.

Then it was perceived that monopolies were bad things; that lack of healthy competition meant that the consumer might be overcharged by profiteering and uncompetitive industries. Trundle in the great god—choice. Break up all those providers, make them compete for our business and we will get better value for our money, won't we? And if the information we received enabled all of us to see where the best value truly lay, that would undoubtedly be true. But those fragmented industries are charged with making profits for their shareholders, rather than saving the customer money, so enter the flimflam men, the three-card tricksters who shuffle the facts around so quickly and so impenetrably that finding good value that lasts for more than a few months would defeat everyone except radio and TV moneyman Martin Lewis, who has devoted his life to panning for monetary gold in the torrents of misinformation that engulf us today.

But I don't want to have to spend hours on comparison websites every time I renew any insurance policy, or get a new phone, or pay for my energy supply. But when the difference can be measured in thousands over a year, those who are able to do so sigh heavily and embark on the great journey into the labyrinth of obfuscation and despair to try and circumvent their traps, snares and delusions. I am about to change my electricity supplier again, because the introductory offer has lapsed and the charges have rocketed. I suppose they hope that the complexity of the task will result in a large proportion giving up and staying put.

I suspect the same fear of brain-fade will result in millions looking at the whole Europe In or Out dilemma in a similar way, and allow the status quo to endure rather than immerse themselves in the barrage of information and misinformation we will have to endure between now and June.

18th March 2016

With all its faults, our political system in the UK seems positively sensible and straightforward when compared to the five ring circus that grinds out the parties' nominees for the Presidency of the USA every four years.

And then when he or she is finally elected, the Senate and Congress of the day seem to decide whether they like the cut of their jib and will pay any attention whatsoever to their policies.

At least our system, whereby the party with the most votes chooses its leader (well, sort of), results in an administration that can function and get stuff done.

I am in Baltimore for a few days, and to while away the time waiting for my luggage to join me, have been following the inexorable march of Donald Trump towards securing the Republican nomination, as it now seems inevitable that he will.

The thought that this ludicrously-coiffed, intemperate billionaire, with his xenophobic and bar room rhetoric, could conceivably become the leader of the most powerful nation on Earth invites one to come up with a domestic comparison. But it is impossible.

There is no one quite so bizarrely inappropriate in this country that might be used to highlight the awfulness of the prospect. I suppose if Bernard Manning were still with us, he might have been a candidate for worst idea for Prime Minister, but he at least was occasionally funny.

It is perplexing and alarming that there are sufficient

citizens in the USA who think Trump is a good idea to encourage him to rabble-rouse so vigorously. Having said that, his competition frankly seems to be only slightly less militaristic and intolerant. They just use more palatable language. They all seem to have God on their side, they all want to have more guns, more soldiers and their attitude to immigrants is somewhat strange in a country where every other surname betrays ancestries well removed from the shores of the Potomac.

But whatever you may think about Cameron or Blair or any of their predecessors, I cannot imagine them using the words 'bimbo', 'dog' or 'fat pig' to describe women, or suggesting that supporters beat up hecklers. We really are two nations divided by a common language sometimes.

25th March 2016

I hadn't fully realised until Gareth Ainsworth, Wycombe Wanderers' manager, brought the subject up this week that referees in all four divisions of the football league were not professional. It appears that only the Premier League has access to full-time professional referees and that the other three divisions are provided with officials who, during the week, are employed in other jobs.

It certainly would be entirely logical, when the players and clubs are professional and football is their living, that those who can have such a profound influence on their career and living should be similarly able to concentrate on what they are doing, rather than turn up after a hard week selling insurance or servicing cars.

Being professional is no guarantee of getting it right, and it is quite surprising, given the sums of money generated by our national sport, that the advantages that technology can offer have been so slowly deployed.

It might be costly, but after that initial hit providing the equipment and the necessary training, the potential for those relegation/promotion injustices could be removed forever, and players crowding round a referee to influence him to send someone off would be forever pointless.

I do wish there could be some way of stopping forever the aggressive barracking of referees. I have always been an advocate of the sin bin as a means of benefiting the aggrieved team at the time, rather than whoever plays the offending team the following week. If a player crowds a referee and says the things we can all lip-read so clearly to them, send them to the bench for 15 minutes. Managers will soon give them the hairdryer treatment if that happens on a regular basis.

The quality of football and behaviour on the pitch could be greatly improved if the referees were brave enough for one season to consistently deal firmly with behaviour that diminishes the great game.

And if the fans are not seeing that behaviour regularly on the pitch, then maybe the undesirable elements of fan language and behaviour might be lessened, enabling parents to bring their young children to matches, confident that what they will see is a game being played fairly with respect for the officials.

In turn, those young people will not be emulating their 'heroes' behaviour when they play football themselves, nor will they have to deal with out of control parents on the touchline.

1ˢᵗ April 2016

I have always been a pushover for gadgets and innovative technology. As a child, for instance, I was fascinated by magnets that behaved in a way that contradicted all the accepted rules of scientific knowledge. When the ability to record television programmes came along, I was one of the first people I knew who simply had to have a VCR—remember them? Thankfully, I didn't go down the Betamax route at a time when my wiser technophile friends were bigging that up as the only way to go. Now, however, I have boxes of VHS recordings, mainly of children's shows that were popular when my daughters were young, that I cannot bear to dispose of the only sensible way—the rubbish tip.

Then—mobile phones. I have fond memories of my first half-brick with a preposterous aerial. They all diminished in size and have now started to slowly get bigger again, though I doubt they will ever go the distance back to the first, less appropriately named 'mobiles'.

I acknowledge that it is a boy thing. Mobile phones, tablets, computers and tech are rarely subjects for discussion with my daughters, but when their boyfriends visit there is no stopping us. I have recently, like a big kid, been showing off my latest acquisition: virtual reality goggles. Just pop your mobile phone into them, armed with the appropriate app, and off you go wandering round the haunted house or riding a big dipper.

Too long with a screen millimetres from your eyes and without awareness of the real environment you are in can only be ultimately fraught with danger for health and security, and they will, I suspect, be a short-term fad, like the Tamagotchi digital pets of the 1990s (and I remember having to feed one of those wretched things regularly for my daughter while she was at school).

The latest fad is sleep-replacement headset/goggles. We all need sleep, but research has established that the benefits of a good night's sleep can be neurologically mimicked by stimulated light and benign radiation through the eyes, so that twenty minutes of targeted emissions can stimulate the areas of the brain that is refreshed by REM neural activity in a normal seven-hour sleep. Handy for the Trumps and Thatchers of this world. But I like my sleep too much.

As they say in France, it is the day of the fish!

8th April 2016

Usually when I am in Wycombe town centre, I am on a mission of some kind, with a schedule to follow. I am not one for aimless wandering, so like to have my route planned so as to minimise wasting precious time. I believe that I am not unusual among men in that respect. Visiting the shops, bank, barber, etc. are not activities to dwell on, but to be transacted swiftly with the minimum of fuss. So this week I found myself in Wycombe with more time than usual to spare, because I had to wait for the mobile phone repairman to put a new screen on my daughter's dropped phone, and I ran out of things that needed to be done in the hour I was told it would take. This is how I came to be ambling around our town centre, getting more than a little depressed, as I realised just how much the town centre experience has changed over the four decades that I have lived in the area. The High Street is a forlorn, depopulated wasteland compared to its former busy self. So many shops closed, or (dare I say it) replaced by decidedly downmarket variants of what was there before.

There was a time when cheap and cheerful Woolies was as downmarket as it got. But now that chain store of my childhood seems like Selfridges by comparison. Take away the fast food outlets, charity shops, hairdressers, opticians, banks and building societies, and you are left with WHSmith and shops that sell stuff for a pound. Even good old reliable Greggs is having a refit or closed; I am not sure which.

The Chiltern Centre is similarly unexciting and has lost its Post Office. So the Eden Centre is the only 'go-to' shopping area. All of which would be fine, if the High Street didn't seem so unloved and a natural habitat for those who choose to drink beer and cider in the street and camp out in the Little Market House, making the rest of us scurry past and avoid eye contact.

I only hope that the new town centre plan approved this week does more than take traffic away from the High Street and flyover, but serves to contribute to restoring the undoubted former architectural and cultural appeal of our town centre. Wycombe deserves it.

15ᵗʰ April 2016

As a self-confessed technophile, my default position is to embrace the new. I had noticed that seasoned travellers now seem to favour the mobile phone version of the boarding card when flying, so I have joined them. I couldn't bear to be left behind, and after all it is more ecologically sound, surely, to dispense with all that paper and ink. On only my second foray into modern travel, however, I hit a glitch. The first leg of my flight to Maine was delayed, so instead of having nearly five hours to negotiate the terminals at Philadelphia, I ended up with around 45 minutes, tight but not impossible. It was 8.15-ish pm., USA time. My luggage had to be collected and then checked on to Bangor Maine. Immigration and baggage checking was a matter of ten minutes, remarkably. The connection was doable. Then I met Ms Implacable on security outbound. I presented my phone, with its facsimile of a boarding card bearing a square data matrix barcode. 'We can't read a BA barcode; you need to get a paper one,' she said. I explained I had only minutes, even seconds, to make my connection, and surely she could read that the boarding pass was appropriate for the flight? She repeated her demand, and already there was an edge of 'If you try to get past me again without a physical boarding card, I will get to use my considerable array of weaponry under this desk.' Where was the check-in desk? Two floors down, other end of the concourse. There was no one there. My plane left without me.

I spent twenty minutes arguing with the reps of American Airlines, who were the lucky providers of my next flight, about where I could spend the next twelve hours, hoping to get on the next (currently full) flight. The inbound flight, though a BA one, had been booked via American, and I had to remind them of their much vaunted One World partnership before I was eventually given a voucher for a distant one-star hotel that was badly in need of a clean.

So my desire to join the 21st Century travel vanguard has waned. The barcode readability in the USA can't have just been discovered that day, so why was I given the option of printing it online? Be warned. Stay simple and ecologically unsound.

22nd April 2016

Each time I travel up to London, I say 'Never again.' I'm not sure whether I forget how awful it can be, or think that somehow this time it will be better. Last week was no exception to the increasing curve of awfulness. I was invited to the press night of *Guys and Dolls*. My daughter insisted that I should go and take her with me. Because I never learn, I decided to drive, blithely reassuring my daughter that of course I would find somewhere to park. And indeed I did, about half a mile from the Phoenix Theatre in Charing Cross Road at a cost of £28 for the evening. Gulp.

The show was wonderful, despite the fact that my seat, in common with most theatre seats, seemed to have been made for a Victorian person of small stature without legs. If you think coach class on transatlantic flights is cramped, try the stalls of a West End Theatre. Just as we reached the gold-plated car park, my daughter realised that she must have left her mobile phone in the theatre. I decided to drive past so she could run in and check if it had been found. Mistake number one. It took forty minutes to drive half a mile in Soho at 10.30 p.m. Roadworks at Tottenham Court Road and thousands of people who didn't have beds to go to. We got there. She ran in to discover it hadn't been found. I then put my phone down on the spring-loaded cover of a storage place behind the gear lever of my car. The cover sprung up and projected my slim phone down the narrowest of gaps behind it into the depths of the fascia. Two phones gone in less than an hour, quite an achievement. After we had glumly negotiated our way out of the gridlocked theatre district and were plodding homeward, I remembered that my phone was attached by Bluetooth to my car radio. I tried ringing her phone, and to our surprise it was answered by the surprised theatre fireman who had just found it. We got home at 1a.m. The next day, my local garage took my dashboard fascia off and delved into the depths to retrieve my phone. I would rather drive on the M25 than in the centre of London. And I suppose that is what 'they' want too.

29th April 2016

For some reason, I was not expecting the celebration of the 400th anniversary of Shakespeare's death to be as magnificently celebrated on the BBC as it was, with the live show from the Royal Shakespeare Theatre in Stratford. Sometimes, getting the greatest and most talented performers together to rehearse, for instance, can be problematical. But on this occasion we were treated to some wonderful and inventive interpretations of the work of that remarkable man, produced for aristocracy and peasant folk alike four centuries ago. And in the right hands, his words and creations can still captivate a modern audience and inspire across the board.

Anyway, if you too are keen on good music, drama, art, literature, crafts, walks, talks or local history, then over the next month in Wycombe you will be spoilt for choice as the 52nd annual Wycombe Arts Festival unrolls its ambitious and eclectic programme. There is unarguably something for everybody.

As an aficionado of brass bands (my northern roots showing there), I was sorry that I was unable to attend the Great Marlow Bandfest last Saturday in Marlow Parish Church, but there are many other musical offerings between now and the end of May that present the talents of our local young (and not so young) musicians, as well as professional musicians from home and overseas. But in some cases, choices may have to be made. If you wish to hear our own consistently excellent orchestra, Wycombe Sinfonia, playing the Mendelssohn Violin Concerto in the Parish Church in Wycombe, you'll have to miss out on seeing Les Baladins de Marly-le Roi perform Noel Coward's very English play, *Hay Fever*, in French, in Bourne End!

I certainly plan to go to one of the lunchtime concerts at Marlow Parish Church, where there are several opportunities to hear the resonant and sublime tones of their splendid church organ. There are also Wednesday lunchtime recitals at the Union Baptist Church in Easton Street for those of you who, like me, enjoy the luxury of freedom in the daytime— although they are all timed to fit in with the normal time allotted by most employers for lunch, starting at 1.10.

Check online at http://www.wycombeartsfestival.org/ where you can download a programme or pick one up at many local outlets. Tickets for events can be acquired at any of our local information centres or libraries. I promise you'll find something irresistible.

6th May 2016

This week we voted (or didn't) for the 41 police commissioners who sit above our police forces in England and Wales and control their budgets, which have a combined total of around eight billion pounds. They also set the policing objectives for their area, having the power to hire and fire chief constables. In the words of the Association of Police and Crime Commissioners (membership 41, presumably?), they are 'responsible for the totality of policing'. That is quite a responsibility.

It seems a shame that a post of such crucial importance, at a time when policing is under such scrutiny and some forces are being held to account for historical shortcomings, has attracted so little interest in the media and will probably have attracted even less interest at the ballot box on Thursday. The numbers voting this year are unknown at the time of writing this, but at the last election in November 2012, less than 17% of eligible voters thought it worth a stroll to their local polling station to have a say in how their police forces are run. And whilst the day to day activities of the police are controlled, quite rightly, by the Chief Constables, the parameters within which they can operate are laid down by the elected Police Commissioners.

I also wish that this particular electoral process was not yet again decided along party political lines. Our four candidates in the Thames Valley were all attached to political parties, when if there were ever an electable appointment that could benefit from being filled by an independent candidate with appropriate qualifications and work experience without having to toe a party political line in order to carry out the job, surely this it. Ian Johnston, a former policeman (who won in Gwent in 2012 by promising to 'Keep Politics out of Policing'), believed it was impossible to do the job if you don't know anything about policing.

It is debatable whether the new, much more expensive system is an improvement on the old Police Authorities, which may have had no mandate but were made up of more than one person and could therefore have less opportunity to impose eccentric policies. A Police Commissioner appoints all his own staff, including his deputy, and to some extent is one of the most powerful individual appointments in the country, arguably on a par with London's Mayor.

13th May 2016

There are many lessons to be learned from the decades of deceit and denial that followed the tragedy of the deaths at Hillsborough in 1989, but the biggest may be that corruption is potentially endemic in every power structure, from Nairobi to Colombia via Sheffield and FIFA—check your history books and prove me wrong, if you can. For that reason, we should continue to name and shame and vilify, even if there may be limited opportunity now for punishment of those who so cruelly slandered the dead to save their own skins.

Nowhere can be guaranteed to remain honest and decent unless every level within every organisation feels free to tell the truth and question those above them without fear of dismissal or reprisals. When, at the highest level, there is pressure downwards to save face, to preserve a fragile status quo, to avoid Pandora's box opening up again and letting Hope escape as well as everything else, then it is a battle against the odds to make things right again.

The fact that all those family members and their supporters from Liverpool contrived to remain strong after innumerable knock-backs is welcome evidence that David can still topple the institutional Goliaths that try to corral us into subservience. The perpetrators may not all be bad people, the ones that try to cover up the unpalatable truths, but that in many ways makes it worse. Weak, fearful, self-protecting people who don't want to upset the owners of national newspapers who had bought into and promulgated the lies and excuses of the incompetent; a blinkered 10 Downing Street that had benefited from the South Yorkshire Police's assistance in breaking the miners' resistance, so were happy to characterise the dead as 'tanked-up yobbos'—the complicity in the lying and covering-up spread throughout the ranks of the powerful, and yet the truth has finally emerged, which is the one shining light to give us hope.

The British people will still stand up for justice. This is why I continue to tell my family to stand up against the unreasonable, the unkind and the plain wrong. They have always known that if they don't, I will. Bullies, cheats, the incompetent and liars can only triumph if we let them. However hard, it is better to blow that whistle until someone pays attention than allow them to crush our spirits and bear false witness.

20th May 2016

Very few things that we used to take for granted are easy today. The great god 'choice' throws up a whole host of wrong paths to go down, and traps for the unwary. A whole-page advert in a popular daily paper induced me to buy five bags of miracle grass seed that would produce 'visible results in 6-7 days'. Well, 21 days after seeding, the only visible result is the seeds lying there on the bare surface, leering at me indolently. Telephoning the marketing company elicits a sympathetic 'Oh dear—I'll get them to call you back about that.' Three times now, and the only vegetation on show is tumbleweed.

Then there's the new, all-singing, all-everything TV system that will revolutionise my life. Being a sucker for new technology—sigh, four weeks in and we still have fewer TVs working at Baker Towers than we had with the old system. Three different technicians have tried and fled, promising imminent remedies. More tumbleweed.

Replacements for our south-facing, wooden cottage

windows? Less than a year it took for them to peel and crack. Apparently, the subcontractors weren't up to snuff a year ago. I am slowly beginning to realise that individual local craftsmen is the only way to go—the local builder who recently turned our decrepit conservatory into a sunny palace ticked every box and 'snagged' quickly and completely. The bigger the company, the less chance you have to nail them down and get value or be able to contact someone who can really sort your problem out, as you gradually move up the levels of (in) competence.

The timing of the Eurovision Song Contest—a month ahead of the Great Escape Vote—has served for many to underline how the UK is perceived in Europe. It cannot be denied any longer that voting is in no way related to the tunefulness or otherwise of the songs, but the cultural and emotional connection between voter and country. If my choice ever wins, it is because it comes from a country that its neighbours love. This year, The Netherlands and Poland floated my boat, not the depressing Russia-bashing ditty from the Ukraine.

But what do I know? The only UK song I ever really loved, last year's electro-swing 20s-type number, garnered 5 votes from Ireland, Malta and San Marino. The abbreviation for the European Song Contest is ESC.

Brexit, anyone?

27th May 2016

In the same week that a petition bearing more than 10,000 signatures was presented to the Chancellor of the Exchequer, asking that 'Buckinghamshire not only receives the national average in funds, but also receives enough public funding so that key services are restored to Wycombe Hospital,' we learn that our local hospital may have its provision reduced even further. Apparently, a ward that cares for the frail elderly is next on the hit list. The aim, apparently, is to enable them to recover in the 'safety and comfort' of their own home. A worthy aim, if a sufficiently high level of care can be guaranteed, but one has awful memories of the care in the community available to those released into a far from caring or prepared community when mental hospitals closed in the wake of of the Mental Health Acts of 1983 and 1990.

It is all about money. But Wycombe is a big enough town to justify an Accident and Emergency Unit, despite what our own MP says. Steve Baker (no relation) insists that the 'return of an old-style A&E would take medical care backwards'. Well, maybe we want a new style A & E department, Mr Baker. We are not asking for a Victorian medical service, and understand that some emergency care can require larger centralised units, but something more sophisticated that the understaffed minor injuries unit and the childbirth facilities currently available in Wycombe is not a big ask. Mr Baker went on to say that 'more people would die in such a unit and that is why it's not going to happen.' With the greatest respect to our serving MP, it is somewhat disingenuous to suggest that anyone is asking for that kind of provision. What we are asking for is a better service than we currently have, and indeed than we had ten years ago when it was closed. It may be that some patients still have to make that horrid, slow journey to Stoke Mandeville, which also might lead to people dying, but let us repeatedly tell our political masters (for that is how they behave, despite pretending to be our servants) that we want better for our children, our mothers and our old people, and if that means a couple of pence extra tax, then so be it. If it is about money, then let's use those millions Mr Baker will save us by leaving the EU.

Friday 4th June 2016

I made the mistake of driving to London again this week. I was working in Kensal Green, where parking is by tickets issued by meters at the roadside, controlled by the Royal Borough of Kensington and Chelsea. I had come armed with a bag of pound coins. I started to feed them into the machine adjacent to my car, and having put three pounds in, I realised that it hadn't registered on the screen, so I pressed the button to eject the coins. Several times. I tapped the machine. I smacked the machine. I jiggled it, pressed the button again several more times and decided, somewhat irritated, to write the loss off and find another machine. I crossed the road, put £7.80 into that machine, printed the ticket, placed it on the dashboard under the windscreen and went to work. In the afternoon I returned, put the ticket for that day and the previous day in my bag (to claim the VAT back) and, as I was driving back to leafy Buckinghamshire, noticed something fluttering under my nearside windscreen wiper. I stopped. It was a Penalty Notice for £80 (£40 if I paid straight away) for parking without clearly displaying a valid ticket. Without having an illuminated arrow pointing at the blasted thing, I am not sure what else I could have done. So I am now going to have to join an undoubtedly long queue of motorists, dancing the ritual fandango of producing my valid ticket and convincing them of my probity. But whereas I was minded to overlook the purloined three pounds from the first dilapidated, graffiti-bearing roadside bandit, I am now going to demand that back as well. In fact, if they are obdurate, and I fully expect a version of 'the computer says no' to assail me when I write enclosing my evidence, then I shall certainly go to court to defend this one and counterclaim for my three pounds. Time consuming? Undoubtedly, and I would have written it off had I not felt so aggrieved about the injustice of fining me for something I haven't done.

I have paid parking fines in the past when I have overstayed my welcome by mere minutes, on the basis that I have no actual grounds for contesting them; this time I am digging in.

Wish me luck. I suspect that I will need it.

11th June 2016

I am not sure whether our membership of the EU has impacted either way on our access to healthcare. Brexiteers would have it that GPs were more accessible before we joined the EU. Pro-Europeans would try to convince us that without our membership of the European juggernaut, we would have even worse health provision than we have now. All I know is that my GPs' surgery will no longer allow me to make an appointment for a future date online or on the phone.

Appointments are only available on the day, by phoning the surgery at 8 a.m. And we all know that the likelihood of getting through as the second hand sweeps past the number 12 at 8 a.m. is less than the likelihood of England beating Germany on penalties. Yes, it could happen, but don't bet your pension on it. Bear in mind that in order to visit the doctor, many people would have to book a day off work. Imagine you had done that, and the phone call lottery for you to make your non-urgent appointment failed to result in success.

The alternative is to do what someone I know, whose doctors have a similar restriction, recently did. Turn up at the surgery at 8 a.m. and pre-empt the phone. Seven or eight people got there ahead of her, and she only just succeeded. I don't think that this is what Aneurin Bevan had in mind, especially as only those physically capable of getting themselves on the doctors' doorsteps at 8 a.m. stand a fighting chance of seeing a doctor. Well, of course they don't want the halt, the lame and the unfit cluttering up the waiting room, do they? Makes the place look untidy.

And then there is the matter of compliance with nonsensical regulations designed not to help us but to avoid litigation. When I visited my consultant, until recently I would pop my appointment letter in a box outside his door. Now the boxes have gone from Wycombe outpatients department and a free for all has ensued. Why? 'Data protection concerns', apparently.

The letter contains my name and the time of my appointment. Any would-be data purloiner can see me sitting there waiting, and if they can tell the time will have a pretty good idea about when my appointment is. Who on earth could derive a benefit from peeping at the letters in full view of a queue of bored people?

I despair.

18th June 2016

As I totter towards senility, the list of things that I am prepared to do myself is dwindling. Some activities I must confess to being relieved to relinquish. Believe it or not (and I struggle now to believe it) I used to happily do all painting and decorating, putting up shelves, electrical wiring and all things to do with nails, screws, brackets, hinges and wires. As some of those things got more technical and/or arduous and my income allowed it, I boosted the local economy by hiring professionals. The majority did better jobs than I would have done. Some were as rubbish as me, but that's another story. In the garden, I used to mow, cut hedges and tidy up, leaving the creative stuff to the female members of my family. In other words, everybody else.

My creaking and ample frame now makes hedges and their maintenance a task too far and fraught with osteopath-employing potential. Tidying up involves too much bending. Ouch. So my dear old English-made ride-on mower remains my sole active connection with the Baker Towers wild outdoors. This week I mowed our grass within a centimetre of its life. We like to call it grass. Horticulturalists might argue that the majority of what I mow is vegetation of an entirely different name. But mowed, it looks fine. I then drove in behind the bushes to my tipping point (without any help from Ben Shepherd). I backed in, and the wheels spun on the rotted grass underneath, and after many minutes of trying to extricate the machine I had to concede defeat; especially when my wife and brother-in-law's added muscle power failed to shift the recalcitrant brute. 'No problem,' I reassured them. 'I'll tow it out with the car.'

Clearly, my mechanical engineering skills were not sufficiently honed at school. I tied a rope to the front of the mower and the tow bar and gently pulled it out. I couldn't see behind me, so failed to see that what I was in fact doing was turning the mower over and spinning it onto its side into bushes and nettles. Stout-hearted local builder friends effortlessly restored it to its wheels the following day, and I have bowed to necessity. I shall mow, but I will not tow. Well, not without completing a risk assessment. I never thought I'd say that!

25th June 2016

And one of the least edifying few weeks in modern British political history is finally over. We now await learning the decision of the British public. How anyone could possibly arrive at a fully informed and dispassionate decision based on the mass of contradictory and bizarre non-information available defeats me and I suspect thousands of other citizens. Each side, fortified by the almost messianic certainty that it is right, has produced figures, projections and doom-laden predictions that have been carefully massaged to support their case rather than cast any light on the debate. This was completely predictable, of course, but decidedly unhelpful. It is the gut feeling of the majority of voters, unmoved by the passion, rabble-rousing, lying, threats and cajoling that will have either kick-started a tortuous process of disengagement or maintained (rather than cemented) a less convincing status quo. Either result, I predict, will leave us less united, less optimistic and less secure as a nation. And either way we will not be detecting much in the way of improvement in our national health provision, our funding for education or the employment prospects for the next generation.

Maybe most of us didn't expect the process to be as frankly unpleasant as it has been. When the old party divide is working in a general election, the ritual dances and hustings sabre-rattling are more familiar and therefore less unsettling. This referendum has turned our expectations for political debate on their head and spun them through alternative dimensions.

The question has divided parties, families and friends more comprehensively than a mere general election or a family whose members support opposing football teams. And the spokespersons for both camps and their supporters have indulged in far more character assassination and sheer unpleasantness than I have ever witnessed in public life before. There are many figures on both sides of the divide whom I will never view the same way again, so tainted are they, for me, by the way they have conducted themselves. And to be fair, there are also, on both sides, unexpected figures who have behaved with dignity when their previous reputations might have suggested otherwise.

I just wish that their pluses, rather than the minuses, of their adversaries had been at the forefront of all the arguments. We would have had more of a chance to arrive at a reasoned decision.

1st July 2016

One of the biggest tensions in modern life—well, my modern life anyway—is achieving some sort of balance between the effects of nostalgia and the demands of available space in the home. My daughter is home from university for the summer and trying to assimilate the contents of her student flat in London into her bedroom for the next few months. Clearing out her cupboard, she found some old newspapers and handed them to me for recycling. As I was doing so, I noticed that they were quite old—in fact, they were the newspapers I bought on the day she was born, thinking that that might be a nice thing for her to have one day, forgetting perhaps that you have to wait until your late middle-age for nostalgia to start nibbling at your resolve to keep a tidy home. I have been working intermittently on tracing my ancestors, so have learnt to value such windows into the past. To be fair, my daughter had not noticed the date, and of course is now happy for me to retain them, pending her desire to claim them back one day. Headlines don't change much, by the way. 'Bishop had £2M, claims Mistress', 'The Bugging of Britain', and 'Police face sack for incompetence' were the three from her natal day.

My late mother was a clutter-phobe, and prone to discard our treasured possessions if she thought we wouldn't notice. Some years after leaving home, I asked about my childhood teddy bear, having suddenly remembered my former best friend (shades of Winnie-the-Pooh and Christopher Robin, there). She informed me with some surprise and a little irritation, as I recall, that she had assumed I didn't want him, as I had left him behind and given him to charity. I can still reproduce the look and feel of his much-loved worn fur in my imaginings, and much though I loved my mother, it did cast a brief shadow over our relationship, I must confess.

Perhaps as a result, I am loath to discard anything that might sit in the memory box of life. School reports, exercise books, games, toys, photographs, general 'stuff' that reminds me of my childhood jostle for space at Baker Towers and try the patience of my long suffering wife, who is thankfully aware of the Great Teddy Bear Tragedy and has thus far resisted her urge to cull.

15th July 2016

Any student of democracy in action examining British politics for the first time might well be more than a little perplexed by its contortions over the last few weeks. We have had a referendum; it had been promised by the incoming Conservative government. There was a demonstrable public will to have the opportunity to vote on our membership of the European Union, and David Cameron's government duly delivered what the public had asked for. He, of course, hoped that the result would go the other way and campaigned to remain, but I am at a loss to understand why the person we elected to lead our country failed to accept the decision of the referendum he enabled and declined to lead us through the turbulent waters of Brexit. His reasons for ducking out of that responsibility have never been fully explained. So who has replaced him? A member of his cabinet who absolutely agreed with everything he did and similarly campaigned to remain a member of the European Union.

Logic would have suggested that someone who believed in the impending amputation might make a better fist of managing it, if the originator of the referendum exited unexpectedly stage right. But no, a like-for-like replacement (gender aside) has been preferred by the Conservative members of Parliament.

Conversely, the leader of the main opposition party has arrived in his position of power by a vote of party members outside Parliament, and allegedly has little or no support within the parliamentary party. He clearly therefore cannot lead them in any meaningful way, but refuses to make way for someone who might be able to, although his tenacity unarguably renders his party unelectable.

Speaking locally, our Wycombe MP was a prominent member of the Brexit faction within the Conservative party. Although the constituency boundaries are slightly different, his constituents did not agree with his passionate commitment to Brexit. Many MPs will have voted differently to the majority of their constituents, and it remains to be seen whether in 2020 the constituency selection committees will remember that. It is rare, of course, once an MP is elected, for there to be an opportunity to compare their votes 'in action', as it were, with the will of the citizens they serve. But it does highlight an interesting point of principle. We now wait to see how the shenanigans of the Shakespearean co-conspirator Brexiteers pan out for them career-wise.

22nd July 2016

In the late 80s I met a remarkable couple. We were accepting cheques for our respective charities. I was Chairman of FSID, the cot death charity, and they ran a Wildlife Hospital from their estate house in Aylesbury. They were Sue and Les Stocker, and we hit it off immediately. I visited them and was astonished to find that their garden was clearly much bigger on the inside, given the amount of sheds, pens and runs they had crammed in to further their mission to save and rehabilitate injured and sick wildlife. The charity they founded expanded to be the Aylesbury Wildlife Hospital, better known as Tiggywinkles, in honour of hundreds of hedgehogs the trust has saved and treated. Since then, I have been privileged to support their work and see Les evolve from being an accountant who couldn't understand why a vet couldn't help an injured hedgehog in 1978, so cared for it himself. He then set about trying to ensure that wildlife had the same survival chance as our domestic animals. Thirty-some years later, his name is celebrated worldwide.

He has an MBE for services to wildlife and in 2002 was made an honorary associate of the Royal College of Veterinary Surgeons—an extraordinary acknowledgement by the veterinary profession of the countless techniques and procedures that Les discovered, invented and improvised over tens of years to achieve his passion of helping our wildlife to survive in a world that we humans make increasingly hostile for them. And Les was a robust and practical animal lover, who knew and understood that his patients were not always going to appreciate his efforts on their behalf. Anyone who has tried to shampoo their cat will understand.

I once helped him release a swan that had been injured by hooks and lead but had been restored to majestic health. I carried it to its new lake in a 'swan jacket', with its sinewy neck wrapped gently around my shoulders, and then saw it preen and sail away. It was a sensation I shall never forget. Les got that feeling every day. I write about him because he is an exact contemporary whose life ended far too soon, suddenly last week. He will be massively missed by all who loved and respected him, especially his wife and son, Colin, who will carry on his excellent work.

Les Stocker was the best of men, a modest, gentle genius.

29th July 2016

Having had our biennial four-day holiday (can't go away for longer when you have a menagerie at home), my wife and I were reminded of the challenge to hotels in offering dining spaces where human interaction can progress in any kind of normal way. Restaurants fall into two main categories, with the optimum sitting between them. We dined at a 'fine dining restaurant' in the hotel in which we were staying on our first night. The ambience and table layout did not permit anything resembling normal conversation.

The faint-hearted stared glumly into space while accepting

their amuse-bouches and offered only desultory thanks when the next large plate of modern art arrived; and the more adventurous spoke in quick bursts or mumbled whispers in the forlorn hope that no one else could hear them, saying, 'What does 'a la foscinato' mean?' when referring to a potato, or 'Do you have any ketchup?' And it's not just about tables being too close together either, although that doesn't help. Sometimes the acoustics of a room are just resolutely unconducive to gentle chats. Add to that a kind of churchlike reverence induced by a menu that lurches from the impenetrable to the downright pretentious and over-attentive waiters needing constant reassurance, and you have a recipe for a pervasive unease, with no one prepared to point out that the king is in the altogether. It is also perhaps partly attributable to the fact that most diners are couples or families on holiday, rather than the great variety of diners to be found in most restaurants the rest of the year.

Other restaurants try to overcome this cathedral tendency with the use of music, instantly running the risk of alienating those who don't like their choice and causing an increase in vocal levels throughout the area. Being of an age when the parameters of my hearing have compressed, entering a cacophonous pub or dining room results in a swift about-turn and departure. Not being able to hear what your fellow diner is saying, unless they're Brian Blessed, is not my idea of an enjoyable dining experience.

The safest option at holiday time, which is dependent upon the weather, is to dine outside where that option is available. We did that on our last night, as the horsefly bites will attest.

They never promised me a rose garden.

A la foscinato? I made it up.

5th August 2016

On Monday morning I rang my doctor's surgery and the receptionist, whom I had known for years, offered me an appointment that evening with my doctor. I then cycled into town, where I left my bike in the rack by the post office. I had forgotten my combination lock chain, but I knew that I needn't worry; it would still be there when I came out. It was. I then went into the library, where there was quite a queue of people returning books and recommending in a whisper to each other the ones they had just read.

When I came out, I saw a little girl crying on the pavement. She had lost her mother. I took her by the hand and led her to the spot where I had just seen the policeman by the Belisha beacon in the town centre. He was still there, and as I was explaining where I had come across her, the child's mother ran up and thanked us all profusely for looking after her daughter. She had just popped into the Electricity Board shop to pay her bill and arrange for an electrician to come and sort out a problem, and hadn't noticed that she had wandered off.

I dropped a shopping list off at our local grocer for him to deliver later that afternoon, and started to cycle home. It was late summer and the council were cutting back the hedges and verges which were encroaching on all the lanes out of town, and a couple of co-workers were bagging up the thorny branches and leaves. If it wasn't for them, in a very short time the roads would have been lethal.

In the afternoon, I visited a friend in the local hospital who had just had his appendix out. The nursing staff were very friendly and even had time to make us both a cup of tea, until matron appeared to make her cleanliness inspection and I had to make myself scarce. I walked to the doctor in the evening and on the way back, I bumped into our local beat policeman, who had stopped at his blue police box, and we had a chat. I asked him what was inside. He said, 'Aha! You would be really surprised if you saw! It's top secret.'

'Wake up Colin! Wake up! Were you dreaming about the 1950s again?'

Apparently I was.

12th August 2016

When I was young one, of the most successful theatrical venues was the Whitehall Theatre in London, where Brian

Rix was the star of a succession of farces over decades. Having acted in a few myself, I know just how difficult it is to earn the kind of laughs that he could command at will, it seemed. He retired in the late 70s, having also appeared in over ninety made-for-television farces. A couple of years later he became secretary general of MENCAP.

His first child had Downs Syndrome at a time when little help was available for any kind of mental disability, and he was a lifelong campaigner for the mentally disadvantaged. His life peerage in 1992 enabled him to dedicate himself to innumerable causes and charities. During that time, he voted in the upper chamber against the decriminalisation of euthanasia or assisted suicide.

It is therefore telling that now that he is on his deathbed, he has taken time out from his own pain and misery to write to Baroness D'Souza, the Lords' Speaker, (who also has a history of working in Human Rights), asking her to allow the question of assisted dying to be considered again. His words are compelling, as one might expect, and even whilst he would like to depart himself, he wants to make some sense out of his prolonged pain and discomfort by helping others in the future to avoid it. He writes, 'My position has changed ... I have been dying now for two months. I have wrapped up my affairs ... they won't let me die and that's all I want to do. I am constantly woozy and hazy but I can't sleep. The doctors and nurses do their best for me, but their best is not good enough because what I want is to die, and the law stops them from helping me with that. I think it's wrong that people like me are stranded like this.'

Those who are members of religions that proscribe assisted dying are entitled to live their lives and die their deaths accordingly, but I believe it is beyond cruel to impose those values on the many millions of us who feel entitled to slide peacefully into oblivion when that is our considered choice and when remaining brings unendurable and protracted suffering.

As the play title had it, *Whose Life Is It Anyway?*

19th August 2016

Next week, I shall either be glad to get my life back or I will be suffering from Olympic withdrawal symptoms. I realised during the late nights and long days of watching the square box—well, it is very rectangular these days, and even curved—but anyway, I realised that in past years I have been gainfully employed and therefore only able to watch the sportsfest piecemeal. Last time was in the UK, of course, so the timings were friendlier. But I have immersed myself in the bars, the rings, the floor and the horse.

I have cheered on the Rugby Sevens, the divers into the green slime of unknown origin, the sailors, shooters, archers and boxers. I have marvelled at the human ingenuity displayed by the creators of the arcane mysteries of the Keirin and the all-consuming Omnium. My curiosity got the better of me, so I discovered that Keirin is Japanese for 'racing wheels', and that the strange orderly pursuit of that motorised bicycle (known as a Derny after the name of its original Parisian creator) started out as a Japanese gambling sport.

But, for me, the main attraction of the Olympics is the unending supply of people who are prepared to go to quite extraordinary lengths to achieve excellence in their sports, sacrificing years to the endless daily pre-dawn hours of practice and training before the rest of us clog up the swimming pools, racetracks and sporting arenas, to the relentless physical toll it takes to maintain the levels of fitness and performance required to achieve even more than anyone else has before in their sport.

And it is with enormous pride that we see how our athletes have conducted themselves in Rio. Great Britain historically wasn't anything approaching a major player on the world stage of sporting activity, achieving gold medals in single figures for decades, the lowest being Atlanta in 1996, when without Sir Steve and Matthew Pinsent, we would have had no golds at all. It may have been lottery funding that helped make the difference or the build-up to London in 2012, but now we take great pride in our national sporting prowess, and quite right too. If honours are given out to retired prime ministers' cronies and hairdressers, then there are many returning athletes who deserve even more for taking such obvious pride in their country at a time when many are demonstrably less supportive.

26th August 2016

Well, thank goodness we can now settle down to watching what we want to watch on television without changing channel every few minutes. I greatly enjoyed watching the Olympics, and was delighted that our national broadcaster the BBC carried all the programming so that it was advertising free and celebrated the totality of the action in Brazil, and not just our opportunities to medal (unlike the case in many other countries, apparently).

I was in America, for instance, back when Ovett and Coe were battling for either the 1500 or 800 metres final, and it wasn't broadcast live as there were no USA medal opportunities, so the basketball was on. And I thought the animated promo film was inspired and beautifully put together. But given the number of channels available to the BBC, why, oh why, did we have to constantly flip between them to watch a particular event from beginning to end. I began to feel sorry for poor Clare Balding, who had the earpiece of doom constantly telling her to order us to switch channels to carry on watching the hockey, the rugby, etc.

Would the world have imploded if people who usually expect a particular programme to be on a particular channel had been told that all non-Olympic regular programming would be on either BBC 1 or BBC 2 throughout the Olympics? Yes, I am sure Disgusted of Leighton Buzzard might have voiced their irritation, but millions upon millions of us had to struggle out of our armchairs in search of the remote when Clare—not a woman to brook disobedience, I suspect— ordered us to switch yet again at the crucial moment. Add to that the cat on your lap that objects to being dislodged, and you can see why the BBC needs to rethink its major event scheduling to something more user-friendly. I know they will say that there are some things like the *News at Ten* or *Ten O'Clock News*, or whatever they call it now, that are sacrosanct, and viewers have a right to expect them to be in the same place at the same time every night, but occasionally they did go to the news late, so why not remove that possibility by separating scheduling completely?

Mind you, next time it will all be early morning from Tokyo, so no one will care. It will all be over at lunchtime each day.

2nd September 2016

The National Health Service, once the best in the world, is being trampled in the mud, and it seems that no amount of screaming and shouting by the bereft population will sway the political will to do anything about it. As soon as a party gets elected, their horizons are blotted out by a large banner saying, 'Make sure you get elected next time, too'. My dream government would try to do what is right, even if it meant a short term of office only. What the NHS needs is mainly investment. You can tinker with streamlining services, reducing waste and decimating superfluous administration (please), but money is needed now and staff are needed now, and the will to bite the bullet and tell the truth should also come now.

I do believe that a public that was told that a number of pence added to the standard rate of Income Tax would be used only and accountably on improvements to the service offered by the NHS, to increase staffing and bring down waiting lists, would be prepared to grit their teeth and endure the pain.

My writing this has been provoked by a recent conversation with a consultant's secretary. I had a scan as a result of ongoing problems that I won't bore you with. A month later I rang for feedback and to make a follow up appointment. The consultant had seen the scan and dictated a letter which, after going to India to be typed, would eventually reach me, contents unknown to the secretary (didn't secretaries once type letters?). I suggested that I make an appointment 'so as not to have to wait weeks' to begin any treatment. A brief shocked silence. Apparently, I may well have to wait a year for an appointment in this doctor's speciality. 'Whatever the result of the scan?' I asked incredulously. I was reassured that if my demise was imminent, I would be seen sooner.

There are many people in much, much worse pain and discomfort than me; I am merely using my example as a springboard for a wider debate which starts with a desire to restore the NHS to its former beacon status without reference to the short-term popularity of the government asking for higher taxes in order to provide it. If they ring-fence it, I have no doubt an increasingly ailing and older population will see the logic and stump up.

9th September 2016

NASA has launched an Osiris rocket, intended to land on an asteroid (that someone has decided should be called Bennu) in 2018, in order to gather information about it before it passes close to Earth's orbit in 2035.

It is now widely accepted that the dinosaurs were probably made extinct by a large asteroid strike some 65 million years ago. But it is not just my former association with space travel that makes me applaud this attempt to learn about something with the potential to cause havoc, albeit temporary, in the distant future. And it is worth mentioning that Bennu, passing through our orbit every six years, is only 500 metres long, unlike the six-mile monster that put paid to the dinosaurs and an awful lot else.

It is a possibility, apparently, that the 2035 pass might be close enough for our gravity to affect its path, so that subsequent visits might get uncomfortably closer. Osiris will gather information, land and take samples, and return to Earth in 2023. The exercise will be invaluable, not least in enabling the formulation of avoidance measures by the scientists of the future.

It is certainly true that at some point, our descendants, if they haven't wiped each other out, will need to find other planets to call home, and we are at the very beginning of thousands of years of that exploration, but now is the time that we should be starting, which serves to highlight the inescapable fact that in terms of what we need to do to help our wounded planet to survive the depredations of homo sapiens, we are starting decades too late and need make a superhuman effort to claw back lost time. If the USA and China see the need to sign up to the Paris Climate Agreement—and both of those nations have historical economic and commercial reasons to avoid doing so—then we know that the fat lady is not only singing but screaming her head off. We need to reverse the effect that untrammelled industrialisation has had on the developed world and support the emerging industrial nations who may not have the chance to catch up if we do what needs to be done to make the impact of a large asteroid a very minor catastrophe by comparison.

As Barack Obama put it, 'Is this the moment that we finally decided to save our planet?'

16th September 2016

If Theresa May introduced the possibility of expanding grammar school education as a means of distracting us from Brexit, she has succeeded. From the reaction of some commentators, you would think she was proposing the return of workhouses.

I was educated at a grammar school. When I sat the test, I do not recollect any anxious build-up, or indeed preparation of any kind. It was seen by all of us then as a means of identifying which of the schools available was more suitable for a child's needs. Parents did not bribe their children for demonstrating their 'cleverness', nor did they employ tutors, though whether the tutor can do more than nudge a child to a slightly higher mark is debatable; furthermore, children so nudged often struggle to keep up with their un-nudged contemporaries in the grammar school.

The problem that has arisen in the intervening years has come from use of the words 'pass' and 'fail' when secondary school selection occurs. The grammar school is sadly seen as a 'better' education, rather than an academic education for those for whom that is more appropriate. Two of my children were selected for grammar education and the other two attended an upper school. The latter two benefited hugely from the less pressurised pace, and I believe achieved better grades than they would have done had they had to compete within the more intensely focussed academic environment of a grammar school.

The perception that all children should aspire to a university education has not helped. When plumbers, electricians, carpenters and builders earn more than most office workers and are in short supply, the redevelopment of courses relevant to those trades and professions for those whose talents lie in those directions seems a no-brainer. But some aspirational parents are more concerned about social status than what is truly appropriate for their child in the system we have in Buckinghamshire. The growth of tutoring for the 11-plus selection, rather than just to help the child through the stickier moments of maths and English, demonstrates this abundantly. And the selection examination is, as far as is possible, intended to measure the way the examinee's mind works and not what they know.

Teachers differentiate within lessons and streaming takes place within all schools, so that unnecessary stress is minimised and each child can maximise their potential. The current system here is merely differentiation by building.

23rd September 2016

Of course, child rearing isn't always easy, and it is the one job that offers no training other than our subjective experience and observation of certain aspects of other people's successes or disasters. But I am brave enough to offer some very simple advice to any parent or would-be parent who is ready to hear it. Be consistent. Don't issue threats you have no intention of carrying out, and don't bribe your way to a peaceful life. And a good rider is: never undermine your partner—even if what they have done is different. Unless it is life threatening or exposes you or your family to prosecution, allow the error to play out.

I am at the point now when many contemporaries are grandparents. I see serene families with happy, outgoing children that are ruled not with a rod of iron but a firm and loving care. But I also see children of all ages who have been indulged to the point where they know that if their complaints and demands are relentless enough, they will get what they want. The resultant brat has acquired that status through no fault of its own, but because harassed, exhausted parents succumb to the temptation of a quick fix and give way; and it is rightly the nature of a child to test its parameters. Capitulation is never worth it. Never. A young lady of my acquaintance has been helping a single working mother for a few weeks and been completely unable to achieve any sensible rapport with the children (of middle school and secondary age), because they have learned that they can completely ignore the most reasonable requests of any adult, as there is never any meaningful sanction if they don't. A shrugging mother—who backtracks on her own instructions to the temporary minder/chauffeur/home help when her children decline to do what the minder has been instructed to ask of them—is only systematically denying them the ability to develop into reasonable adults. Adding to that the provision of mobile devices to keep them quiet, and the chance of civilised redemption decreases yet further.

If you let a child believe that your wishes or those of any other adult are of less value than the gratification of their own immediate desires, then you and they are frankly doomed. As adults, we should know that, and help them to value and respect the needs and wishes of others.

30th September 2016

Sam Allardyce always gave the impression that he was a man in a world of callow youths. He was a big presence. It is sad that his common sense seems to have lagged behind his other manifest attributes. Let us dismiss the suggestion that millionaires don't need or shouldn't want more money, which is demonstrably false. I have no personal experience of that kind of wealth, but I imagine the more you have, the more you suspect it will all evaporate and you will be back where you started. Also, why not investigate all offers? Why do film stars make more movies when they are already multimillionaires? Because the job is fulfilling and a challenge, and why they became performers in the first place.

It seems to me that Big Sam's terminal mistake was to show off. He nose-tappingly suggested that the rules of the FA, his employers, about the third party ownership of players, could be circumvented. And the biggest evidence of his lack of common sense was his preparedness to speak disparagingly, to people he had only just met, about his predecessor, Roy Hodgson, about Gary Neville and the grandsons of the Queen, and others. Showing off. We all say stuff to our nearest and dearest that we wouldn't want the subject of the comments to know about. But most of us have the nous to be wary with strangers.

I am frequently asked by *Doctor Who* fans at conventions what I think about my predecessors and successors, personally and professionally. Outside the running gag that Sylvester McCoy and I have about his stealing my role and some humorous badinage based on that, I have never and would never presume to comment other than favourably about my colleagues. Mercifully, that is quite easy, as I respect and admire all of them, and in the event that I did have any knowledge of what they had done or said that might surprise an audience, I would keep it to myself, as I hope would they. And my mother always inculcated in me the maxim that if you had nothing positive to say, then say nothing.

Big Sam's mistake was a rather naïve desire to impress, combined with a feeling of invulnerability as a result of his new position. He had two advisors with him. I should imagine they are now jobless too. They should be. At least he has a 100% success record.

7th October 2016

As the money for local councils shrivels and inexorably reduces their ability to provide the level and number of services we have come to expect, it underlines the need to reassess how many levels of service provider we actually need for local government. A local school was recently asked to by the Council to cut back trees that were obscuring road signs. The school told them that the offending trees were in fact not on its land but that of the self-same council. Months later, the trees remain unlopped. The council can't afford it, any more than schools can, and trying to shift the burden to another pot of the taxpayer's money is pointless.

Back in the summer, Bucks County Council, which is also financially challenged by dwindling government funding, approached the district councils with a sensible proposal to save money for everyone by joining with them in preparing a business case for a single unitary council for Buckinghamshire.

The four local councils were disinclined to join that particular exploratory dance, which might lead to their being subsumed by the larger predator, and have instead instituted their own joint study to decide how they can provide the best service for us all. This is a familiar pattern. The curse of the long consultation process rarely achieves much beyond enhancing the bank balances of those who conduct the consultation on their behalf. There have been several such processes in the last few years in Wycombe, and each time the process resulted in more money being paid to consultants then was ever saved, when the results were subsequently disregarded or found to be impractical.

I have a great respect for those among us who put themselves forward as councillors. They don't do it for financial reward, certainly, and most of them are genuinely motivated by a desire to serve the public at a time when few are prepared to do that. Many of them, in fact, serve on both District and County Councils, but beneath them is a large body of salaried employees who advise them and might not unreasonably find themselves avoiding being the turkey that votes in favour of Christmas. If you ever want to see your roadside verges and hedges cut again, or community and library services fully restored—the list is endless—let us hope that a reduction in the massive bureaucracy and combining of resources will make that possible.

14th October 2016

How lucky are we that our political system, which may have its faults and historical anomalies, does not usually produce spectacles quite as dispiriting as the recent presidential debate in the USA? It is indicative of something in the American psyche that a billionaire belligerent locker room bully, with no political credentials or history or evidence of altruism, can appeal to so many people that they are prepared to overlook his undeniable xenophobic, misogynistic greed and arrogance. It appears, sadly, that the mainstream politician with a credible history of functioning calmly and sensibly at the sharp end of politics for a decade or two is so unpopular with some Americans, disenchanted with the established political scene, that she is having to fight quite so hard to stave off the most dangerous candidate for world power in a long time.

Hillary may be 'more of the same', but I would have thought that not being Donald Trump would be enough to get almost anyone else elected President. The only slight consolation is, perhaps, that for all its vicissitudes, the US constitution does give the Senate and Congress President-blocking and limiting powers, as Barack Obama has discovered repeatedly and dispiritingly for eight years. And Hillary being the wife of Bill Clinton should be a big plus for her, despite the retaliatory mud-throwing in the aftermath of Trump's 'Locker-roomGate.' Many of us have good reason to be grateful for Bill's assistance in bringing about the Good Friday accords in Northern Ireland, in brokering peace between Israel and Jordan and in Bosnia Herzegovina and bringing about nuclear stockpile reduction worldwide.

It is interesting that America appears to like the dynastic approach to political power, something less familiar here since the Pitts two hundred and fifty years ago. But Roosevelts,

Kennedys, Bushes and now Clintons have proved attractive to the American voter and political scene, whereas we have been spared sons or daughters of Churchill, Thatcher or Blair so far.

I have a sneaking suspicion that, given his ability to surf the unseemly evidence of his misogyny and greed on waves of adulation from his non-PC admirers, Trump's opponents will spring some evidence of even worse solecisms at the last moment, so that the scales will fall from the eyes of those admiring the would-be Emperor's clothes and he will be sent back to sneer, sniff and wave his quiff on *The Apprentice*. We can hope.

21st October 2016

As a result of appearing in popular TV shows, some of them years ago, I am lucky enough to have a large number of people who have seen my work and profess to approve of it. This is a luxury denied to most members of what politicians like to call 'hard-working families.'

Not many car mechanics or insurance salesmen get stopped in the streets for selfies, accompanied by outpourings of delight about an ancient repair or a brilliant car insurance policy. Sometimes I do, and am amazed that something I took part in three decades ago has continued to please others after all these years. Even though sometimes the interruption may be an inconvenience (I have had an autograph request while in a urinal—a real 'in convenience'), it is a minor one in the grand scheme of things. I am therefore very disappointed when I hear of tetchy actors or writers who spend as much time refusing to give an autograph, or summon up a smile for a selfie, than it would have taken to oblige.

It may be that fame was never the spur. It certainly wasn't in my case. It never occurred to me. It was the doing of the work that was the golden objective. Fame is sometimes an unlooked for by-product of your work reaching a wide and appreciative audience. If your fame reaches Beckham or McCartney levels, you may need some protection or a buffer, otherwise any movement in a public arena becomes impossible. But most of us who ply our trade in the media can endure stoically the occasional fan who needs our attention briefly. I am therefore disappointed when I hear stories from friends of their experiences with irritated or plain rude celebs.

An eminent producer told me this week that I had been kind to him when he was a teenage fan at a stage door in the 80s, and then told me of another actor (whom I knew well) who had testily brushed him aside when seeking an autograph at another theatre. Both incidents were firmly lodged in his memory. I know which memory I would like to engender. A young author friend recently got very short shrift when approaching a grumpy well-known children's author at a charity event. She will never forget it. We all have our down days, but when you're in the public eye they can come back and bite you.

28th October 2016

Like many readers of this newspaper, I have to endure the frustrations of the M25 on a regular basis. Despite the frequent delays, it remains the only practical way of circumnavigating London in a vehicle. Whatever the time of day I travel along it, traffic slows to a stuttering crawl past Heathrow and regularly grinds to a halt in both directions as the five lanes fail to cope with all the traffic from the M3, A30, M4 and M40 merging within a few miles and the thousands accessing our major airport hub. Lorry drivers talk of the volume of commercial traffic trying to gain access to the freight terminals and, when unable to do so, being obliged to drive, sometimes for an hour or more, round and round the internal perimeter roads before they can gain access to facilities already stretched way beyond their originally projected capacity.

So it was somewhat of a shock to learn that the volume of that traffic is to be increased by 50% potentially by the addition of a third runway at a location where, were you starting from scratch, you would probably not put an airport at all.

Whichever location is chosen will, of course, galvanise

opposition in the area surrounding the development, which will cause chaos locally for years and blight thereafter. Were it planned in my bit of this green and pleasant land, I would be there manning the barricades, but we all have to endure temporary privation for the greater good in a 21st-century world. I have the M40 as a backdrop to my bit of rural England and am praying for low-noise asphalt.

But there are so many alternatives—not just Gatwick, which is arguably inconveniently placed geographically—to satisfy the demand. I was recently diverted to Birmingham Airport, which is served by excellent rail links and access to several motorways and which is more centrally placed. It is also surrounded by land and facilities (supporting the NEC) much more conducive to servicing an expanding airport. Boris' dream of an airport in the Thames estuary seemed an excellent plan to many, and massively less disruptive. There is a disused airport at Greenham Common which once had the longest runway in the UK as far as I am aware. Why not Stansted or Luton, which are both closer to London than most international airports are worldwide to the cities they serve?

4th November 2016

There was a news item this week about a turkey farmer in Berkshire preparing his birds for the sound and fury of 5th November by letting off fireworks intermittently around his farm in the preceding month when he could keep them calm, gradually increasing the frequency and proximity, so that when the Guy Fawkes frenzy kicks off this weekend, the poor creatures won't be so spooked that they thrash around and damage or suffocate each other before their date with destiny next month.

Clearly, the farmer's motivation is more commercial than anything else, but it serves nonetheless to remind us all of the toll that the sudden onslaught of noise and light can have on wildlife, farm animals and pets. We will have to calm one of our dogs all night as he becomes frantic when the bangs and flashes start and for some reason tries to escape and hide in the neighbouring woods at precisely the time that logic dictates that he should stay near us and be protected. Dog psychology is complex, it seems. Especially for Henry, who needs to be constantly assured of our love and devotion most of the time, to the extent that although he is perfectly capable of negotiating the pet flap, he occasionally demands that we get up and open the door to prove our continuing love for him. But when the fireworks start, he heads for the hills, even though that means he is usually running towards the danger. But he is the same dog who won't eat his dinner unless he thinks someone else wants it, so why am I surprised?

It is a strange time of year with trick or treat and symbolically-burn-the-traitor in quick succession, offering marketing opportunities for the supermarkets and irritants to those of us whose children are all grown up and have forgotten the excitement of the flames, flares and nocturnal adventures. Now it is just a confirmation that summer is really over and spring is a very long way away. But if you are running an event that involves bonfires and bangs, do please check the bonfire you have made before lighting, as until ablaze, those great piles of brush and wood make very desirable residences for our smaller wildlife. And do make sure you're far enough away from farm stock and homes with animals to minimise the terror and panic that can be induced.

11th November 2016

Commitment to a political party in the UK is not always simple because our system can lead to strategic rather than commitment voting. If you live in a safe constituency for a party you don't care for, then it is tempting to vote for whichever alternative might unseat them. And this has played a large part in what has just happened in the USA. It may be that Donald Trump is at heart no more a Republican in the traditional sense than he is a Mexican or a champion of gay rights, but he knew which buttons to press in an environment of endemic distrust of politicians and the establishment in order to make his manifest imperfections, rampant misogyny, prejudice and arrogance less important than his Pied Piper-like beguiling of vast numbers of citizens who thought themselves forgotten and disenfranchised.

He is the man who said in 1998 that if he were ever to run it would be as a Republican, because they were 'the dumbest group of voters in the country.' QED, you might say. The reality may prove less terrifying than we fear. But the signs are not propitious. A Republican party that has all three branches of the administration in its grasp for the first time in almost a century will be unlikely to champion the causes of gun control, global warming, gay and transgender rights, a woman's right to terminate a dangerous pregnancy, tolerance—the list goes on. The lesson of the Berlin Wall has not been learned, either. If the Mexican Wall becomes a reality then it will be the most retrograde step in international relations since the Cold War. That Putin, Le Pen et al have welcomed the Trump accession says it all, really.

And the political malaise that has produced this result in America is not limited to that country. There is a global trend towards nationalism that has produced unrest and political extremism throughout the entire world. Brexit is a symptom of this. When surrounded by intolerance and terrorism, there is a very natural tendency to withdraw into the corral and look after your own. We voted to be a little island again with the sole responsibility of looking after ourselves, please. If only we still had a strong agricultural and manufacturing base, we would have more chance of success in that 'Don't mind us, we'll just be quiet over here in the corner' ambition.

18th November 2016

It's that time of year again, when another motley bunch subject themselves to deprivation and humiliation in the name of entertainment, as Ant and Dec supervise the modern equivalent of the spectacles in the Roman Coliseum in *I'm a Celebrity Get Me Out of Here.* I did it four years ago, and am therefore riveted to the unfolding events as a new group of the intrepid, the curious and the beguiled expose themselves to the three-week examination of their resolve and courage.

Why would anyone do it? Well, of course, it is a job, and therefore there is a fee involved, which certainly has the potential to persuade anyone who isn't implacably averse to the idea. In my case, I was the same age as Larry Lamb is this year. My career as an actor was arguably mainly behind me and I wasn't risking making myself unemployable; it would probably have been unhelpful to have done such a programme when I was a twenty-year-old wanting to be taken seriously as an actor. As usual, the participants are either 'celebs' whose future won't be damaged by doing more of the kind of thing they have already become famous for doing, or those who think the risk is worth taking for the experience or the rewards.

I think I was persuaded by the enthusiasm of my family as much as I was by the prospect of paying off what was left of my mortgage. And even though it probably ensured that an invitation to join the Royal Shakespeare would probably not be heading my way after all, I have never regretted taking part. It sounds trite, but I really did learn an awful lot about myself and what was really important in my life. I also got to meet a great bunch of folk that I would have been very unlikely to have met, or perhaps even wanted to meet, otherwise. And of course, the most unlikely relationships were formed very quickly, although the intentions behind exchanging of addresses afterwards soon morphed into memory when real life resumed. But I am still in touch with two of my merry campmates and remain fond of the others.

I watch with a tinge of envy. I know that jungle clearing so well and would love to have another go and try and do better next time. I could have been a contender!

25th November 2016

This Wednesday was the 53rd anniversary of the arrival of the blue police box on our screens as something other than just a handy point of contact and storage facility for Her Majesty's constabulary. I know exactly where I was on the evening of

23rd November 1963, as do many others of my generation. We were all still reeling from the awful killing of John F Kennedy the day before, and the airwaves and media were full of reaction to that terrible and memorable event when William Hartnell made his first appearance as the Doctor.

In fact, the BBC repeated that first episode the following week (at a time when repeats were about as rare as they are all too common now). They were aware that the viewing public may have had other things on their mind when the first one was aired. But I don't think anyone believed for a second that we would still be talking about the programme two generations later. I watched it, leaning on the banisters of the stairs down into the Bayswater flat I then shared with three fellow law students. The transmission started as I entered and I was still leaning there, riveted, when it finished. However hard it may be to believe, it was state-of-the-art in 1963. I know many people say that they loved it because of the silly low budget props and shaky sets, but they are, I'm afraid, deceiving themselves. All television looked like that then. That was the best that could be done with the technology half a century ago. And all science-fiction programmes (not that there were many) offered up imaginings of the future that inevitably look laughable or bizarre when that future arrives. People just can't accept that they could possibly watch and believe something that bears little comparison, visually or audibly, with what can be done now, so they subconsciously invent a nostalgic affection for the manifest inadequacies of the time.

But here we are in 2016, eagerly awaiting the return of the excellent Peter Capaldi in this year's Christmas offering of what is arguably the most loved and most successful television programme ever. And I really like Peter's version of the Time Lord. He is grumpy, intolerant, angry and rude—not unlike my own version of the role in the 1980s. He's twice the man I was, though. Me—six; him—twelve.

2nd December 2016

The excellent garage that services my family's cars offers loan cars when available to assist us to continue to function in an area where public transport provision is rudimentary rather than rural-friendly. Last time I availed myself of this service, I was surprised to find that the fuel gauge indicated that there was not much more than a cupful or two therein. I was told that this was not uncommon.

However much is in the car when loaned, there is invariably less when returned. I suppose some people only use the car to get home and then back to collect their own vehicle, so don't see a need to splash the cash or indeed the petrol. I know that car hire firms with petrol pumps solve that dilemma by letting the cars out full, and then topping up and charging extra to the renter if they are not returned in a similar condition. A small garage without pumps doesn't have that option. On that occasion, I made it and put in half a tankful, as I knew I would be using it all day. I returned the car a quarter full, offering some peace of mind to the next driver, who might value and replicate the thoughtfulness. I do not intend to paint myself as a saint by telling this story, as the sum of money is a tiny fraction of what it would cost to hire a car from a third party for a day.

This week I had occasion to need a courtesy car again, and my first port of call again had to be the petrol station, as the petrol gauge gave me no confidence that I would even make it home. Once again, I will return the car with a quarter tank at least. The folk at the garage clearly do not want to antagonise the reluctant petrol purchaser by checking the mileage and the petrol gauge in and out every time, and indeed they should not have to do so.

But it would be nice if the recipients of the extra service provided could respond to that good service by thinking of the next person to drive the car, even if it costs them a few pounds at the pump. It will much less, in most cases, than the cost of a taxi to their home and back after dropping off their cars.

9th December 2016

It is Advent again; the advent of all those adverts on television that inform us what Christmas is actually (rather than really) about. You would think from the present saturation on all channels that our noses were all of mendacious Pinocchio dimensions, because perfume—or should I say scent (even though the advertisers don't)?—appears to be what we all want to be informed about. An endless succession of impossibly chiselled, slim and glamorous models jostle with your actual Hollywood A-listers to walk on water, descend from Mount Olympus, inhabit surreal baroque landscapes or drive cars that exist only in magazines along ludicrously empty and gleaming roads to tell us, accompanied by seductive French tones, how a squirt of their own particular concoction will render you irresistible to the point of divinity.

I suppose they have to adopt this approach rather than tell us that their very expensive product is made from the poo of a sperm whale, the private parts of a deer, a beaver's bottom, the fossilised excreta of a hyrax or the glandular secretions of a civet cat. Apparently, none of these beguiling substances are that delightful at the point of creation, and the mammals themselves are probably as happy to get rid of them as the perfumers are to benefit from the said summary expulsion. How it was ever discovered that the assorted processes involved could turn the contents of animals' cesspits into the most expensive liquids on the planet, when measured by the millilitre, is lost in the mists of time. Maybe a caveman who had fallen foul of a civet cat's wrath spilt some primitive alcohol on himself and found the resultant combination endeared him to his neighbours.

Wind the clock forward a few millennia, and the country's largest holiday celebration seems to require that we all smell better than we did for the rest of the year. The adverts are invariably lavish, and per minute would probably cost more than the majority of feature films.

Then there's the supermarkets and department stores. We all look forward to seeing how they can better that one we liked so much last year. Make way, lonely grandpa on the moon, for trampolining badgers being watched by envious Buster the boxer; two old teddy bears coming home to see their families; and here come the lorries full of sugary, fizzy drinks.

It must be Christmas.

16th December 2016

Christmas cards. We might have fondly imagined that the paperless society would have resulted in a lightening of the annual burden carried by our postmen, but I suspect that technology hasn't made a jot of difference. We still seem to want to send each other these pieces of folded cardboard with hastily scrawled and highly optimistic promises of jolly meetings next year, despite the likelihood of our actually ever doing that being about as high as it was when we made a similarly well-intentioned promise last year. If we are being really thoughtful, we tailor the design of the card to fit our intended recipient. No nativity scenes for atheistic friends and no foxes gambolling in the snow for poultry farmers. The opportunity to let those we have lost touch with know that we haven't forgotten them is to be embraced, but how many do we only send out of guilt, I wonder?

We have all had that last minute scramble, demanding a first class stamp, when someone has slipped through the net, however detailed our lists may be of last year's cards out and cards in. For several years, I have failed to send a card to someone I like a lot, because his address had disappeared in a series of computer updates. I finally solved that problem by searching the hard disk of the discarded computer, and my friend in Chichester will no longer think I have forgotten him. A minor victory. But I really do not mind at all if you don't send me a Christmas card, even if we are really good close friends. Well, especially in that case, really, because we presumably see each other from time to time and can assure ourselves of our mutual affection in so doing.

But if you do receive a card from me, it will be at least a year old, as the other thing that happens every year is the purchase of dozens of new charity cards, having forgotten that there are still a hundred or more languishing from previous years in that box in the loft. Because I am not doing pantomime this year (it's behind me!), I approached the whole festive farrago in a more leisurely way and remembered them. And I remain eternally grateful to the unnamed genius who came up with the sticky-backed stamp. No more post-licking aftertaste and no more paper cuts on the tip of the tongue!

23rd December 2016

Every year, we read of some bloke who did all his shopping on Christmas Eve in two hours flat and doesn't understand what all the fuss is about. I suspect if we look at what this burst of generosity comprised, we would not be as impressed as he would hope. A few boxes of discounted chocolates, some flowers from the petrol station and a bottle of Cava does not a Christmas make, and I suspect that Mr Last Minute has a wife who has been running ragged for several weeks to make his leisurely approach possible.

Even an average-sized family with a small circle of friends wrestles with lists and schedules for weeks. In Baker Towers, we resolved that this year we would get Christmas sorted by the end of November. When we said it, we really meant it. But the detailed lists went AWOL, the gifts purchased early were forgotten and have now re-emerged to make us seem the most generous of givers when more than was intended is handed over, thereby making the recipient feel somewhat shamefaced by their perfectly adequate gift to us.

In past years, I have escaped much of this stress and anxiety, because I have been gainfully employed twice daily throughout December in the gaudy glitter of pantomime. Being available to assist has proved much more stressful than the familiar territory of fairies, villains and inappropriate pop songs being sung by scantily clad young men in caves in Arabia. I have just returned from a panicked dash to get something that we both thought the other had already got for someone whom we are seeing today. There will doubtless be others. Someone will turn up on Christmas Eve, hand-delivering the most enormous and generous gift, for whom we have nothing to offer in return, unless we rip the label off someone else's gift and postpone the inevitable. And to be blunt, there are only so many tins of Quality Street, Cadburys Heroes, Celebrations and Roses that one can amass without fearing ending up like Terry Jones' exploding gourmand in *Monty Python*. I suspect many of those tins get passed on to other lucky recipients. My wife once received a gift from a friend, bearing the original tag wishing the donor a happy Christmas from her niece. We rather liked that, and of course shared the joy with the hapless friend. Happy Christmas, all.

30th December 2016

In common, I suspect with many others, I removed myself from the roads for much of the Christmas build-up by shopping online. Of course, I merely replaced my pollution of the air and the highways with that created by the many drivers, with varying familiarity with the English language, who delivered the plethora of parcels of Christmas joy to me so that I could then pass them on to others, or occasionally directly to those others, cutting me out of the equation entirely. Most of them arrived on time. One or two are still clogging up someone's van or warehouse and will hopefully turn up eventually. But all of the companies concerned have emailed me, asking for feedback. I used to think it was quite charming that customer service was so important to them that they wanted to check that I was happy via a detailed questionnaire.

Now I am less sanguine about their motives. We are merely free customer research that can be used or ignored as the company chooses. Of course, whereas they can rely on the fact that we will most certainly let them know if they let us down, we are unlikely to unilaterally send a glowing tribute to their ability to send us four pairs of thermal socks within the time frame promised and reasonably well-packed. I used to dish out my stars with careful and judicious consideration as requested, but am now more inclined to allow the Internet (and more importantly, myself) some time off. This decision was hastened by several companies' importuning me to rate stuff I have sent to third parties as gifts.

The last thing I am going to do is ring up the recipient and ask them all the questions about packaging, timeliness and appreciation of the gift itself, so that I can pass it on to the firm I bought it from. So my first resolution for the New Year is to apply Occam's very useful razor to requests from companies for feedback and simply let them know when it is not to my satisfaction.

So all of you suppliers of goods out there, please be assured that I am perfectly happy unless I contact you to the contrary. Furthermore, when I do so contact you, please deal with it as expeditiously as you do when you send out your requests for feedback, which often arrive in my inbox before the item itself.

***

If you have enjoyed Colin's view of life, keep up to date with his regular column *Look Who's Talking* in the *Bucks Free Press* each week and online at www.bucksfreepress.co.uk

About the Author

Colin Baker describes himself as actor, columnist, writer, husband, father, Wycombe Wanderers fan, grumpy old man, and amateur zoo keeper.

For many he *is* Doctor Who, having played the role during the 1980s and still happy to meet fans all over the world at conventions and fan gatherings.

With many acting credits to his name including *The Brothers*, in which he played the ruthless Paul Merroney, he is a well-respected figure equally at home on the stage or a television screen, and in more recent years starring once again as the Doctor in audio plays by the much respected Big Finish Productions.

For the past 21 years, Colin has written a weekly column for his local newspaper, the *Bucks Free Press*, discussing many and varied topics from renewing his car insurance to local government, from football to the state of the world.

Colin continues to write his weekly colum and can also be found commenting on the world at large via his Twitter feed.

Colin Baker website: colinbakeronline.com
Colin Baker on Twitter: @SawbonesHex
Bucks Free Press: www.bucksfreepress.co.uk
FBS Publishing Ltd website: www.fbs-publishing.co.uk
Twitter @FBSPublishing
Facebook: www.facebook.com/FabulousBookS
Instagram: fbspublishing

Lightning Source UK Ltd.
Milton Keynes UK
UKOW01f0322170217
294636UK00002B/12/P